Eric '22

My Up-Close View

Personal Stories from a Longtime Sports TV-Radio Columnist

By Larry Stewart
L.A. Times & L.A Herald-Examiner

D1527257

Cover design: Steve Benke
Editors: Bob Greenamyer and Jill Sanford
Technical support: Jeffrey Lee

ISBN: 979-876-116-3652

Table of Contents

Cover photos:
(1) Me interviewing Curt Gowdy at Dodger Stadium in 1975.
(2) Me with Bob Miller, Chick Hearn and Vin Scully in 2000, when the three L.A. legends appeared together on Fox Sports West 2's "Sports Roundtable" program, hosted by Bill Macdonald.

FOREWORD

By Jim Nantz, CBS announcer

When I started my network television career in 1985, there were only a dozen or so sports television critics in the entire country. These days that number is closer to 100 million. That is, if you count all the trolls who reside in the Twittersphere.

Point is, it's difficult to find someone who doesn't voice a strong opinion about what they are watching or listening to – especially when it comes to sports television. It seems that everyone is a critic. And almost everyone has the vehicle to have their opinions "published." Today, social media is the perfect confluence – with passionate sports fans – to breed so much contempt.

I'm proud to say that, along with my great friend, Al Michaels, we pay little attention to the zealots who attack the broadcast world in anonymity. We remain the last of the holdouts – possessors of zero social media accounts between us.

I guess you could say we are old school in that regard, feeling self-confident about our work, while trusting our instincts. As a broadcaster, you know when you've had a special broadcast. You also know when things could have been better, tighter, or livelier. No one understands the nuance of what makes for a quality broadcast better than the ones who have been in the trenches for decades.

So, while we've been around long enough to ignore the noise of Twitter, we do however appreciate the opinion of those who have dedicated their careers to understanding the intricacies of the medium. The ones who have built relationships, while reporting with integrity. The critics who aren't always praising your work or shining a positive light. With time you grow to understand their job and to respect their opinions, win or lose.

Such a soul for nearly 35 years of his nearly 40 years as a Los Angeles sportswriter was Larry Stewart. He saw my industry grow tenfold during his respected career. When he first began writing about sports broadcasting at the L.A. Herald Examiner in 1973, he was covering a medium that consisted of three networks – CBS, NBC, and ABC. Larry went to the L.A. Times in 1978 and said goodbye to his TV-Radio column in 2007. By then, sports television had become in his own words "a big business with too many networks to count."

In essence, he had witnessed and reported on sports TV's amazing growth, tantamount to seeing International Business Machines transition from a typewriter company to a global tech juggernaut known as IBM.

Larry met this challenge by nurturing contacts at every level from every outlet. Anyone who was anybody in sports television – locally in his hotbed of a market, to the national networks – realized the importance of making a favorable impression with the man out west who wielded tremendous power. No one outworked him, and no one underestimated the value of his opinion.

In January of 2007, I was traveling from my home in Connecticut to San Diego to call an NFL playoff game. The CBS Sports PR team set up a telephone interview with Larry, one that would take place upon my arrival in California.

At the time I was just a few weeks away from embarking on a 63-day journey "unlike any other." I would be calling consecutively for the first time the Super Bowl, the Final Four, and the Masters. I looked forward to my visit with Larry because I had always found him to be cordial and informative. What I liked best was the way he asked questions and sparked conversation. It was never pablum. Actually, his comments were downright thought provoking. You sensed he had a knack for getting right to the heart of the story. The story of his subjects.

On this occasion he asked about my mindset going into that glorious three- event, nine-week sequence. What came next was a perspective that only a venerable observer could offer – immediately comparing my schedule to that of the legendary and hardworking Curt Gowdy. He saw symmetry with the versatility of my career to that of another icon, Dick Enberg. Hearing him draw such parallels to a couple of broadcasting giants was stunning to say the least. But after no more than five minutes the interview was complete. He said he had all that he needed. I was left wondering if there was enough material to even write a story. I should have known better.

The next day I got an early morning call from a friend in Los Angeles excitedly telling me he had just read "the best story ever written about you." I was astonished to learn that Larry had taken our brief conversation and turned it into a nearly half page history lesson.

Back in those days his column was syndicated to dozens of papers around the country. Within a week, his story about my "groundbreaking broadcasting triple" had taken on a life that I never anticipated. It led to me making several radio and TV appearances.

Even more compelling, there was interest by several publishers to author a book about "the journey." To this day I'm certain that if it weren't for Larry's contextualizing, there never would have been an "Always By My Side."

It was a book that in many ways changed my life. Utilizing the three-event backdrop, I wrote the story of my dying father's 13-year battle with Alzheimer's and how I longed for his presence and support during this whirlwind stretch. The book became an instant New York Times bestseller.

Even more, upon seeing its galvanizing effects on the Alzheimer's community, my wife Courtney and I realized it was our "calling" to create and open an Alzheimer's research center in Houston and dedicate it to my father. The Nantz National Alzheimer Center has one of the foremost research institutes in the world. And I truly believe none of it would have been possible without Larry's story triggering the whole chain reaction. Today, I consider the NNAC to be my proudest achievement.

One other observation about Larry – he had a jaw-dropping assemblage of gifted announcers to cover who were locals, including Vin Scully, Chick Hearn, Bob Miller, and Dick Enberg, as well as countless national broadcasters. You will see in the coming pages that there were a few times when things went sideways with some of the broadcasting elite, but eventually differences were mended. Larry always seemed to have a lot of friends.

I saw firsthand a friendship develop with UCLA's all-time winningest football coach, Terry Donahue, who was my broadcast partner on college football in 1996. Larry was generous with his advice to Terry, who had no broadcasting experience. I know that meant a lot to Coach Donahue. Sadly, Terry passed away on the 4th of July 2021. Their friendship was a special one to the end.

As you will experience in this book, Larry is not only a gifted storyteller but also someone who found himself in the middle of some fascinating escapades. Larry has built and nurtured friendships with many of the biggest stars in sports. I consider it an honor to have had Larry critique and report on my career. I trust you will enjoy the many behind-the-scenes stories from a remarkable reporter.

Chapter 1: Riding Along Memory Lane

The limo was headed east on the 134 Freeway approaching the exit that would take us to the NBC Studios in Burbank, Calif. In addition to me, the passengers were Charles Barkley and Greg Hughes. Suddenly we heard a loud pop, and the limo began to sway. We soon realized a rear tire had blown.

"I've told you, Charles, you need to lose some weight," Hughes joked as the limo driver pulled off to the side of the freeway. Hughes, then the sports publicity director for Turner Broadcasting, could get away with such ribbing. He and Charles had that kind of relationship.

The year was 2002. The limo, provided by NBC, had picked the three of us up at the Beverly Hilton Hotel and was taking us to a taping of Jay Leno's "Tonight Show." Barkley, then in his second season as the colorful studio analyst on TNT's "Inside the NBA," was a scheduled guest. Barkley and Hughes were staying at the hotel, and I had driven there from the downtown Los Angeles Times Building, where I had worked since 1978.

After the tire blew, the limo driver pulled over to the shoulder of the freeway. He called NBC to request that someone come and get us. No one came. He also called the Auto Club. Again, no one came.

After we got out of the limo, I stood next to Sir Charles on the side of the freeway. People driving by were doing double takes. This was quite a looky-loo situation. I wondered what these people might be thinking.

"What in the world?" "Is that Charles Barkley?" "Who is that little guy standing next to him?" I am 5-foot-7 if I stretch. Sir Charles, of course, is huge.

This was just one of the many pinch-me moments I had during nearly 40 years as a sportswriter and editor for two Los Angeles newspapers, moments I could have never dreamed of as a shy, insecure farm boy from the tiny, economically depressed town of Strathmore in California's vast San Joaquin Valley.

Eventually, the limo driver replaced the flat tire himself and got us to NBC just in time for Barkley's appearance. Throughout, Barkley was cool and composed. If anything, he had fun with it, continually cracking jokes.

At the NBC Studios, Hughes and I joined Charles in his dressing room. Leno usually talks to his guests before they go on the air, but he only had time to stick his head in and say hello. Barkley was soon whisked away to go on the air.

The first thing Barkley said, after being introduced, was, "Jay, the limo bringing me here had a flat tire on the freeway. NBC was supposed to send another limo to get us. It never showed. Our driver, a good man, had to change the tire on the side of the freeway. What sort of operation are you running here, Jay?"

Charles was grinning and the audience was laughing.

This was second or third of at least a half-dozen times I accompanied Barkley when he came to L.A. to appear with either Leno or ABC's Jimmy Kimmel.

Such experiences came my way as a sports TV-Radio columnist for nearly 35 years. My first column appeared in the old L.A. Herald Examiner on May 4, 1973; my last official column appeared in the L.A. Times on Sept. 14, 2007.

In May of 2001, prior to Barkley's first appearance with Leno, Hughes, a brilliant publicist who in 2011 became the head of public relations for NBC Sports, came up with the idea of me doing a "ride-along."

The first one, a nine-hour adventure, was a huge success on all counts. No flat tires then. And Barkley provided me with a national exclusive by confirming that Michael Jordan was planning to return to the NBA.

Jordan had retired from the Chicago Bulls in 1998 and Rick Reilly, citing a source, had reported in Sports Illustrated that Jordan was considering playing for the Washington Wizards in 2002. Speculation was rampant after that, and it included the possibility of Barkley joining Jordan with the Wizards.

This ride-along started off with Hughes and me, in an NBC limo, going from the Beverly Hilton Hotel to LAX to pick up Barkley, who was flying in from his home in Scottsdale, Ariz. At the airport, he squeezed into the limo and greeted me. Soon his cellphone rang. "Excuse me, it's Tiger," he announced. "Hey bro, what's up?"

Barkley told Woods he would have to call him back. "I'm with a reporter from the L.A. Times," he explained. Nice to know I ranked over Tiger.

Before I could begin interviewing Charles, he had a story to tell. "I recently played golf with Tiger in Vegas," he said. "After our tee shots on one of the holes, Tiger told me they were going to build a Walmart on this site. I asked where, and he said, 'Between your ball and mine'."

When Barkley turned his attention to me, I asked, "What can you tell me about the possibility of you and Jordan returning to the NBA?" I was pleasantly surprised that he gave me a straight answer. He said it was 99.9% a done deal that Jordan was coming back and that it was true that he was planning to join him.

Then he added the four words a journalist hates: "That's off the record."

He then called Tiger back.

Later, during the taping, Leno brought up the rumors about a Jordan-Barkley comeback. "So, who called who?" Leno asked. "Did Michael call you or did you call him?"

Barkley begrudgingly admitted Jordan made the call.

Leno then went on to other topics. However, Charles had said enough to provide me with an opening. I knew I had a big story if I could get it.

The original plan was that after the one-hour 5 p.m. taping of Leno's show, we would go back to the Beverly Hilton, Barkley would check in, go work out in the hotel gym, and then call it a night. However, that post-show plan would change.

In the limo after the taping, Barkley said, "I'm not going back to the hotel and then sit on a stationary bike for an hour." He then asked our driver, "You know of a good place around here for ribs?"

The driver suggested Ribs USA in Burbank. He said he could drop us off there and return whenever we called. Barkley liked that idea. I was now thinking that chances of him joining Jordan in returning to the NBA were slim, no pun intended. And I was right. Barkley remained retired, but Jordan played two seasons with the Wizards, averaging 22.9 and 20.0 points per season.

Once we got our dinner plans squared away, I said to Charles, "I think you just confirmed on national television that Michael and you are planning to return to the NBA. The way I see it, what you told me earlier is now on the record."

Charles smiled. "Yeah, go ahead and use it," he said. "Michael is going to kill me anyway." Now I needed details, and Barkley obliged.

I learned he had gotten the call from Jordan just before Christmas in 2000. After that, Jordan came to Barkley's home in Scottsdale, where the two worked out together. They scrimmaged with Penny Hardaway and some local college players at the gym Barkley uses. After his TNT duties concluded on May 24, Barkley planned to move in with Jordan in Chicago for a month of serious training.

Barkley also told me he had lost 45 pounds since he and Jordan started training. I asked, "So how much do you weigh now?" He said he was *"down"* to 292 and his goal was 265. Barkley is 6-5½.

When we arrived at Ribs USA, it was not crowded. As we walked in, one lady asked Barkley how tall he was. "I claim to be 6-6 but I am only 6-5½," was his polite answer. A few other people noticed Barkley, but they left him alone.

"This is my kind of place, just regular people here," Barkley noted. "If Michael were here, or Tiger, word would spread and this place would be packed, with people going crazy. I don't attract the kind of crowds those two do."

I wrote two stories, which appeared in the Times on Thursday, May 10, 2001. The main story for Page One was about Barkley confirming Jordan's plan to return to the NBA. Everything else about the evening went into a secondary story, known in journalistic terms as a sidebar. It appeared on an inside page.

The Jordan-Barkley news was picked up by media outlets throughout the country, with the Times getting credit. It was particularly big news in the Washington, D.C. area. My boss, Times sports editor Bill Dwyre, and his wife Jill were visiting their daughter Amy and her family in Baltimore, located 40 miles northeast of Washington.

Dwyre called the paper the next morning and, talking to assistant sports editor Dave Morgan, said: "Every local newscast back here is leading with 'The Los Angeles Times is reporting that Charles Barkley has confirmed that he and Michael Jordan plan to play for the Wizards next season.' Who broke that story?"

It was a win-win-win situation. I got a big story, Hughes got lots of publicity for his network, and Barkley, well, he got those ribs he was craving – and he had a good time too. As I got to know him, Barkley seemed to always have a good time, no matter the circumstances. To him, even a flat tire is a fun experience.

The success of our first ride-along led to the others. We usually would start off from the hotel where Barkley was staying and, after the tapings, have dinner at someplace more upscale than a ribs place. One time it was The Ivy in Beverly Hills; another time it was Morton's Steakhouse in Burbank. Oftentimes, other people would join us. At Morton's, Ernie Johnson and Kenny Smith were there. So was my daughter Jill, who would develop a nice relationship with Barkley.

Once when Barkley was on with Kimmel, Jill was also there for the taping. She was then working for the Disney Channel and had her own contacts to get backstage. When I visited the free buffet in the green room, Barkley joked with Jill. "Look at your dad, a typical freeloading sportswriter," he said. I was within earshot. Defending myself, I said: "Jill, tell Charles that I'm not a cheapskate, that I'm a generous guy."

"My dad is generous," Jill said, "but he also likes free stuff."

I never knew what Charles would come up with next. Here is an example of what I mean. When Martha Stewart was released from prison in West Virginia in 2005 after serving five months for insider trading and was under house arrest at her home in Maine, Charles offered this: "Why would Martha Stewart have to wear an ankle bracelet? She is living in a mansion on a 150-acre estate with maids and butlers. What is she going to do, make a break for Mexico?"

For years people would ask me who was my favorite person to interview. Before C.B., it was difficult to say. Now it is easy. That person is Charles Barkley. He was always quotable – and fun.

Chapter 2: With Time on My Hands . . .

At the start of the COVID-19 pandemic in 2020, with time on my hands, I decided to resume work on a book I had started in 2012. My idea then and now was to get down on paper many of my experiences as a sports journalist interwoven with biographical material explaining how I went from a tiny central California farming community to a career far beyond anything I could have ever imagined.

I did farm work as a youth, but farming was not a lifetime goal. Instead, at a young age, I set my sights on sports writing. Through twists of fate and a concentrated focus, I ended up spending 30-plus years at the Los Angeles Times.

That run ended on July 14, 2008. It could have been just another routine day. It was eight days before my 62nd birthday. I was on the 10 Freeway on my way to work at the Times, my employer since May 23, 1978, following an 8½-year stint at the L.A. Herald Examiner, which folded in 1989.

Randy Harvey, who had succeeded Bill Dwyre as sports editor in 2006, called me on my cell.

"Where are you?" Harvey asked.

"I'm on my way in," I said.

"Good," he said. "Come and see me when you get in."

I knew why he had called. There had been a series of layoffs in recent years, and we had been given word that on this day there were going to be many more.

"Am I getting laid off?" I asked Harvey.

There was a pause before he meekly said, "Yes."

I was part of the biggest layoff in the history of the L.A. Times – some 350 people, including 14 in the sports department.

The end came quickly after I arrived at work. As requested, I went into Harvey's office in the old Times Building at First and Spring Street in downtown Los Angeles. Harvey stood by as a young man from human resources who, just doing his job, checked off a list on his clipboard as I handed him my security badge along with my Times-issued laptop and cell phone.

When the HR person told me that I would not be able to return to the building to clean out my desk, and that it must be done now, Harvey finally spoke up.

"Larry, you can return anytime you like," he said.

Then, to my astonishment, he added: "Larry, you've had a great career. In fact, I can't think of anyone in sports writing who has had a better career."

The cynic in me wondered how he could say such a thing after pegging me to be laid off. Maybe he meant it was a great career for someone with mediocre writing ability. Or maybe he was just trying to make me feel better.

But you know what? I thought about it later. It *was* a great career.

My attitude was not so upbeat immediately after we finished the bookkeeping that abruptly ended my career at the Times. I walked out of Harvey's office not sure what to think or what to do.

Although horse racing was now my main beat, I was working on a story previewing television coverage of the 2008 Summer Olympics at Beijing. Now I did not have to finish it, which was somewhat of a relief.

ESPN publicists Chris LaPlaca, Josh Krulewitz and Rob Tobias were in town for the 2008 ESPYs. As previously scheduled, I met them that afternoon for a beer at the downtown Biltmore. When I found them at a table in the hotel bar, I sat down and announced: "Guess what, guys? I just got laid off."

It was good to have people to kibitz with. They were confident that I would be fine. I was beginning to feel that way too, on Day One of my new life.

The next day, I did not stay home and mope. I played in the ESPY celebrity golf tournament at Industry Hills Golf Club east of L.A. The celebrity in our foursome was actor Bruce McGill, who has been in a million TV shows and films. His first notable role was as D-Day in the 1978 National Lampoon movie "Animal House." I was not familiar with his name, but immediately recognized his face.

When we introduced ourselves on the first tee, I said, "I'm Larry. I was a sportswriter at the L.A. Times for 30 years until yesterday. I just got laid off."

McGill said, "That may be the strangest introduction I've ever heard at one of these golf outings."

I stayed in touch with McGill and later did a freelance story on him for a golf magazine. I have occupied my time with freelance writing and charity work ever since I got laid off and began my "semi-retired" life.

I never felt depressed about losing my dream job. I figured it might hit me later, but it never did. I realized the job had been going downhill amid a constant stream of layoffs. I do not want to say getting laid off was a blessing in disguise, but neither was it the end of the world.

It led to another chapter in my life.

Chapter 3: L.A.'s Big Three:
Scully, Chick, Bob Miller

A few years after my tenure at the Times was over, I spoke at a journalism class on the Orange County satellite campus of the University of San Francisco.

One student asked, "What was the best part of your job? Did you love to write?" I said, "No, writing is work. The best part was dealing with people."

The next question, from another student, caught me off guard. "What was the worst part of your job?" I paused for a second, then said: "The answer is pretty much the same: dealing with people."

Covering sports broadcasting gave me a connection to all sports and thus a wide variety of people. Some people I liked, some I did not, and some of course fell in between. I tried to be objective. There were times I criticized people I liked and other times I praised people I did not like. But I am human, and I will admit that remaining totally objective was impossible.

I no doubt at times made the mistake of getting too close to people I wrote about. However, I was in a different position than simply being a critic who observed from afar. I was also a reporter who needed to cultivate sources to do my job. That meant socializing with sources.

I am glad I developed relationships with such people as the great L.A. trio of the Dodgers' Vin Scully, the Lakers' Chick Hearn, and the Kings' Bob Miller, plus many national sports broadcasters.

I also became close with other sports figures, such as Terry Donahue, the former UCLA football coach; Don Klosterman, the former Ram general manager who, as you will read later, was tight with the Kennedys and people of that stature; and Bill Sharman, who is in basketball's Hall of Fame as both a player and coach. Bill was one of the nicest, if not the nicest, person I have ever known.

I considered legendary UCLA basketball coach John Wooden a friend too. Late in his life, my wife Norma and I had several dinners with him and his daughter Nan. Our last meal with those two was at the Bistro Garden restaurant in Studio City when Wooden was 98 and in a wheelchair. He had to be lifted into my car when we picked them up at Coach's condo in Encino. Later in the evening, when we were

leaving the restaurant, the valet was helping Nan and me get her father into my car. I realized I was a dollar short for a sufficient tip and asked my wife for the dollar. Wooden, while hanging onto a handle above the passenger seat, motioned for us to stop. He pulled out a money clip from a pocket, peeled off a dollar bill and called Norma over to the car. The photo above shows Norma with Coach Wooden.

"Norma, this is for you," he said as he handed her the dollar bill. "A lady should never have to pay."

A true, old-school gentleman.

Wooden died on June 4, 2010, three months before his 100th birthday. Nan, who remained a close friend, died Sept. 14, 2021, at the age of 87.

During my career, I had hundreds of conversations with Scully, with one bump in the road. In 1983 I got a glimpse of another side to the *almost* always gentlemanly Vin Scully. I'll get into that more later, but that was just a blip on what was an otherwise good relationship. Scully, in my view, was the greatest sports broadcaster of all time. In May of 2020, Scully was voted L.A.'s all-time No. 1 sports icon by readers of the Times. Magic Johnson finished a distant second.

Here is what might be my favorite anecdote involving Scully.

In March of 2007, at a Paralysis Project of America fundraiser at a downtown hotel, Wooden was the honoree. I was somewhat surprised to see Scully in the VIP room. Scully rarely made public appearances.

Scully said he was there because of Wooden, whom he called a good friend. Scully then told me an amazing story.

Scully said when the Dodgers moved to L.A. in 1958, owner Walter O'Malley rented him and his wife an apartment in Brentwood. A few days after moving in, Scully walked to a grocery store and returned carrying two bags filled to the brim.

"When I reached our apartment building," Scully said, "a gentleman appeared out of nowhere and opened the gate on the wrought-iron fence. The gentleman also offered to help me with my groceries, so I handed him one of the bags. After we set the bags down in my apartment, the man, who told me he lived in the same building, asked if we were new to the area. I said we were.

"I introduced myself and explained I was an announcer for the Dodgers, who had just moved here from Brooklyn. The man said he was a baseball fan and fully aware of that. He then introduced himself, saying, 'My name is John Wooden, and I coach basketball over at the nearby university, UCLA.' That is how we met."

I called Wooden to get his version, and it was pretty much the same. It made for great fodder for my next TV-Radio column.

A Times copy editor, handling that column, called me over to his pod. "Is this for real?" he asked. I assured him it was.

I also had many conversations with Chick Hearn throughout my tenure on the sports broadcasting beat. He was a brilliant yet complex and insecure character.

A vivid memory I have of Hearn came when he worked his 3,000[th] consecutive Laker game on Jan. 19, 1998. He was honored with elaborate gifts and received two rousing standing ovations during a halftime ceremony on the court at the Forum. When it was over, I interviewed Chick as we, just he and I, walked together in the bellows of the building.

The first thing he said to me was: "Do you think they like me?"

Knowing Chick, he could have been kidding. But I think he was serious.

"Yes, Chick, I think they like you," I assured him.

On Dec. 16, 2001, Chick's consecutive game streak ended at 3,338 due to scheduled bypass surgery. His return was scheduled for March 1 but was delayed when he fell at a service station and broke a hip on Feb. 17.

Chick was hospitalized and was going to need surgery.

I went to the hospital where Chick was and talked with his wife Marge. She provided most of the details I needed for a story, including the location of the service station. I went there and found the employee who called for an ambulance and helped Chick until the paramedics arrived.

Chick was able to return to work late in the season. At a Laker game in April of 2002, while sitting with Marge, she told me she wanted her husband, then 85, to announce that the next season would be his last.

Marge and I came up with a plan in which she would get her wish and I would get a scoop. I'd come to their home in Encino to ostensibly do a routine interview, but the hidden objective was getting Chick to announce his retirement.

The day I was scheduled to go to the Hearns' house, I told Bill Dwyre that, with Marge's help, I may get Chick to announce his retirement.

"That is not going to happen," Dwyre said assuredly. "Chick will never announce he is retiring."

Dwyre knew Chick. In fact, the two were related.

"Your new boss is my cousin," Chick had informed me not long after Dwyre became sports editor of the Times in 1981. When I asked Dwyre about it, he explained the connection. To put it simply, they were distant cousins.

After I arrived at the Hearns' home, I exchanged greetings and small talk before Chick invited me to sit down on the living room couch. Marge took a seat in a nearby chair.

"Chick, have you finally realized that you are truly liked?" I asked, even though beloved would have been the appropriate word.

"Yes, the outpouring I received after I broke my hip convinced me," he said.

Eventually, I got around to asking the key question: "Chick, have you thought about announcing that next season will be your last?"

Said Chick emphatically: "No, I am not going to retire! You've been talking to Marge, haven't you?"

That was that. Our scheme had failed. Tragically, it did not matter. On Aug. 5, 2002, Chick died several days after he fell at his home in Encino, sending shockwaves throughout L.A.

A month or so later, Norma and I took Marge out to dinner. Afterward we went back to Marge's home, and she showed us exactly what happened. Chick was trying to move a large potted plant in the back yard when he fell on the side of their swimming pool and hit his head. He was taken to a Northridge hospital and had brain surgery, but doctors were unable to save him.

Chick was posthumously enshrined into basketball's Hall of Fame in 2003.

In December of 2002, my friend Harvey Hyde, a former college football coach, asked if I could get Marge and the legendary Keith Jackson to come to a Pasadena Quarterbacks Club luncheon at Brookside Golf Club, located adjacent to the Rose Bowl. The club wanted to honor Chick, posthumously, along with Jackson. The club planned to send a car to pick up Marge and another car for Keith.

I said only one car would be needed because their homes were located only about two, maybe three, miles apart – one west of the 405 Freeway in southeast Encino, the other east of the 405 in Sherman Oaks. The Hearns and the Jacksons never realized they were neighbors. Not next-door neighbors, but neighbors by L.A. standards.

Marge and Keith and his wife Turi Ann came to the luncheon in one car.

Marge was the first to speak. She opened with, "Keith, we had never met before today, but your name was often mentioned around our house."

She then pointed at me sitting at a table near the dais and cited something she had read in one of my columns.

"Keith, when Larry asked when you might retire, you said, 'Well, look at Vin Scully. He is going to go on forever. As for Chick Hearn, someone is going to have to shoot him.' So, whenever I would get upset with Chick, I would tell him, 'Keith Jackson is right, I am going to have to shoot you'."

Marge had remembered the Keith Jackson quote perfectly.

Norma and I remained close to Marge for years, and periodically got together with her until finally one time she said, "I'm sorry Larry, I'm just too old to still enjoy going out."

A year or two after that, our grandchild Theodore "Teddy" Lawrence Sanford was born on what would've been Chick's 96th birthday, Nov. 27, 2012. I called Marge to let her know. "Maybe your grandson will be a sports broadcaster," Marge said. Could be. Teddy already loves sports.

After Marge died on Jan. 31, 2016, at age 98, Norma and I attended a memorial for her at Staples Center. Stories told there also established that a good portion of Chick's wit had come from being married to Marge for nearly 64 years.

Scully, Hearn, and Bob Miller are generally recognized as the three greatest L.A. play-by-play announcers of all time.

Dick Enberg's name is often thrown in with that group because of his affiliation with the Angels, Rams, and UCLA basketball before making a name for himself nationally at NBC, and then CBS. The difference is that Scully, Hearn, and Miller spent nearly their entire careers with an L.A. team.

Enberg called the delayed UCLA basketball telecasts at KTLA Channel 5 for eight seasons, beginning in the fall of 1966, before bowing out and being replaced by a young Al Michaels in 1974. Enberg was the radio voice of the Angels and Rams for 11 seasons, from 1968 through '78. He left that position after signing a second contract with NBC, thus breaking a direct tie to L.A.

Scully worked for CBS (1975-82) and NBC (1983-89) but thanks to a deal worked out by team president Peter O'Malley, he continued to announce Dodger games as well. Scully's 67-year tenure with the Dodgers ended in 2016 when he retired at the age of 88.

As for Bob Miller, he was with the Kings for 44 years. He is in the Hockey Hall of Fame, the Kings' Hall of Fame, the Wisconsin Hall of Fame, and the Southern California Sports Broadcasters Hall of Fame.

I will have more on Miller coming up. But first an item on Enberg. I wrote about him at various times over the years, but what I remember most is what I did not write about him.

In August of 1983, after working the World Track and Field Championships in Helsinki, Enberg went to visit a friend in his hometown of Armada, Mich. NBC Sports publicist Kevin Monaghan called to tell me Dick wanted to talk to me and gave me the phone number in Michigan where he could be reached. Monaghan did not offer many details beyond the fact that Enberg was upset.

When I got a hold of Dick, he was more than upset. He was angry. He had worked the 1982 baseball playoffs and World Series with Joe Garagiola and Tony Kubek and had been promised by NBC brass that he would be the lead baseball play-by-play announcer, beginning in 1983. But in February of '83, he was informed that Scully had been hired away from CBS and had been given the top baseball announcing job. Scully would work with Garagiola. Kubek would be relegated to the B team. Enberg, with baseball out of the picture, had no idea where he fit in at NBC.

"I was blindsided," Enberg told me.

Arthur Watson, NBC Sports president, and his rough-on-the-edges lieutenant, Ken Schanzer, were the ones who negotiated the Scully deal. But it was left to executive producer Mike Weisman to inform Enberg. "I remember making the call, but not much else," Weisman told me when I asked him recently about that conversation.

Making matters worse was that Enberg and Scully had the same agent, the legendary Ed Hookstratten. Enberg remained mum for six months. But then Hookstratten was a no-show for a scheduled meeting to discuss Enberg's future with Watson in New York. Now Enberg was ready to go public with his frustration.

"We were supposed to discuss my future – and my agent was not there!" Enberg said. "I think I have no choice but to fire him."

Enberg explained that he had called Hookstratten's office and left a message about the meeting. He never heard back but assumed Hookstratten would be there. It turned out he was not. Enberg sat alone in Watson's office and futilely waited for Hookstratten to show. Eventually he got up and left. He did not feel comfortable negotiating without his agent there.

My conversation with Enberg took place on a Thursday evening. I was at the Times and had already filed my column for the next day's paper. But now I had an exclusive involving three major players in sports broadcasting – Enberg, Scully and Hookstratten. I planned to rewrite my column, but first had to call Hookstratten.

Known as "Hook," Ed Hookstratten was a noted power broker. His list of clients, besides Scully and Enberg, at various times had included Elvis Presley, Johnny Carson, Bryant Gumbel, and a bevy of big-name newscasters such as Tom Brokaw. Hookstratten, who died of heart failure at age 83 in 2014, was an old-school agent with the reputation of being a tough but brilliant negotiator.

I reached Hookstratten at home in Beverly Hills and told him what I had. "Don't write that," he barked. "Where is Dick? I have been trying to reach him."

I gave him the phone number in Michigan. Hook soon called back. "Your story is dead," he said. "I've got everything settled with Dick." I told Hook I would first have to call Enberg back. When I did, Dick had changed his tune. "Hook has done a lot of good things for me," he said. "And he has worked out a deal for me that I did not know about. He said he has been trying to reach me. Larry, please do not write what I said before."

Hookstratten, unbeknownst to Enberg, had gotten him financial compensation, believed to be $100,000, and a promise of prime assignments. Enberg became NBC's lead play-by-play announcer on the NFL, calling eight Super Bowls through 1998. He also worked the Rose Bowl, Wimbledon and French Open tennis, U.S. Open golf, the Breeders' Cup, boxing, and the Olympics.

Enberg left NBC in 2000 for CBS and was with that network through 2010.

I wrote a full-length feature story on Enberg prior to the 1993

Super Bowl between the Dallas Cowboys and Buffalo Bills at the Rose Bowl. It would be the fifth Super Bowl he would work as the play-by-play announcer.

The photo on the previous page was taken prior to the 1983 Super Bowl. Enberg, who worked that game with Merlin Olsen, signed and sent me the photo.

My 1993 story on Enberg included his salary, which then was $1.9 million. The next time I saw Enberg, he said, "That was a nice story, but I wish you would not have included my salary. I don't want my neighbors to know how much I make."

Not sure why he was concerned. He was then living in upscale Rancho Santa Fe and was probably the poorest person on his street.

Maybe around 2006 or '07, Norma and I went to the North Coast Repertory in Solana Beach to see the one-man play Enberg wrote about Al McGuire, the Marquette basketball coach turned broadcaster. Cotter Smith starred as McGuire. Enberg was there and did a Q&A session with the audience after the play.

I took the opportunity to tell a story involving McGuire and Bill Dwyre. Those two developed a close relationship when Bill was at the Milwaukee Journal. My story was about the first time I met McGuire. When I told him I worked in Sports at the L.A. Times, he said, "Your boss is my best friend in the whole world." Then, after a pause, he asked: "What is his name again?"

That, apparently, is vintage Al McGuire. A true character.

McGuire died in 2001 at age 72 after battling leukemia.

Enberg died unexpectedly from an apparent heart attack at his home in La Jolla on Dec. 21, 2017. He was 82. Dwyre, in a tribute in the Times, aptly referred to Enberg as "broadcasting royalty."

I never heard anyone say a bad word about Dick Enberg.

Bob Miller, who was with the Kings from 1973 until his retirement in 2017, became more than just someone I wrote about. Bob became a good friend and ranks up there with Bill Sharman in the nice-guy department.

In my semi-retirement, one of the things I began doing was helping charities put on celebrity golf tournaments. Miller, not a golfer, came to one in Glendora in 2012 that benefitted a La Verne-based food bank, Sowing Seeds for Life.

This was not long after the Kings won their first Stanley Cup. Miller, wearing a Stanley Cup shirt, signed autographs, rode around with tournament host Vicki Brown during play and stayed to see sportscaster-entertainer Roy Firestone perform. Firestone, who earns as much as $20,000 from corporate clients for his one-man show, did this one for free.

During the tournament's live auction, a man who was in the process of bidding on Dodger package that included meeting Scully, approached Miller and said: "I will up my bid from $2,000 to $3,000

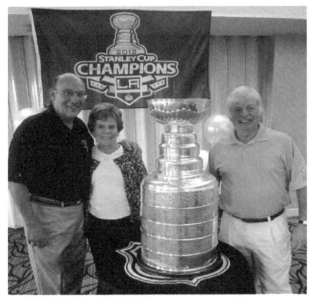

if you give me your Stanley Cup shirt." Miller was taken aback. "What would I do for a shirt?" he asked.

"I'll trade you the shirt I am wearing," the man said. Miller stood up and both men stripped off their shirts as the audience, seeing these two topless, roared with

laughter. Norma, sitting next to Bob, had the best seat.

When I called Bob the next day to say thanks, he told me his wife Judy noticed he was wearing a different shirt. When he told her what happened, he said she asked, "Well, are those your pants?" His response: "Yes, I do have my limits."

The top photo on previous page shows Norma and me with Bob after the Kings won the Stanley Cup in 2012. The other photo shows Bob after he briefly went topless at the Sowing Seeds for Life golf tournament.

When Bob was the president of the Southern California Sports Broadcasters, a position he held for six years, he recruited me in 2010 to write the SCSB newsletter. I recruited my good friend Martin Leon, a tech expert, to design it.

Those moves impacted the future of the SCSB. In 2016, when longtime UCLA radio announcer Chris Roberts was the SCSB president, Martin and I became SCSB board members.

Two years later, Martin was elevated to SCSB vice president/executive director. Martin brought the organization, founded in 1958, into the 21st century.

Chapter 4: His Mule Was Named Pearl

In November of 2011, before I was a SCSB board member, I asked Keith Jackson, often referred to as Mr. College Football, and Roy Firestone to speak at an SCSB luncheon. College football viewers often associated Jackson with the phrase "Whoa, Nellie," but I knew the real story behind it. It was *not* Keith Jackson's signature call. The line was a Firestone creation. Firestone began using it when impersonating Jackson as part of his act.

"My mule while growing up in rural Georgia was named Pearl (not Nellie)," Keith had told me years earlier.

At the luncheon, Firestone admitted he had never heard Jackson use the phrase. He said he got it from Roy Rogers' sidekick Pat Brady, who would yell "Whoa, Nelly," while bouncing along in the jeep named Nellybelle. "I thought it sounded like something Keith would say," Firestone said.

Jackson did use the phase on occasion, but only after Firestone had tagged him with it. Nevertheless, "Whoa, Nellie" will always be associated with Keith Jackson, even though he was not the first announcer to use it on the air. Dick Lane, who in the 1960s called roller derby and professional wrestling for L.A. station KTLA Channel 5, often interjected a "Whoa, Nellie" for dramatic effect.

Not long after working the 1998 Rose Bowl for ABC, Keith Jackson announced he would retire after one more season. But he changed his mind six months later and un-retired following some changes among the top brass at ABC Sports. He worked seven more years before finally retiring for good in 2006.

However, his retirement announcement in 1998 was big news. ABC scheduled a media conference call with Jackson, but I told network publicist Mark Mandel that I would prefer interviewing Keith in person at his home in Sherman Oaks. When Mandel put in my request, Keith said no, that he was tired of all the hoopla.

When Mandel told me Keith's response, I said, "Mind if I give it a shot?"

Mandel said to go ahead.

When I called Keith, I initially also got shot down. Several times.

"Can we at least send a photographer to your house?" I finally asked. When he reluctantly said yes, I asked if I could accompany the photographer. "I guess that would be all right," he said.

The photographer and I drove separately but arrived at the same time, around 11:30 a.m. After the photographer did his thing, I stuck around. As Keith and I talked, I realized I was getting an in-person interview after all.

His wife Turi Ann made us lunch and Keith opened a bottle of wine. At one point, Turi Ann asked, "Keith, why isn't the phone ringing? Did you turn it off?"

Keith said he had. This meant I had Keith all to myself, and I filled my notebook. It was close to 4:30 when I got up to leave. "Where are you going?" asked Keith as he brought out a second bottle of wine.

"I'd love to stay, but I do need to get going," I said. "And I certainly don't need any more wine. But thanks for the offer and thanks for the time."

When I was no longer with the Times, around 2010, I got a call from Keith Jackson, who invited me to play golf with him the next day at the L.A. Country Club. This was a first. He had never invited me for a round of golf when I was writing my sports TV-Radio column. I believe he would have felt uncomfortable doing that. Now there was no agenda, or an appearance of one, so no problem.

When I told Norma about the invitation, she said, "I thought we were going shopping tomorrow?" I politely explained playing golf with Keith Jackson at the exclusive LACC wins out over shopping.

That first round of golf led to others. I enjoyed playing with Keith, although our skill levels did not compare. When he was 67, he shot his age on the easier south course at the LACC. That was not the only time he would shoot his age.

After health issues put an end to golf for Keith, I visited him several times at his home. Norma and I also hosted Keith and Turi Ann, pictured here, for lunch at Spago in Beverly Hills in 2016. Not pictured, but also there, was our good friend, longtime track and field promoter Al Franken.

Keith died Jan. 12, 2018, at the age of 89. On Dec. 14, 2019, a Keith Jackson statue was unveiled at the Rose Bowl. He had dubbed the annual game there "the Granddaddy of Them All."

I'm glad we got to know each other later in life outside of our professional connection. I learned there was a very nice man under that sometimes-gruff exterior.

Chick Hearn and Keith Jackson, besides unknowingly being neighbors, were similar in that both could be crusty on the outside but were mush on the inside. I once described Chick in print that way, and he concurred. Jackson also had an undeniable soft spot, along with a penchant for generosity.

At the 1998 Rose Bowl game, featuring Washington State against Michigan, Jackson was in the broadcast booth long before the kickoff when he discovered two 50-yard line tickets in his coat pocket. Tickets were hard to come by, mainly because Washington State had not been to a Rose Bowl game in 67 years, and scalpers were getting top dollar. But Jackson chose not to sell the two tickets.

"Go downstairs and give these tickets to someone who looks deserving," he told ABC Sports publicist Maxine Lewis.

Maxine picked out two young men looking for tickets. "Here's two on the 50," she told them. "How much?" one of them asked. "Nothing, they're free," she said. "They're Keith Jackson's personal tickets and he told me to give them away."

Those two guys ended up with free tickets and an unbelievable story to tell.

I was at that 1998 Rose Bowl game to do a sidebar on ABC commentator Bob Griese, who was calling the game with Jackson. The story here was that Griese's son Brian was Michigan's starting quarterback.

Although Bob was reluctant, I was able to arrange to talk with him before the game, again at halftime, and of course after the game. I had planned to watch the game from a press box seat, but publicist Maxine Lewis arranged for me to be in the suite adjacent to the broadcast booth. One plus about that is I got to meet Bob's wife and Brian's stepmother, Shay, who became part of my story.

Bob's late wife and Brian's mother, Judy, died from breast cancer in 1988.

Before the game, I asked Bob if he had grown tired of doing interviews about himself and Brian. "Yes and no," he said. "I know it is a nice story."

That nice story became an incredible story. Michigan won and Brian was named the game's most outstanding player. In the broadcast booth after the game, I asked Bob if he was going to the locker room. "Yes, as soon as the crowd thins out a little," he said.

I volunteered to run interference, which turned out to be a difficult task. When we left the press box, the crowd had not thinned out much. As we made our way through the masses, Bob was nearly mobbed by Michigan fans.

When we got to the entrance of the Michigan locker room, I was told to go to the adjacent media interview room. My credential did not allow me in the locker room. But Bob got me inside.

I was the first to spot Brian. "There he is, Bob," I said. We both walked over to him, but I stepped back to give them some room. They hugged for about 30 seconds without speaking. When Bob pulled away, he had eye black on his cheek. Brian wiped it away with his thumb. It was an unbelievably touching moment.

Brian was then taken to the interview room. Bob and I followed and found two seats up close. When Brian was asked if he had spoken with his father, he said that he had. When asked what was said, Brian hesitated before saying, "He told me he loved me and how proud he was of me."

I nudged Bob. "You two didn't say a word," I noted.

"Words weren't needed," he said. "He knew and I knew."

That was the tagline on my story.

Chapter 5: A Blip in Scully Relationship

Dating back to my days as the Herald Examiner's sports TV-Radio columnist, I regularly attended Television Critics Association press tours held in L.A. Initially, it was a three or four-day affair held at the Century Plaza Hotel, but as cable television took off, the TCA press tours gradually increased to three weeks, twice a year. One was held in January at what is now the Langham Hotel in Pasadena and another at a westside hotel in July.

There would be daytime media sessions followed by nighttime parties. The reporters there for the full three weeks no doubt got tired of the parties, but I could pick and choose the ones I wanted to attend. It gave me an opportunity to meet and chat with many big-name television stars. Some of them welcomed talking to me because I would let them know I was a sportswriter and not there looking for a story from them. That enabled them to talk freely.

More than 200 journalists who belonged to the TCA would come to L.A. for each session and file some 40,000 stories and bank others to be used later.

During an NBC Sports media session in the summer of 1983 at the Century Plaza Hotel, on the dais was Vin Scully, his broadcast partner Joe Garagiola, and executive producer Mike Weisman. They were there to promote the upcoming baseball All-Star Game telecast.

This was Scully's first year as the lead baseball play-by-play announcer for NBC after spending eight years at CBS as a pro football and golf announcer.

When he joined CBS in 1975, it appeared his career as a Dodger announcer was over. But as I mentioned earlier, team president Peter O'Malley, recognizing the importance of Scully to his organization, asked Scully, "How about if you stayed with us and just work games when you are available?"

Scully had the same deal during his seven years at NBC Sports.

At that TCA session, Garagiola, who had switched from play by play to commentating upon Scully's arrival at NBC, was asked, "How do you like commentating as opposed to play by play?" Garagiola said all the right things, indicating he enjoyed his new position.

Then came a question for Scully: "How do you like working with a commentator?"

I do not know if the journalist who asked that question realized its significance. Scully, throughout his long career with the Dodgers, worked solo. He was taught to do it that way by his mentor, Red Barber, and always said he preferred talking directly to his audience, not to a commentator.

Scully was steadfast against a two-announcer format on Dodger broadcasts.

Years later I learned that in 1988, new Dodger announcer Don Drysdale suggested he and Ross Porter work a spring training broadcast as a two-man team. Peter O'Malley heard them, called the broadcast booth, and instructed them to go back to one-announcer format. Drysdale told me he thought Scully might have complained.

At the TCA session in 1983, when Scully was asked how he liked working with a commentator, he, like Garagiola, said all the right things while noting the advantages of having a commentator in the booth.

Scully hurried off stage when the session ended, so I was not able to talk to him then. But I did the next night at Dodger Stadium.

"What did you think of that TCA media session?" I asked.

"I'll never do another one of those," he said.

He complained about some of the questions being asked. Scully was particularly bothered by this question regarding Dodger pitcher Steve Howe's cocaine use: "If you were aware of it, would you report it on the air?" Scully's philosophy was always to only talk about what takes place between the chalk lines.

I listened to a few more of Scully's beefs before telling him there was one thing I wanted to follow up on.

"You pointed out the advantages of working with a commentator," I said. "Would you ever want to go to a two-announcer format on Dodger broadcasts?"

Scully, in answering my question, explained that he saw no need for the Dodgers to change what he called a "winning formula," but he did see a need for a two-announcer format on a national network.

"When you are talking to someone in Dubuque (Iowa), you have to supply more information than when you talk to someone who listens to the Dodgers every night," Scully told me. "Two announcers can help provide that additional information."

I thought that was a good answer. I used it in my next column, which appeared under this headline: *Scully Still Prefers Working Alone*. A more accurate headline would have read: *Scully Still Prefers Working Alone on Dodger Broadcasts but Sees Need for a Commentator When Working for NBC*.

Of course, there was not room for all that.

The next week I learned through the Times' Dodger beat writer, Richard Hoffer, that Scully was upset with my column.

The Dodgers were in San Diego, so I called the hotel where they were staying and asked for Vin Scully's room. He picked up on the first ring.

I figured the always gentlemanly Scully would calmly explain what bothered him, and that would be that. I was wrong.

"I was extremely upset by your column, and I still am," he said in harsh terms. He then proceeded to unload with both barrels.

In a nutshell, he claimed that the headline made it sound as though he could not work with anyone.

I said, "You know the writers don't write the headlines?"

"The headline writer read the column the same way I did," he said. "Your column was an insult to Ross Porter, Jerry Doggett, Joe Garagiola and everyone else I have ever worked with. I have always returned your phone calls and talked with you whenever I've seen you in person at the ballpark or elsewhere. But we have had our last conversation."

For me, this was like a break-up call from a girlfriend. I had trouble sleeping for the next few nights. It certainly was not the only time someone complained about what I wrote, but this time I had unintentionally angered an icon.

I was in the office when I made the call to Scully and told assistant sports editor Dave Moylan about it. "You should write it," Moylan said. He was close with Chicago announcer Jack Brickhouse, so never a Scully fan. But I knew better than to take on Scully in L.A. That could be career suicide. I also knew that I should not let the phone call affect whatever I would write about Scully in the future. That would be ethically wrong.

No one is perfect 100% of the time, not even Vin Scully. I had touched a nerve. During the baseball playoffs a few months later, I would learn why Scully was so upset and who was the real target of his anger.

After giving Scully and Garagiola a positive review for their work during the 1983 playoffs, I received a letter from Scully. He often sent hand-written thank-you notes. But this was not just a note.

"I appreciate the fact that you wrote what you did, particularly since we crossed swords earlier this year," Scully wrote. "You mentioned the preseason speculation about two giant egos in the same booth, a speculation for the most part made by a Boston writer whom I have never even met.

"It was this negative, almost spiteful attitude, that I found appalling, as if writers were wishing for the failure of a marriage before the vows were even taken. How very sad."

The writer he was talking about was Jack Craig of the Boston Globe. I had seen the column where Craig had written there was not enough room in one broadcast booth for the two giant egos of Scully and Garagiola. But I had not mentioned that, or anything like that, in my column. I think Scully must have read that into my words. But I was grateful that Scully had sent the letter.

Bottom line, my relationship with Scully was back on track.

Scully, as a Dodger announcer, had grown accustomed to positive press. But when he went national on CBS and NBC, Jack Craig was not the only sports TV columnist who took shots at Invincible Vince. Negative press was something he had never experienced before.

Throughout his long career, Scully was always a perfectionist. One does not become as good as he was at his craft without being driven to succeed. Perfectionists generally do not handle criticism, or perceived criticism, well.

During a casual conversation in the Dodger Stadium press box many years later, Scully told me that for the most part he was no longer granting interviews.

"We've known each other forever, so I will always talk to you," he said. "But the way I see it, the best I can hope for with any profile is to come out even.

"There might be nice things, but there will also be something that bothers me. I just turned down Esquire Magazine, who wanted to do a cover story on me."

Except for that one phone call, I have only positive memories of my long relationship with Vin Scully.

I cannot tell you how often I took people into Scully's broadcast booth at Dodger Stadium to meet him. It was usually part of a charity auction prize. Initially I would simply just go into his Dodger Stadium broadcast booth and ask if I could bring a few people in. He might grumble a bit but then warmly greet the group, pose for photos, and charm them for what seemed like five minutes.

Toward the end of Scully's career, so many people wanted to visit him in his booth, the Dodgers set up a special room right outside the press box where there was more space and easier access. I was in that special room with auction-prize winners only once. There were other people waiting their turn. After that, I felt that I had bothered him enough.

Scully did me a huge favor in 2011, coming to a charity golf tournament for the Sunland-based Tierra del Sol Foundation, which  helps people with developmental disabilities. Scully was there for an hour and a half, posing for photos and signing autographs. With us in the adjacent photo is former Dodger shortstop and manager Bill Russell, another invited celebrity guest of mine.

We had a car service bring Scully to Angeles National Golf Club in Sunland, and he offered to pay for that. But, no, we did not let him pay for the car service.

Bill Dwyre had a charity golf tournament the same day as mine. The day after Scully agreed to appear at mine, Dwyre called him to request his presence at his tournament. Scully, to his credit, stuck to his original commitment.

Dwyre sent an email saying, "You beat me to the punch."

I became involved with Tierra del Sol because our daughter Kelly, born in 1975, has Asperger's Syndrome, which falls under the autism spectrum. The older of our two daughters, Kelly was in special education classes as a youth. As an adult, with marvelous help from Tierra del Sol staff member Keri Giddens, Kelly was able to move out and live on her own. She resides in a nice apartment building in Duarte, an easy four-mile drive for her to our home.

People with Asperger's often have special skills. Kelly's is data entry. She is an extremely fast and accurate typist. Among people who have hired her are former Dodger president Bob Graziano, now an executive with JP Morgan Chase, and his wife Wendy Wachtell, president of the Joseph Drown Foundation. They hired Kelly to input contact information for some 6,000 people. They raved about the job she did, much of which was made possible thanks to the work of Tierra del Sol and selfless donors and contributors to the cause like Vin Scully was that day.

After I got Scully to come to the Tierra del Sol tournament, I got more involved in charity golf tournaments, mainly lining up celebrities and auction items. One such tournament benefits a Northridge-based charity, formerly Angels Nest and now JOBE TLP. The TLP stands for transitional living program, which involves housing, feeding, and supporting former foster care youth who are attending college.

In 2016, I recruited Laker legend James Worthy, pictured here, to be the featured guest at the organization's annual charity golf tournament, and Big Game James came through big time. He was so great the organization asked me to invite him back in 2017, and he gladly accepted.

At that post-tournament dinner, Worthy was introduced by Marquis Williams, a JOBE alum who now works with foster care youth and is the author of an autobiography titled "Beating the System: My Life in Foster Care."

In introducing Worthy, Williams talked about his life in foster care. When Worthy got to the podium, he hugged Marquis and proceeded to talk about a friend named Eddie he had in the fourth grade in Gastonia, N.C. Worthy said one day Eddie was taken away by the county and Worthy never saw him again.

As Worthy talked, the tears started to flow. "I didn't know I had this in me," he told the audience. "It was in the recesses of my mind, but it all came back to me at this moment." Eventually, someone handed him a box of tissues.

Worthy's tears were not the only ones flowing that night. Foster care isn't something that gets talked about in public spaces much, and to see a larger-than-life celebrity like James Worthy break down like that was extremely powerful.

Chapter 6: Rekindling Memories

At the start of the COVID-19 pandemic of 2020, I spent several days cleaning out overloaded closets and desk drawers. I read through clippings and email printouts and found photos I had forgotten existed.

One folder contained printouts of the more than 700 emails I received after saying farewell to the TV-radio beat in a column that appeared in print on Sept. 14, 2007.

Reading through some of those emails along with others I had saved, and skimming through old clippings, many organized in scrapbooks, made for quite a trip down memory lane. It was enough to inspire me to consider finishing my memoirs.

One thing that caught my eye was a column I did on Bryant Gumbel in 1974, when he was 26 years old and working at KNBC, the L.A. affiliate of NBC. I had Bryant's personal email address, so I scanned the column and sent it to him.

That led to a series of email exchanges that also included former Dodger general manager Fred Claire and former Dodger announcer Ross Porter.

Bryant and Ross were colleagues at KNBC in the 1970s, but they had not had any contact with each other in 45 years. I was glad to put those two together.

Around the same time, I had an email exchange with one of my all-time favorite people, CBS' Jim Nantz, who has remained a good friend. Nantz was among the people who encouraged me to revisit my book project.

Nantz often reminded me how a column I wrote in January of 2007 – the first year he would work the Super Bowl, the Final Four and the Masters – helped inspire him to write his 2008 bestseller,

"Always by My Side: The Healing Gift of a Father's Love." The book was both a tribute to his father and an autobiography.

Here is an excerpt from my 2007 column:

The Super Bowl marks the start of an amazing 63-day run that also includes the NCAA men's Final Four and the Masters. He could write a book, which he might do. When he called, he had just come from a meeting at IMG, the agency that represents him, where a book possibility was discussed.

Here is an excerpt from Nantz's book:

Larry Stewart, the well-respected columnist for the Los Angeles Times, who has followed the evolution of sports broadcasting over the past four decades, set this three-event sequence into historical context. The results of his research appeared under a big headline: NANTZ'S CBS LIFE BECOMES A SERIES OF MAJOR EVENTS.

Nantz's book at one point was ranked No. 3 on the New York Times' bestseller list, which was the highest ranking for a hardcover nonfiction sports book in 2008. To get a mention in that book was quite an honor.

I knew that after I was no longer with the Times there would be some relationships that endured and some that would not. My relationship with Nantz, which dates to 1985, is one that has endured, making him an obvious choice to write the foreword for this book.

I learned firsthand just how strong our friendship was at the start of 2017. After my wife and I spent New Year's Eve in Cambria, we drove up Highway 1 to Monterey, located near Pebble Beach where Jim and his family lived. Jim took us to breakfast at the Pebble Beach Lodge, but his hospitality did not stop there.

First there was a tour of the area in his golf cart, then a visit to his beautiful home there. We got to see the famous golf hole in his backyard, a replica of Pebble Beach's par-3 seventh hole. When we visited his wine cellar, Jim presented us with several of his best bottles of wine. He and partner Peter Deutsch, a veteran of the wine industry, produce excellent wines branded The Calling.

Jim had a special surprise for me, giving me a bottle not intended for drinking. It was his last commemorative engraved bottle that he got when he was inducted into the Pro Football Hall of Fame in 2011 as the winner of the Pete Rozelle Radio-Television Award. That bottle has a special place in my home office.

I saw Jim again in the latter part of January 2017 at the Farmers Insurance Open at Torrey Pines in La Jolla. I was there for just the Saturday round. While there, I visited my friend Don Rodriguez, the CEO of the Long Beach Boys & Girls Club, as well as chairman of the board of governors for Farmers Insurance, in his room at the Torrey Pine Lodge.

Rodriguez's room overlooked the 18th green and was near the CBS booth where Nantz and commentator Nick Faldo were stationed.

While Rodriguez and I were standing on the room's balcony, I sent Jim a text. He texted back that he could see us. "Impressive!" he wrote. He also invited us up to the CBS booth.

I used the text from Nantz to get us past security. We walked into the booth during a commercial break and Jim got up to greet us. He then went over to a woman wearing headphones. She was sitting in front of us. Nantz tapped her on the shoulder and said, "Larry Stewart is right behind you." The woman was LeslieAnne Wade, former head of publicity for CBS Sports who was then Faldo's longtime manager and live-in girlfriend.

LeslieAnne, a demonstrative type, turned around, took off her headphones and came over to give me a big hug and plant kisses all over my face. We had not seen each other in maybe 15 years. I had enjoyed some great and memorable times with LeslieAnne and her longtime sidekick, CBS publicist Robin Brendle. As I was getting kissed, Rodriguez noticed Faldo mouthing, "What the . . .?"

I think Faldo was more perplexed than angry. He gladly posed for a photo with us and Nantz. Besides getting a photo, we also had a story to tell.

This photo shows me and my friend Don
Rodriguez, right, with Nick Faldo and
Jim Nantz in the CBS booth at the 2017
Farmers Open at Torrey Pines. At right is
an photo of me with two of my favorite
network publicists, LeslieAnne Wade,
left, and Robin Brendle. Those two
worked together at CBS for many years.

Chapter 7: My Dealings with Cosell

In the previous chapter, I made note of being mentioned in Jim Nantz's book. I got more than a mention in Howard Cosell's 1985 autobiography, "I Never Played the Game." Cosell devoted almost two pages to his version of how I got a national exclusive in 1984 that he was quitting ABC's "Monday Night Football."

That led to me making it into several other books, including "Monday Night Mayhem," by Marc Gunther and Bill Carter, and a 477-page Cosell biography by Mark Ribowsky, published in 2012. "Monday Night Mayhem," published in 1988, was turned into a made-for-TV movie, which aired on TNT in 2002.

A key scene in the movie is when Cosell, played by actor John Turturro, gets a phone call he thinks is from ABC Sports president Roone Arledge. His wife Emmy, played by Patti LuPone, shakes her head. "It is a reporter from the Los Angeles Times," she says. Cosell asks, "Stewart?" Emmy nods to indicate it is. Cosell says, "All right."

Emmy hands the phone to Howard, who says: "Yeah, Larry, what's up? You hear I am not going back to 'Monday Night Football.' Where did you hear that?" There is a pause. "Well, I suppose I should confirm that," Howard says.

That is nowhere close to an accurate account of the phone call. Not completely the fault of the screenwriter; Cosell, Mr. Tell It Like It Is, also fudged with the facts in his book.

Cosell wrote he did not know how I obtained his home phone number. I did not have his number. Cosell returned my call after I called his office and left a message with his assistant. But I guess he could not admit that he would return a call from a lowly print reporter.

Here is what Cosell wrote in his book: "Stewart's story broke the next day – and all hell broke loose. Without knowing it, I had given him a scoop. My company had yet to make an official announcement about my departure from 'Monday Night Football.' How Stewart got his information is beyond me. Maybe he was just fishing."

I was not fishing – or bluffing, as Ribowsky claimed in his book – but following up on what Howard told me over cocktails prior to the start of the 1984 Los Angeles Olympics. Cosell had advised me to call his office a week after the Olympics because he might have a decision by then. I called his office two days in a row and left messages with his assistant. He called back the second day.

My first interaction with Howard Cosell was a phone interview in 1973, about three months after I began writing the "Sports on TV" column for the Herald Examiner. Cosell was in L.A. to appear as a guest on NBC's "Dean Martin Show," the precursor to the highly successful "Dean Martin Celebrity Roast." NBC publicist Bud Tenerani set up the interview.

I called Cosell at his hotel, and he was civil. During the interview, one thing he talked about was his interest in politics. He told me, in all seriousness, that he planned to run as a New York Democrat for the U.S. Senate in 1974 against Republican James Buckley, the older brother of William F. Buckley.

My column ran on Aug. 9, 1973. The headline read: *Will Cosell Be Our Next President?* The headline, which I wrote, was intentionally facetious. Usually, at newspapers, copy editors write the headlines. At the Herald, partially because of a skimpy desk staff, writers often wrote the headline on their own column or story.

Cosell was never going to be our next president. To refresh your memory, after Richard Nixon resigned on Aug. 9, 1974, he was replaced by Gerald Ford.

My first in-person dealing with Cosell was on Dec. 10, 1973. There was a luncheon that day at the Hollywood Palladium featuring Cosell, Frank Gifford, and Don Meredith prior to the Rams playing the New York Giants at the Coliseum on ABC's "Monday Night Football." I attended the luncheon with Herald Examiner colleague and friend Barbra Zuanich, now Barbra Zuanich Friedman. Barbra covered entertainment television for the Herald.

At a pre-lunch VIP reception, the two of us approached Cosell. He was civil. I believe he took a shine to Barbra. It appeared obvious to me that he was flirting with her.

During our conversation, Howard told us he was not feeling well. "I felt so bad yesterday that I went to the UCLA Medical Center," he said. "I'm still sick."

"That's awful," Barbra said, "Are you going to be able to go on the air tonight?"

"No, I'm just going to let those other guys handle it," Cosell deadpanned.

My immediate thought was there was still time to call the paper and get a short story in the afternoon edition.

"Are you serious?" I asked Howard.

Howard's mood flipped on a dime, as he went from civil to indignant.

"Are you an immature little baby?" he shot back. "Don't you understand, young man, I am 'Monday Night Football.' Without me, there is no show. Who would do the intro? Who would provide any reportage beyond the game itself? Who would provide the humanization of the players? Who would do the halftime highlights with the drama that I provide? . . . "

Barbra and I stood there dumbfounded as he continued to rail on about how important he was. He finally paused and said, "I remember the column you wrote about me. It was terrible and grossly inaccurate."

His bellowing voice drew a crowd. He then pulled out a tattered letter from his coat pocket. It was from a college professor who supported him in his attack on what he liked to call the bought-and-paid-for print media.

He shoved the letter into my face and told me to read it so the people around us could hear. I glanced at the letter and handed it back to him.

"I'm not going to get into a verbal confrontation with you, Howard," I said, more than a bit rattled. I was only 26 years old.

I turned and started walking away when he said, "Come back here young man, I'm not done with you yet."

Stupidly, I walked back, giving him an opportunity to blast away.

"You have to get out of that corrupt business you are in," Cosell said.

This was not fatherly advice; it was venom. And it was now showtime for Cosell.

I cannot recall his entire onslaught, but it was not pleasant. Fortunately, he eventually wandered off, presumably looking for someone else to harass.

ABC Sports publicity director Irv Brodsky, who had heard about my encounter, called me at the Herald Examiner later in the day to apologize for Howard's behavior. I am sure Brodsky was well-versed in apologizing for Howard.

That evening in the Coliseum press box, Larry Merchant, then a nationally known sports columnist for the New York Post, found me and introduced himself. I recognized the name, even though this was five years before Merchant left sports writing to embark on his long career as a boxing commentator for HBO.

"I understand you got a brow-beating from Cosell today," Merchant said. "Don't feel bad. He finds a young sportswriter in every town to attack. You just happened to be his target today."

A year or two later, I saw Cosell again at an ABC function in a private home in Westwood that had a pool table. After I re-introduced myself, he surprisingly invited me to play a game of eight-ball. But once an audience converged around us, I never got a shot. Cosell wanted to show off his skills with a pool cue and did not want anything, or anyone, to interfere with that.

In 1976, during an ABC press junket in Montreal a month prior to the Summer Olympic Games there, Brodsky, who was on the junket, invited me to sit with him and Howard and his wife Emmy for a drink.

Howard at first was semi-civil, but then he started in on sports TV critics and became visibly angry. I interrupted him to point out that he had a great job that paid well and made him famous. "Can't you just enjoy all that?" I asked.

That had no impact on his tirade.

Brodsky later told me that Howard must have a network of people letting him know whenever something bad is written about him.

"When we were in Munich for the '72 Olympics," Brodsky said, "I was asleep in my hotel room when Howard called and screamed about something in the Des Moines Register that day. Anytime there is something negative written about him, Howard somehow knows about it."

This was long before the internet made articles easy to find.

A couple of days before the start of the 1984 Summer Olympics in Los Angeles, I was at the Universal Hilton, the ABC hotel. I had gone there hoping to stumble on a story. I certainly did that – and more. I hit the jackpot.

While walking through the hotel lobby, I ran into my esteemed colleague and friend Jim Murray, the Times' Pulitzer Prize winning sports columnist, and Brodsky, the ABC publicist.

"Irv and I were just at dinner with Cosell," said Murray, one of the few journalists Cosell liked. "We talked about your column. I told Howard that you wrote that he would be missed if he quit 'Monday Night Football.' He liked that."

The column Murray was referring to was balanced. I had pointed out the good and bad about Cosell, who was undecided about returning to "Monday Night Football" for a 15th season that fall. But since Murray had led Cosell to believe the column was all positive, I thought Cosell might talk to me.

I asked Murray where he was.

"I think he was headed toward the hotel bar," Murray said.

Of course.

Murray helped me find Howard, who was sitting at a little bar table with several of his ABC colleagues.

"Howard, look who I found, Larry Stewart," Murray said.

Murray said he had to get going, but Howard invited me to sit down in the empty chair next to him and told me to order a drink. That was around 9 p.m. Since my family, like a lot of Southern Californians, had left town to avoid the Olympic traffic congestion that never materialized, I stuck around sipping on gin and tonics until closing time, which was approximately 1:30 a.m.

During that 4½-hour span, with Howard holding court and enjoying his vodkas on the rocks with a twist of lemon, the group at the table was constantly changing. But Mike Pearl, the executive producer of ABC Sports, stayed for the duration, and Mike Eruzione hung around for most of the night. Eruzione, captain of the gold-medal winning U.S. Olympic hockey team at the 1980 Winter

Olympics, had been hired by ABC to work the L.A. Summer Games in an unspecified role as a broadcaster.

When we were told it was closing time, Howard was the first to get up and leave. When the bill arrived, Pearl grabbed it and I saw him say something to the waitress. I offered to contribute, but Pearl said, "Don't worry about it. I told the waitress to put it on Howard's room. Howard always gives his room number to waitresses and invites them to come up after closing. But they never do."

Maybe that was just a joke. Not sure.

At one point during that evening, after more drinks and time to allow Howard to get more comfortable with my presence, I asked him about rumors that he was going to retire from "Monday Night Football."

He initially told me no decision had been made and offered no other details.

After softening him up by feeding into his ego, he told me he was taking the week after the Olympics off but planned at some point to talk with ABC Chairman Leonard Goldenson. He said there might be a decision by Monday, Aug. 20.

"Can I call you to see what you have decided?" I asked.

"I don't know if I'll take your call," he said, "but you wouldn't be doing your job if you didn't try." When I asked for his number, he said to call his office at ABC in New York.

On Aug. 20, as planned, I called Cosell's office and his assistant said Howard was at his summer home in Westhampton, N.Y., and would not be in.

The next day, after a source within ABC Sports told me Howard had decided to quit "Monday Night Football," I tried his office number again. This time I was more persistent and told his assistant that it was imperative that I get ahold of Howard. I also told her that he was expecting my call and gave her my home phone number.

She said if he called in, she would give him my message and phone number.

It was morning in L.A. I waited patiently for a call until finally deciding to go for my daily run. I didn't get very far before coming to my senses and returning home. Less than 10 minutes later, the phone rang. When I picked up, the first thing I heard, in Cosell's distinct voice, was: "How are you and Mike Eruzione getting along these days?"

During the Olympics, I had been critical of Eruzione's role. ABC had him doing offbeat, light features from such places as Rodeo Drive in Beverly Hills and I complained in print that this Olympic hero was ill-suited for such assignments.

Cosell obviously remembered our night together with Eruzione and liked what I wrote. He often complained about what he called *jockocracy* – the networks hiring sports commentators based solely on their marquee value. I ignored his Eruzione reference and said, "Howard, I understand you have decided to retire from 'Monday Night Football'?"

I was not fishing. It was a legitimate question.

Cosell's answer was: "It's the end of a chapter."

He then went on to provide me with the details I needed for a full story. "I'm not retiring from ABC," he said. "I'll work what I want to work. I got it down to what I wanted." Cosell was 64.

Cosell had met with Goldenson, ABC president Fred Pierce, and ABC broadcast group president Tony Thomopulous the previous Thursday. Conspicuously absent from that meeting was Roone Arledge, the president of ABC Sports.

After I was done talking with Cosell, I immediately called the office. Bill Dwyre was not there, so I told assistant sports editor Dave Moylan what I had. "Do you think it is exclusive?" Moylan asked.

"I am pretty sure it is," I said.

I then headed for the office to write my story. It got a banner headline in large type that read: *It's Official: Cosell Is Staying Home on Monday Nights.*

I did not know the true impact that story had until a year later when a copy of Cosell's book arrived in my mailbox at work. I scanned through it to Page 165, where I learned that my story caused "all hell to break loose" at ABC.

Howard's version of how I got the story confirmed that I had a true scoop. After reading it, I made a beeline into Dwyre's office to show him. He read through it, looked up and said, "Way to go."

Chapter 8: And Then There's Chet Forte

My last contact with Cosell was in May of 1990. I called him when I was in New York working on an in-depth story on Chet Forte, the former award-winning director of "Monday Night Football" whose life had been turned upside down by a gambling addiction.

This story was easy to pitch to sports editor Bill Dwyre, whose strong ethics platform included a stand against sports gambling. That meant, under Dwyre's direction, the sports section had no betting odds or horse racing handicaps.

Dwyre had to give a little after the Herald Examiner folded on Nov. 2, 1989. Upper management wanted to attract Herald readers who bought that paper for its horse racing coverage, so the Times began carrying a handicap, a consensus and full race charts. But Dwyre stuck with his edict about no sports betting odds.

I told Dwyre that to do the Forte story properly, I should go to New York.

In 1990, the Times had unlimited budgets and tons of space for stories. Classified ads alone were bringing in close to a billion dollars a year.

Dwyre gave me a week to work on it. I flew to New York, on a Monday and returned to L.A. on a Friday, flying out of Philadelphia.

The week was capped off when I was able to interview Chet after a court appearance in Camden, N.J., located across the Delaware River from Philly.

After that interview I knew I had the makings of a great story. And I would get the space to tell it.

During my week in the East, I got to see what it is like to be an investigative reporter. I poured over court documents. I did a ton of interviews, some in person, some on the phone. I befriended Forte's public defender. The prosecutor in the case faxed me information but declined to be interviewed. But I went to his office anyway. I waited for more than an hour before the prosecutor invited me into his office. He ended up offering a few off-the-record nuggets. One was that Forte had lost $210,000 in one night at an Atlantic City casino.

I talked with a lot of people who knew and/or worked with Forte, dating back to when Forte was an All-American basketball player at Columbia. He used to say he led the nation in scoring in 1957, but his scoring average of 28.9 ranked him third, behind University of Seattle's Elgin Baylor (29.7) and Kansas' Wilt Chamberlain (29.6). Good company there, though.

I called Cosell at his office in hopes of setting up an interview. Cosell had been Forte's best man when he got married in Las Vegas. When Cosell answered my call, I immediately knew an in-person interview was not going to happen.

"Why are you calling me?" he bellowed. "I'm in an important meeting." He then told the person he was meeting with, "This is a reporter from the Los Angeles Times." Cosell loves to name drop.

I explained the reason for my call.

"Why would I care about Chet Forte?" Cosell asked. "Yeah, he got himself in some trouble, but what does that have to do with me?"

I said, "Weren't you his best man when he got married?"

"Yeah, but I just happened to be in Vegas at the time," Howard said, showing a total lack of compassion.

But he did calm down enough to give me a usable quote: "Everybody at ABC knew he was a compulsive gambler. But there was nothing anybody could do to get him to stop."

A key for me that week was taking Forte's public defender, Lawrence Lustberg, out to lunch at a deli in downtown Newark, N.J. Judging from his dingy second-story office, Lustberg probably did not get many lunch invitations. We hit it off, and he told me if I showed up for a court appearance in Camden, he would let Forte talk to me if he was willing. The court appearance, according to Lustberg, would be brief and would take place first thing on the upcoming Friday morning. I figured it was worth a shot, even though it meant finding a way to Camden, which is located near Philadelphia.

I had recently gotten to know Vince Wladika, who then worked for a PR firm that had NFL Films for a client. Wladika volunteered to pick me up at my New York hotel at 5:30 a.m. and drive me to Camden. The plan was that we would go from the courthouse to NFL Films headquarters in Mount Laurel, N.J., located near Camden, for a tour and lunch with NFL Films President Steve Sabol.

Everything clicked. Wladika, who later became a PR executive for NBC Sports and then head of PR for Fox Sports, got me to Camden on time. We were waiting on the courthouse steps when Forte, accompanied by Lustberg, emerged.

Forte came over to me and we shook hands.

"Larry, I'm willing to talk to you because I am desperate for a job," he said. "I'm hoping that talking to you might help me get a job."

One thing I wanted to know was, in his words, how he ended up $1.5 million in debt.

"Most gamblers might make two or three bets a day," he said. "But when you are a wacko like me, you make 10 bets a day."

He said he was betting $10,000 a day, but others told me it was more like $30,000-$40,000 a day. When I asked him about dropping $210,000 in one night, he was taken aback. "How did you know that?" he said. "Actually, there were two of us that lost that much."

My story, which got great play in a Sunday paper on May 20, 1990, may have indeed helped get Chet a job.

He was facing fraud and income tax charges that could have landed him in prison for 11 years. But a little over a year later, a judge thought he had suffered enough and let him off with five years' probation, 400 hours of community service and an order to pay $39,000 in back federal taxes.

The job Forte got was on the other side of the country for him – at San Diego-based sports talk station XTRA (690), where he was paired with Steve Hartman. Billing themselves as "The Loose Cannons," their show became a hit.

But in 1996, only five years after getting another shot at life, Chet Forte died of a heart attack. He was only 60 years old.

Chapter 9: To Be Frank About It

Yes, Howard Cosell was a jerk. Frank Gifford was the opposite.

The "Monday Night Football" announcing team of Gifford, Cosell and Don Meredith seemed to be together for decades. But Cosell's tenure was only 14 seasons and Meredith's 11. Meredith missed three seasons, 1974-76, when he went to NBC hoping to become both a football commentator and a dramatic actor.

Gifford, meanwhile, was on MNF for 27 seasons – 15 doing play by play and, beginning in 1986, 12 doing commentating alongside Al Michaels.

I had a special kinship with Gifford because of our San Joaquin Valley roots. He graduated from Bakersfield High in 1949, and Bakersfield is roughly 60 miles south of my hometown. I lived with my parents and an older brother among orange and olive trees on a 20-acre farm west of Lindsay through the fifth grade. In the summer of 1957, we moved to a 20-acre piece of property east of the one stoplight community of Strathmore, which I consider my hometown. Lindsay is four miles north of Strathmore and the "big city" of Porterville is six miles south of Strathmore. Access to that area in Tulare County is via Highway 65.

I first saw Gifford when he came to the annual Lindsay Orange Blossom Festival in 1956, when I was 9. The other celebrity guest that year was Lucille Ball.

I always wondered how little Lindsay could attract such big names. I once asked Gifford about that.

"I don't know about Lucy, but I had an offseason job serving as a spokesman for a fertilizer company that paid me to make appearances," Gifford said. "The fertilizer company set up my appearance in Lindsay. Back in those days, professional athletes needed offseason jobs to supplement our incomes."

Cosell often publicly criticized Gifford. What would he have done had he known Frank was a spokesman for a fertilizer company? I can only imagine.

Gifford always returned my calls, no matter the reason I was calling. I think it helped that I was familiar with all the little Valley towns where Frank lived as a youngster, places such as Taft, Shafter, Avenal, Coalinga and super tiny Alpaugh.

The first time I interviewed Gifford he told me that prior to entering junior high school he and his family, which included a brother and a sister, moved 43 times. In a later interview, he said it was 47 times. Whatever, it was a lot.

He said his family was continually moving because his father worked in the oil fields and went wherever there was work.

"I don't remember ever completing a single grade in the same grammar school," Gifford told me. "I hated school and never tried to make any friends because I knew we would soon be moving. I spent the first day of school in Avenal, then we moved to Coalinga. We were there for one week."

Gifford spent his junior high years in Hermosa Beach, when his father worked in the San Pedro shipyards. Then it was back to Bakersfield, but the constant moving stopped. His mother saw to that, even though it meant at times young Frank had to live with relatives. As a freshman at Bakersfield High, he went out for the lightweight football team and got cut. As a sophomore, he was a third-string end on the lightweight team.

He still hated school, and his grades showed it.

"I even failed woodshop," Frank told me.

Gifford grew between his sophomore and junior year, and Bakersfield's varsity coach, Homer Beaty, spotted raw talent. Gifford became a reclamation project.

Beaty planted the idea that Frank might be able to get a football scholarship. He never gave college a thought until then. But first he had to get his grades up.

He had to attend Bakersfield Junior College for one semester but went on from there to become an All-American at USC and a Hall of Famer with the New York Giants prior to his 27 years on "Monday Night Football."

After a column I did on Gifford in 1993, I got a hand-written note from him on engraved personal stationery. It read:
Enjoyed visiting with you the other day and I also enjoyed reading the article you wrote!

I sat with Frank at the wake for our mutual friend Don Klosterman at the Bel-Air Country Club in June of 2000. Frank reminisced about his youth in the Valley as another man at our table, a friend of Frank's, listened.

"When was your life better, back then or now?" the man asked.

Frank had to think about it. "One thing for sure, I have a lot more money now," he finally said.

I always believed that he was uncomfortable in the limelight. And the limelight was not always kind to Frank.

Gifford died on Aug. 9, 2015, at age 84.

As for Don Meredith, my first contact with him was a phone interview in early 1974 after he left "Monday Night Football" and signed with NBC. Meredith's agent, Ed Hookstratten, set up the interview.

Meredith's grandiose plans of being a commentator and actor did not quite work out, so he returned to the MNF booth in 1977. ABC let his contract expire after the 1984 season, the first without Cosell. With no Cosell there, Meredith's schtick did not work. I wrote: *Meredith without Cosell was like Laurel without Hardy or Abbott without Costello.*

Meredith brought personality to the booth, offsetting Cosell's lack of it. What made it work was Cosell not knowing how to react when Meredith would say something like, "Howard, you are just a plethora of insignificant information." Cosell's nonresponses made it funny. And made Meredith popular with viewers.

I did an interview over lunch with Meredith in 1977 in Chicago, when I was still at the Herald Examiner and on a trip with the Rams for a Monday night game. The Rams and the ABC crew were staying at the same hotel, and we met at the restaurant on the top floor. He was pleasant enough, but I had the feeling he was there because he felt he had to be.

Around 1990, I tried to get ahold of Meredith at his home in Santa Fe, N.M. I got his home number from Don Ohlmeyer, who told me, "If his wife answers and asks where you got the number, don't tell her. She is sensitive about that."

Sure enough, Meredith's third wife, Susan, answered the phone and asked where I got the number. When I froze, she told me to never call there again, and then hung up. I bring this up because of what happened in 1994, when I was on vacation with my family and we stopped in Santa Fe to spend time with my uncle, Harry Alexander. To fully see Santa Fe, we took a bus tour of the city.

While slowly going through a residential section, our tour guide said: "We are about to pass the home of Don Meredith, the famous football player and announcer. We need to be as quiet as possible because Mrs. Meredith always calls to complain when we go by their house." When the tour ended, I told the guide, a nice middle-aged woman, about what happened to me when I called the house. "That doesn't surprise me," she said.

I heard that Meredith had become a recluse, and it was apparently true.

Meredith died Dec. 5, 2010, after suffering a brain hemorrhage. He was 72.

Chapter 10: Jordan and Other 'Legends'

In August of 1987, I spent a day with Michael Jordan at the La Costa Resort in northern San Diego County when he served as the guest host of the nationally syndicated show "Greatest Sports Legends." Jordan, over a two-week period, taped nine of that season's 10 shows at La Costa. The other one was done at Walter Payton's home in Chicago, with CBS' Jayne Kennedy hosting.

My day with Jordan started off with breakfast. He was late and Berl Rotfield, the creator and executive producer of "Greatest Sports Legends," was nervous. "He's got a full day of work ahead of him; he should be here," Rotfeld complained.

Jordan arrived about 15 minutes late. "It's about time," Rotfeld said as Jordan joined the two of us with a big smile and a firm handshake for me. He was three seasons into his NBA career and at this point was still friendly with the media. "How can I be mad at someone who smiles like that?" Rotfeld said.

Jordan had been picked third by the Bulls in the 1984 NBA draft behind Hakeem Olajuwon (Houston Rockets) and Sam Bowie (Portland Trail Blazers). Charles Barkley (Philadelphia 76ers) was the fifth pick in that draft.

In the 1986-87 season, Jordan led the league in scoring during the regular season with a 37.1 points per game average, but the Bulls were swept by the Boston Celtics in the first round of the playoffs. Meanwhile, Magic Johnson was named league MVP, NBA Finals MVP, and the Lakers defeated the Celtics, 4 games to 2, to claim their fourth title of the 1980s.

There had been rumors that Jordan was frustrated in Chicago and might join Magic on the Lakers. That was the key question I had for Jordan. But I chose to hold off asking about that right away, giving Jordan time to feel comfortable talking with me. I knew there would be down time during his interview sessions with that day's guest, former New York Jets wide receiver Don Maynard.

An advantage print reporters have over broadcasters is that we can ease into the most important questions.

Over breakfast, I started off with simple questions such as this one: "Michael, what was your first impression of Chicago?"

"I hated it," he said. "It was freezing my very first night in Chicago and the heater in my hotel room wasn't working. I asked myself, 'What am I doing in this place?' I was so homesick that night I cried."

Later, during a midmorning break, I sauntered over to Jordan and said, "Michael, I'm sure you are aware of the talk about you coming to the Lakers and teaming up with Magic. Do you see that ever happening?"

"Nope, never going to happen," he said. "The Bulls are my team, the Lakers are Magic's team, and that is how it is going to stay. I'm not going to a team where I would be second fiddle."

We did not talk long. I could tell he was in a hurry to get back to work. That was because he had a standing tee time of 1 p.m. to play the La Costa golf course, site for years of the PGA Tournament of Champions.

One day when he missed his tee time, he complained to segment director Matt Gibson. That prompted Gibson to bravely say, "Mike, are you here to film these shows, or are you here to play golf?" Gibson knew what was coming. "I'm here to play golf," Jordan said.

Many years later, while writing this book, I contacted Gibson, who told me Jordan was kidding and that he actually did a good job.

Besides Gibson, another young member of the "Greatest Sports Legends" crew was Mike Tollin, the executive producer of "The Last Dance," the 10-part ESPN/ABC documentary series on Jordan and the Bulls that aired during the 2020 pandemic. Tollin's first job after graduating from Stanford in 1977 was as a segment producer and writer for "Greatest Sports Legends." Tollin later would become a good friend.

Berl Rotfeld, from the Philadelphia suburb of Penn Valley, was a songwriter – and, among other things, a huge sports fan – when he created "Greatest Sports Legends." The idea came to him after a bar argument in 1971 over who was better, Jim Brown or O.J. Simpson?

Beginning in 1972, 10 new episodes per year were nestled among 42 reruns, mostly on ABC stations. Production stopped in 1993 after more than 200 shows, but old episodes continued to be shown on ESPN Classic and elsewhere.

I first got to know Rotfeld in 1973 when I did a phone interview with Paul Hornung, the show's first host. Rotfeld used an array of celebrity hosts to give the show more media exposure. Subsequent hosts included Reggie Jackson, Tom Seaver, Steve Garvey, and CBS' Jayne Kennedy.

For the first three years, the shows were taped in a six-room apartment on the third floor above an Italian restaurant in Bala Cynwyd, Pa., owned by Rotfeld's second wife Carole. For one year, the site was a casino in Atlantic City before Rotfeld made a deal, beginning in 1976, to film the shows at La Costa, about an hour and a half drive south from L.A.

From 1988 until the end of its 20-plus-year run in '93, the site for the "Greatest Sports Legends" tapings was the Dana Point Resort in Southern Orange County, which meant a shorter drive for me.

Berl would call me each year prior to the 10-day "Greatest Sports Legends" taping sessions to give me his lineup of guests. It was always an impressive one. I would pick the tapings that I wanted to attend.

In 1983, I had one of my most memorable interviews ever when Hall of Fame quarterback Johnny Unitas was the "Greatest Sports Legend" guest.

I was to have dinner with Unitas the night before the taping at La Costa. I left L.A. early to beat the traffic. After arriving, I had time to kill so I went to the hotel bar. The place was empty except for a man at the other side of the horseshoe-shaped bar. A post partially blocked my view. When I told the bartender why I was there, he pointed toward the man and said, "That's Johnny Unitas sitting over there."

With my notebook in hand, I went over and introduced myself. Unitas invited me to take a seat. For the next hour, Unitas talked in detail about how CBS did not prepare him to be a game commentator. "I kept hearing, 'Johnny U, you're doing great,' and then I'd usually get a pat on the back," Unitas told me.

Unitas said at midseason he was called by CBS Sports president Barry Frank and told to come to New York for a meeting. At that meeting, Frank told him, "You're butchering the King's English." Frank then arranged for Unitas to meet weekly with a special tutor in Philadelphia.

"For nine straight weeks, I made the trip from my home in Baltimore to Philadelphia for those tutoring sessions," Unitas said. "I still got fired."

I believe my ensuing column delivered a message to the networks: Do not hire a big name and hang him out to dry. Soon the networks began having training sessions and rehearsals for new commentators before putting them on the air.

Also, that column was plagiarized. A columnist for the Baltimore Sun, a sister paper of the Times, picked up my column off the Times wire service, put his name on it and used it almost word for word. I was stunned. Since Unitas lived in Baltimore, he certainly would see the Sun column, or at least hear about it.

I showed Bill Dwyre the two columns, mine and the one in the Sun. Dwyre in turn mailed printouts of both columns to the sports editor of the Sun. I never heard anything about it after that. Usually, punishment for plagiarizing is a suspension. In cases of repeat offenses, it can mean termination.

I interviewed Hall of Fame running back Jim Brown by phone in 1975 when, as a CBS commentator, he was scheduled to work with

Vin Scully and George Allen on a Rams game against the Green Bay Packers in Milwaukee. It was a surprisingly pleasant conversation.

In 1988, I interviewed Brown again at the "Greatest Sports Legends" taping in Dana Point. Brown, for years, declined to appear on "Greatest Sports Legends," even though he was No. 1 on Rotfeld's list of desired guests.

Reggie Jackson, who was the show's host in 1988, was the impetus in getting Brown to change his mind and do the show. Brown always complained about the pay. The appearance fee was $500 before going up to $1,000.

The above photo shows me with Reggie Jackson, left, and Jim Brown in 1988 at Dana Point.

After arriving in a limo from his home in the Hollywood Hills, Brown told me the reason he was there was because of Reggie. Brown added it was not just that he and Reggie were friends, he also thought Jackson would listen to what he had to say and ask the right follow-up questions.

Reggie was initially the host of "Greatest Sports Legends" in 1977. But after one season, Rotfeld fired him. Rotfeld complained to a Philadelphia writer how Reggie had been arrogant, unreasonable, demanding – and worse. The quotes got national attention.

Rotfeld hired Reggie back in 1988, and he did three seasons.

I asked Reggie about the earlier breakup and was surprised by his answer.

"I was a brash, immature, self-centered 29-year-old," he told me in front of Rotfeld and Brown. "I was full of piss and vinegar. All I cared about was driving around in my Rolls and eating big, thick steaks." He then made a slurping sound.

I got to know Reggie fairly well during the tapings at Dana Point. He could be charming, particularly if he thought what I wrote could do him some good.

One time a girlfriend had just broken off a relationship and Reggie, who was married from 1968-73, talked in detail about maybe giving marriage another chance. I think he might have wanted to convey his regrets to the ex-girlfriend, or maybe he was just emotionally down and was venting. Whatever, it made for an interesting column.

When Harmon Killebrew was the featured "Legends" guest at Dana Point, part of the show was to be filmed at a nearby high school baseball diamond. As most of the crew was piling into a van headed for the high school, Reggie asked me why I was not getting in the van with everyone else. I explained I was driving over to the high school and then going home from there.

"Could you use some company?" Reggie asked.

"Sure," I said. Reggie got into my car, a 1985 Buick Somerset with a stick shift, and immediately asked how I liked my car.

"This is the second worst car I have ever owned," I said.

"You had a car worse than this?"

"Yeah, a 1960 Falcon Ranchero," I explained.

He then made a pitch to sell me a car. He told me that at one time he had owned five car dealerships but was now down to three.

I asked if the two dealerships he unloaded were losing money.

"No, all five dealerships were making money," Reggie said. "But there were too many problems, too many headaches."

He then added a statement that I have since often quoted to other people:

"There is such a thing as too much money."

Steve Carlton, the Philadelphia Phillies pitcher, was infamous for never granting interviews to all media members except Tim McCarver, his former batterymate. But in 1989 at Dana Point, when Carlton was the featured "Legends" guest, I interviewed him.

Prior to the taping of the Carlton segment, Rotfeld and I discussed how we should handle me getting an interview. Rotfeld suggested that I just casually start talking to him. "If I try and set up an interview, he is going to say no," Rotfeld reasoned.

Rotfeld's plan worked. I believe I got the interview because Carlton earlier saw how Reggie Jackson and I got along. When I casually approached Carlton, he was cordial.

Among the questions I asked Carlton was why he agreed to be on the show. He thought about his answer before saying, "I guess I wanted to make up for those years of silence, to show the fans I care about them and appreciated their support."

The last time I saw Berl Rotfeld was in the mid-90s when he was in L.A. on business. He invited me to have lunch at the five-star Bel-Air Hotel, a hidden gem nestled off the beaten path in wooded hills. I never knew it even existed.

Berl said to come straight to his room, which was located on the first floor. As I walked through the beautiful grounds, I noticed there was no one in sight. It was like the place was abandoned. When I got to his room, Berl suggested we eat lunch on the poolside patio just outside his room. There was still no one around.

Soon after we ordered lunch, I noticed a well-dressed man approaching. "Hey, Berl, Robert Redford is headed our way," I said.

Berl turned around to look, then jumped up to go get his wife Carole, who was napping inside the room. As Redford walked by, he nodded and said hello. But he was gone by the time Berl and Carole came out of their room.

An actor I met through Berl Rotfeld years earlier was Dick Van Patten, best known for his role as the father on the sitcom "Eight Is Enough." Dick and his wife Pat attended one of the "Greatest Sports Legends" tapings at La Costa and we all had dinner together.

After that, I would always have pleasant conversations with Van Patten when I would see him at the Santa Anita racetrack in Arcadia. He was there *every* race day. One time in early 2004, I saw him, and he looked terrible. I asked what was wrong.

He said he had a diabetic stroke and was in the hospital at Cedar Sinai for seven days. "My goodness," I said. "When did you get out of the hospital?"

"This morning," he said.

"And you came straight here from the hospital?" I asked.

He did. I knew he loved the sport of horse racing, loved being at the track, and loved handicapping. But checking out of a hospital after a seven-day stay and coming straight to the track put him in a class by himself.

Van Patten continued to be a Santa Anita regular up until his death on June 23, 2015, at age 86.

Mel Brooks was often at Santa Anita with Van Patten. According to Van Patten, Brooks became depressed after his wife Anne Bancroft died in 2005.

"I told Mel, come to the racetrack, it is good therapy," Van Patten told me.

After I began covering horse racing for the Times in 2007, sports editor Randy Harvey suggested I do a feature story on Brooks. When I approached Brooks and asked about doing an interview, Brooks turned me down cold. He was downright rude about it.

After Mike Wallace died on April 7, 2012, "60 Minutes" did a tribute that included a significant segment on Wallace's friendship with Brooks. When I saw Brooks at the track a few days later, I told him I enjoyed the segment.

Said Brooks, sarcastically: "Wow, like no one else has mentioned that."

He turned and walked away. A simple thank you would have been nice.

Early on, I became close with Berl Rotfeld's son Steve, who worked on the "Greatest Sports Legends" show before branching out and creating his own production company in 1985.

Steve produced such shows as "Bob Uecker's Wacky World of Sports" and its spinoff, the "Bob Uecker Sports Show," as well as the "Lighter Side of Sports," which ran in syndication and on ESPN for two decades. He also produced shows for the Golf Channel, including the "Haney Project," and "Donald Trump's Fabulous World of Golf," which ran for two years, 2012 and 2013.

Steve Rotfield eventually got out of the sports business and now does educational and informational programming.

It was through Steve that I got to know Bob Uecker. I can attest he is the same guy off camera as the one in the Miller Lite commercials or the dozens of guest appearances with Johnny Carson. The longtime Milwaukee Brewers announcer made a career out of making fun of himself as a player during seven seasons in the majors, mainly with the Milwaukee Braves and St. Louis Cardinals.

It was always fun to be around him. I spent the good part of a day and evening with him in 1987 when he was taping the "Bob Uecker Sports Show" at a bar in the Pacific Beach area of San Diego. I drove down to La Costa and from there rode in a motorhome with a small group that included Uecker, Steve Rotfeld, and Johnny Bench.

Bench, a scheduled guest, had an interesting experience after arriving at the filming site. A 23-year-old woman from El Cajon approached him and wanted the Cincinnati Reds Hall of Fame catcher to sign the thick scrapbook she had been keeping on him since she was a catcher on her fifth-grade softball team. She said all her friends called her Johnny Bench. The real Johnny Bench was taken aback.

From 1985-90, Uecker, who was also an actor, appeared on the ABC sitcom "Mr. Belvedere" as sports columnist George Owens.

When I told Uecker my daughters liked the show, he arranged for me to bring them to a taping. And after the taping, he invited us to have dinner with the cast.

Uecker also invited me to a "Mr. Belvedere" taping at a softball field in West L.A. featuring some 10 Hall of Famers. Among them were Hank Aaron, Willie Mays, Johnny Bench, Ernie Banks, Hamon Killebrew and Reggie Jackson. I took our daughter Jill along with me. I believe she was 8 at the time. I suggested she get Mays' autograph during the lunch break. He shooed her away and made her cry. A nasty ABC publicist who yelled at Jill did not help matters.

A few years later, in 1990, I was assigned to interview Mays, who came into the Times office to talk about a global youth baseball event at UCLA in which 200 youngsters, ages 9-14, from 23 countries would be participating.

I believe Mays was being paid to promote the event, so he was nicer on this day. After I introduced him around the office, I told him about the first major league game I attended. I went with my mother and her friend Louise Stoltenberg to see the Dodgers and Giants in 1961 in Candlestick Park. I reminded him that he hit a two-run homer off Stan Williams in the seventh inning of a 4-3 Giant victory. He had only a vague memory of that game.

I saw Mays again when my wife Norma and I went to the 2004 Baseball Hall of Fame inductions in Cooperstown, N.Y. We noticed Mays, one of 50-some Hall of Famers there that weekend, attracted the longest lines and got the highest prices for signed memorabilia.

We went to Cooperstown while on a driving vacation through New England and upstate New York. We first visited our son-in-law's father and stepmother, Dick and Laurie Sanford, who live in a rural area of the Catskills. The area's historic weekly newspaper, the Catskill Mountain News, had been owned and run by the Sanford family since 1904. It was sold in 2018 and folded two years later.

From the Sanfords' home in the hamlet of Bloomville, N.Y., it was about an hour's drive to Cooperstown. Once there, we got VIP treatment. That was mainly because I was among the 20 people who voted on the Ford C. Frick Award that goes to a baseball broadcaster.

Our first day in Cooperstown, we went to the Otesaga Hotel to attend a late-afternoon outdoor cocktail party. That is where the Hall of Famers stay, and I noticed several of them as we walked through the lobby. At one point I whispered to Norma, "There's Ernie Banks." He heard me, turned around and engaged us in conversation for several minutes. He was living up to his fan-favorite reputation.

Then I spotted Dodger great Duke Snider, my first sports idol, getting on an elevator. As he held the elevator door open, I reminded Snider that we met in 1992. That is when he served as the Dodger commentator for ill-fated SportsChannel Los Angeles, a pay channel

that folded later that year.

With Snider still holding the elevator door open, I asked Norma to take the photo shown here. I am not much of a memorabilia collector, and I always believed getting autographs was unprofessional. But in my home office, atop a bookcase and next to the wine bottle from Jim Nantz, is an area dedicated to Duke Snider. It consists of an autographed ball he gave me, unsolicited, in '92, a Duke Snider bobblehead, and two photos of me with Duke. One was taken in '92; the other is the one taken by Norma in 2004.

While at the outdoor cocktail party at the Otesaga Hotel, I left briefly to go find a restroom. On my way back, I spotted George Brett and his wife off by themselves having drinks at an outdoor table. I had met George through baseball agent Dennis Gilbert, and was close with George's brother Ken, an Angel announcer who had died 10 months earlier, in 2005, after a six-year battle with brain cancer. When I stopped to say hello, George warmly greeted me, introduced his wife Leslie, and invited Norma and me to join them.

Having drinks with George Brett was cool, and it was doubly cool when George picked up the tab.

The next day, we attended several special sessions at the Hall of Fame Museum. One featured Lou Brock, and we met him and his wife Jackie. Norma and Jackie hit it off because they both worked in special education. Norma, in midlife, went back to school to become a special education teacher. She worked in the Arcadia Unified School District for 20 years, mostly at Camino Grove Elementary School, a half-mile from our house. Norma retired in 2011.

The highlight of any Baseball Hall of Fame induction weekend comes Saturday night. The Hall of Famers have dinner together at the Otesaga Hotel, then make the short trip to the museum for cocktails and dessert where they mingle with invited guests. Norma and I were among the invited guests in 2004.

A personal highlight for me was running into my old friend Bob Uecker (shown here). Uecker was the Ford C. Frick Award winner the previous year and was back in Cooperstown in 2004 because the Brewers' Paul Molitor was one of the inductees. Dennis Eckersley was the other.

Uecker and I hugged as if we were lifelong friends.

Chapter 11: Late Night Show Tapings

Besides my visits with Charles Barkley, I was often invited to the NBC Studios in Burbank whenever a prominent sports figure was a guest of Johnny Carson or, later, Jay Leno.

In all the times I was at NBC, I only saw Carson once, in a hallway. He had his head down as he walked past me, avoiding eye contact. It was known he never interacted with his guests off camera. It was said he was totally comfortable behind a camera in front of a television audience of 20 million and totally uncomfortable in a room in front of 20 people.

In 1976, when I was assistant sports editor of the Herald Examiner, Norma and I were at a swank dinner at the Beverly Hills Hotel put on by the Women's Tennis Association (WTA) and its major sponsor, Virginia Slims cigarettes. The entertainment was Carson and Bill Cosby. I asked Hollywood publicist Charlie Pomerantz if he could introduce us and the couple we were with to Johnny. Pomerantz shook his head, saying: "No, Johnny is not receptive to that."

The previous year, the WTA dinner was at the Beverly Wilshire, with Joan Rivers and Jonathan Winters supplying the entertainment. Before dinner was served, I walked past a table of nine women's tennis stars, including Chris Evert. There was an empty chair at the table and one of the stars who I did not recognize invited me to sit with them. "We need a man at our table," the tennis player said. I was flattered but explained my wife might not approve. When the group was later introduced individually, I learned the player was 19-year-old Martina Navratilova.

Leno was the opposite of Carson. I always saw Leno when I was at NBC, usually in a dressing room. One time I was alone in Barkley's dressing room talking on the phone with my wife when I felt someone grab me by the neck from behind. I looked up. It was Leno, just having fun.

My visits to "The Tonight Show" during the Carson and Leno years provided me with good writing material as well as fond memories.

In 1984, after Jeff Blatnick pulled off one of the biggest upsets at the Olympic Games in L.A. by winning a gold medal in Greco-Roman wrestling, he was a guest when Carson was still the host. This was particularly memorable because of a remote hookup with the high school gym in Blatnick's hometown of Niskayuna, N.Y., located not far from Albany. It seemed the whole town was there to surprise its local hero. Blatnick was still in tears when I interviewed him in his "Tonight Show" dressing room.

Sadly, Blatnick died in 2012 from complications following heart surgery.

When 1985 World Series MVP Bret Saberhagen of the Kansas City Royals was on with Carson, I got more than just an interview for a Page One feature story. I also got a fun night out on the town and developed a friendship with Bret's father Bob, who more than anyone was responsible for me taking up golf.

Saberhagen's agent was Dennis Gilbert, whom I first met in 1969 when I was a news and sports reporter for the Visalia Times-Delta and Dennis was a centerfielder for the minor league Visalia Mets.

After the taping of the show, Gilbert invited me to go to dinner with Bret and Bob Saberhagen, plus a few of Gilbert's other baseball clients. After dinner, we went to the Hollywood Tropicana to watch mud wrestling. It was a popular fad at the time, and there was a line to get in. I boldly went up to the bouncer and told him I was with the Times and was doing a feature story on World Series MVP Bret Saberhagen. That got all nine of us in right away – free of charge.

Bob Saberhagen, who rode with me that night, asked if I played golf. I explained I had given up the game after a couple of bad attempts on difficult courses. Bob suggested we play an executive course in Van Nuys. That is where I bought my first set of clubs. Bob and I played together a lot, even after he and his second wife Judith moved from the San Fernando Valley to Pine Mountain, located 23 miles west of Frazier Park off the 5 Freeway.

I would stop there on trips to Visalia, and Norma and I spent several weekends as guests of Bob and Judith. I lost contact with Bob not long after Judith suffered a fatal heart attack in 1994. In doing research for this book, I learned that Bob, Pine Mountain's postmaster, died in May of 2015 at the age of 71.

In 1993, when Barry Bonds was a Leno guest, I was there. So was Dennis Gilbert, who was also Bonds' agent. After that taping, as planned, Bonds, Gilbert and I went to the Beverly Hills home of Jeff and Gayle Rosenthal for a fundraiser for Pete Wilson, then the governor of California. During the cocktail hour, a photographer took the photo shown here. Yes, that is a slimmed down Barry Bonds. Pete Wilson is on the other side of me.

After the photo was taken, I introduced myself to the governor, simply saying, "I'm Larry Stewart." As we began to talk, I realized I had the governor of the state one on one.

For the next 25 minutes, from 7 to 7:25 – I clocked it – I questioned Governor Wilson about every topic I could think of, from teacher salaries to farm subsidies and water allotments. It was not actually an interview because I was not going to write anything, so there was no need to identify myself as a reporter.

Eventually Gilbert came over and blew my cover, telling Governor Wilson, "I see you have met Larry Stewart from the L.A. Times." The governor pulled away and appeared surprised. "Larry, you didn't tell me you wrote for the Times," he said.

I explained I was a sportswriter, not a political writer. After that, we were friends for the rest of the night. He even singled me out when he spoke in front of the small gathering later in the evening. While complaining about the Times' coverage, the Republican governor pointed at me and said, "But I'm not talking about L.A. Times sportswriter Larry Stewart, who is here with us tonight."

I later met Wilson's wife Gayle, who told me that the man sitting next to her on her flight down to L.A. that day asked to borrow her copy of the San Francisco Chronicle and then complained there was no Sports section. "I told him I had already read the sports section before I got on the plane, so I didn't bring it," Gayle Wilson said. "Sports is always the first section I read."

A few days after the U.S. national women's soccer team won the 1999 World Cup in dramatic fashion, defeating China, 5-4, on penalty kicks at the Rose Bowl, goalie Briana Scurry was on with Leno. Chinese officials had complained that she had illegally stepped forward on one of her penalty-kick saves, and she had taken some heat from the U.S. media as well. In an interview that took place in her "Tonight Show" dressing room, she told me: "It is up to the discretion of the referee. There was no warning, I was never told I was off my line. But I understand China's disappointment. They came within a hair of winning."

Another memorable visit among the dozens I made to the "Tonight Show" was in September of 2006 when former St. Louis Ram and Pittsburgh Steeler running back Jerome "The Bus" Bettis was Jay Leno's guest. He had retired after helping the Steelers beat the Seattle Seahawks, 21-10, in the 2006 Super Bowl and had recently been hired by NBC as a studio analyst for "Sunday Night Football." He had that job for only two seasons.

While with Bettis at NBC, I was impressed by how cheerfully he interacted with everyone. After the taping, inside the NBC complex, he had fun with four or five youngsters who were on an elevated concrete platform, looking down at Bettis as he walked by. They all called out and one of them handed him four football cards to sign.

"I'm only signing one of these," Bettis growled menacingly. "Pick one." He then laughed. "Just kidding," he said, breaking out in a smile. "Give me everything you've got, and that goes for all of you."

One time when I was with Barkley in 2007, Beyonce was the other guest. She had just appeared on the cover of Sports Illustrated. I thought it would be cool if she would pose for a photo with Barkley.

I went into her dressing room, which was packed with her entourage. After finding the right person to talk to, I asked about getting a photo with Beyonce and Barkley. The man I was talking to snickered and said that Beyonce had a pressing engagement and would not have time to pose for a photo for the L.A. Times.

After the taping, I was in the hallway when Beyonce's entourage began leaving, followed by Beyonce. She walked right past me, then suddenly stopped.

"I don't like this dress," she called out to no one in particular. "I've got to go back and change."

She spent about 20 minutes in her dressing room before heading out to that "pressing engagement."

Chapter 12: Navigating the Course

For most of my 30-plus-year tenure at the Times, sports broadcasting was my beat. My weekly TV-Radio column appeared in Sports on Fridays, generally on Page 3. I also usually worked three or four nights a week on the night sports desk as a copy editor and rewrite person. If there was a breaking story not handled by a beat writer, I was often the person who wrote it.

Working the desk, watching sports on TV, listening to sports talk radio, gathering material for my column, and writing news stories about sports broadcasting meant I rarely had a full day off. But I am not complaining. A lot of what I was doing was more fun than work.

In 2000, I got off the desk and became a full-time writer.

That freed me from having a defined work schedule and admittedly I started slacking off. In mid-2003, Dwyre called me into his office for a stern pep talk.

I was aware I might be in trouble after Randy Harvey, then the senior assistant sports editor, called me one day on my cell and asked, "Where are you? Are you on the golf course?" He guessed correctly.

When I met with Dwyre, he said one of the editors under him wanted to take my column away from me and have me instead be the regular writer for the well-established daily Morning Briefing column that appeared for decades on Page 2 of Sports. I knew the editor he was referring to was Randy Harvey.

But Dwyre backed me. "You've got good sources. Bear down and break a few stories and you will keep the column," he said. "But you are still going to have to write the Morning Briefing."

"You mean every day and still cover the TV beat?" I asked.

"That's right," Dwyre said, which meant a heavy workload for me.

In order not to lose the TV-Radio column, I immediately went to work, calling my best sources. One of them told me that ABC was going to have Al Michaels, in addition to working on "Monday Night Football," also be the network's lead play-by-play announcer on the NBA. This was the type of breaking news I was seeking.

But I still needed confirmation, either on or off the record, from Michaels. When I called Al, I told him my situation and said I could use his help.

"I'm sorry, Larry, I can't help you," Michaels said. That was okay, but then he added: "Sometimes change is a good thing."

No, Al, losing my column was not going to be a good thing.

Despite Michaels' unwillingness to help, the scoop was enough to end the threat by Randy Harvey to take away my column, at least for the time being.

I was now writing seven Morning Briefing columns a week, my TV-Radio column and any breaking stories involving sports broadcasting.

I was busting my butt, and it did not go unnoticed by Dwyre. He sent me glowing praise in an email, which was nice. But he also sent it to everyone in the department. For weeks after that, I could feel the resentment from other staffers.

Dwyre soon found a way for me to lighten my workload. For three weeks, I would do Morning Briefing and the TV-Radio column. On the fourth week, I would only do the column. Now, everything was perfect. I still had my column, plus additional exposure via Morning Briefing.

I had a wonderful stretch until Harvey, after a two-year stint as sports editor of the Baltimore Sun, returned to the Times in 2006 to replace Dwyre, who decided to step down as sports editor and become a full-time columnist.

I feared Harvey would take away my TV-Radio column and just have me do the Morning Briefing. But he threw me a curve and said he wanted colleague Mike Penner to do Morning Briefing and have me cover broadcasting full time.

That was a surprise, but nothing like the surprise that came a year later.

In April of 2007, Penner, after taking some time off, wrote a personal column that I believe set a record for number of online hits, at least a record for Sports. In the column he explained that he was a transexual and would now be known as Christine Daniels. The headline read: "Old Mike, New Christine."

The night before the column appeared in print, everyone in Sports was alerted. I was out at the Derby restaurant in Arcadia with executives from HRTV, a horse racing network, when I got two separate calls on my cell phone.

It was stunning news to all of us in Sports. Mike, a terrific writer, was well liked and well respected. He often wrote my column when I was on vacation, and we had worked together on stories. We never had any kind of disagreement.

About a year earlier, in 2006, Mike and his wife Lisa Dillman, also a well-liked and well-respected Times sportswriter, came to our house and we took them out to dinner. I recall being envious of their lives. Lisa covered tennis for the Times and Mike often traveled with her to places such as Paris, Melbourne, and New York.

I would have never guessed there was any sort of turmoil in their seemingly perfect lives. I later heard Mike and Lisa were separated, and that alone was surprising. Then came a bigger surprise.

The first time I saw Christine was in the crosswalk leading to the Times building. She said, "Hi Larry, how are you?"

For a second, I wondered who this tall woman was. Mike was 6-foot-1, not particularly tall for a man but quite tall for a woman. "It's me," she said while offering a hug. Mike and I had never hugged.

Christine returned to being a male in 2008 and tragically committed suicide a year later. A terrible situation all the way around.

Although I continued writing my TV-Radio column, Harvey took the guts out of it. First, he told me not to write about sports talk radio. I told him I got more reaction from that than anything else.

Harvey did not care. Later, he told me not to put any opinions in my column. "Just write about the events coming up over the weekend," he said. I called that "rewriting the TV log." I also called it boring.

In the summer of 2007, Harvey asked if I might consider taking on another beat. He wanted me to cover horse racing. "When they are running at Santa Anita, you'd have an easy commute," Harvey said. He knew I lived in Arcadia, site of the legendary racetrack.

I was hesitant about changing beats. I told Harvey that if I continued covering sports broadcasting until the following April, it would mark 35 years since my first sports media column.

"You could cover horse racing and still do your TV-Radio column," Harvey said. "You don't have to be at the track every day."

That sounded okay to me.

I started on the horse racing beat on opening day of the Del Mar summer meeting. The date was July 11, 2007.

However, two months later, Harvey made the inevitable decision. He decided Christine Daniels would write a column called Sound and Vision that would replace my TV-Radio column. He said I would cover horse racing full time.

I said goodbye to the broadcasting beat on Sept. 14, 2007, with two columns, with one of them only for the Times website. In the website-only column, I wrote, tongue in cheek, that I was not changing genders, I was changing beats. I checked with Christine to see if she was okay with that line, and she was.

The layout for my print-edition column was tremendous. The headline read: *His Time on the Beat Fades to Black.* Inset in the column were the top parts of two of my old Herald Examiner columns, including the mug shot, and a short story I wrote for the Times in May of 1979 about this crazy idea of launching a 24-hour sports channel later that year to be called the Entertainment and Sports Programming Network, or ESPN for short.

A mounted and framed copy of the print column, with 15 signatures dotting the white border, arrived in the mail the next week.

It came from the ESPN PR department, and ever since has been hanging in a special spot in my home office.

When Harvey took away my column, he gave me some hogwash about upper management's desire to put more emphasis on horse racing. It turned out the opposite was true. My new beat was a key reason I was laid off a year later. I had been put out to pasture.

Not only was I laid off on July 14, 2008, so was Bob Mieszerski, the Times' horse racing handicapper. He was later asked to return by upper management but declined the offer. I had hired Bob as a prep writer in 1976 when I was the assistant sports editor of the Herald Examiner. He later became a horse racing handicapper and came to the Times when the Herald folded on Nov. 2, 1989.

Chapter 13: Developing Sources

Establishing relationships, something that is important in most businesses, is very important to journalists. We are collectors of information, and we need sources who know us and trust us enough so that they are willing to help, even when there is no direct benefit involved.

Here is an example of what I mean.

During the CBS-televised 1987 NBA Finals between the Lakers and Boston Celtics, I got a tip that CBS was courting Marv Albert to replace Dick Stockton as its lead NBA play-by-play announcer. But I needed confirmation and details.

I called Marv at his home and although he did not say, "Yes, and it counts," which was one of his signature calls, he did supply me with enough information for an attention-grabbing column after I agreed not to quote him directly.

He told me he had met with CBS Sports president Neal Pilson over breakfast, but the meeting was simply exploratory in nature. There was no offer.

Albert was immensely popular in New York, where he had been announcing Knicks games since 1967, so CBS' interest was understandable. Albert emphasized that the impression he got was that CBS was not unhappy with Stockton.

My ensuing column got plenty of reaction. Stockton, a natural worrier, was among those who called, and I had to figuratively talk him down off a ledge.

Stockton remained at CBS and called the NBA Finals through 1990. After that, NBC held the NBA rights through 2002. Stockton left CBS for Fox in 1994, the year that network began televising NFL games.

I liked Stockton and was also very fond of his wife at the time, former Boston sportswriter turned broadcaster Lesley Visser. They divorced in 2010.

Stockton's broadcast partner during the NBA Finals from 1984 through '87 was Celtic cheerleader Tommy Heinsohn, likely the most hated broadcaster ever among L.A. viewers. Fortunately, he was gone from CBS after the '87 Finals.

Earlier during the 1987 playoffs, in a column on Heinsohn, I noted he was an accomplished artistic painter and added: *There are plenty of people in Southern California, and elsewhere as well, who would like to see Heinsohn paint himself into a corner and never come out.*

As for Marv Albert, I always viewed him as an easy-going nice guy. He never put on any airs, and I always enjoyed his company at various media functions.

I knew his marriage was in trouble after calling his house in the mid-1990s and his wife sternly informing me he did not live there anymore. But still, I was stunned when the news broke in 1997 of his involvement in a sex scandal.

He was fired by NBC but brought back to announce NBA games two years later and at the same time worked out a deal with TNT. NBC lost the NBA package to ABC in 2002, but Marv continued calling games for TNT, reestablishing himself as one of the best, if not the best, basketball play-by-play announcer of all time. He retired in 2021 after calling the NBA Eastern Conference finals, ending a broadcasting career that began in 1963.

Marv Albert's willingness to help me in 1987 contrasts Al Michaels' refusal to help me in 2003. But I think overall I had a decent relationship with Michaels, despite some ups and downs.

I immediately liked him after we first met in 1974. That was when Bob Speck, the sports director at KTLA Channel 5, hired Michaels to replace Dick Enberg on the tape-delayed UCLA basketball telecasts.

Born in Brooklyn, Al moved with his family – and the Dodgers – to Los Angeles in 1958. He graduated from Hamilton High in 1962. When we first met, he was living in the Bay Area and was an announcer for the San Francisco Giants. He moved back to L.A. after being hired by ABC.

Al has a wonderful family. Over the years I got to know his wife Linda, son Steve, daughter Jennifer, and brother David. Our daughter Jill worked for Steve Michaels for a brief period. Steve was producing the documentary sports series, "Beyond the Glory," which aired from 2001 to '06.

My role in Jill getting that job was minimal. I had a face-to-face meeting with Steve in early 2001 and he asked about my family. When I mentioned that my younger daughter was a recent UCLA grad and interested in a career in broadcasting, he said, "Have her give me a call. Maybe I can help her."

Steve more than helped her. He ended up hiring Jill as a production assistant. I knew this could create an appearance of a conflict of interest, so I told Dwyre about it. "Okay," he said. "Just don't write about any episodes that she works on."

Jill soon moved on to the Disney Channel, where she worked in children's programming. When she was the network executive for the popular Disney series "Phineas and Ferb," a trade publication in 2011 put her on a list of the 40 top TV executives in the country under the age of 40. Jill later held executive positions at Nickelodeon and Netflix and now is an independent producer and consultant in family programming. Yeah, I am a proud dad. And a proud grandpa. She is now Jill Sanford and, as I mentioned earlier, she and husband Courtney have a son, Theodore "Teddy" Lawrence Sanford. Note the familiarity of that Lawrence name. Since I never had a son Jill wanted to carry on the family legacy in that small way.

But back to Al Michaels. Our relationship hit a rough patch in 1990. Dennis Swanson, a tough former Marine officer who in 1986 took over from Roone Arledge as the president of ABC Sports, apparently sought to take Michaels down a notch or two when he suspended Michaels for an unspecified amount of time in February of 1990. Al did not miss any assignments because none were scheduled during his suspension, which I believe was two weeks. There may have been a dock in pay, but I was never made aware of that.

It was all over a seemingly minor offense. Michaels' then 15-year-old daughter, a sophomore in high school, had worked the 1990 U.S. Figure Skating Championships in Salt Lake City as a runner, a job that paid $50 a day. Swanson cited a company policy against nepotism as the reason for the suspension. I tracked down the son of an ABC cameraman who told me that, from his experience, the nepotism policy did not apply to runners.

There obviously was a problem between the head of ABC Sports and its star announcer. Media attention was warranted. I called the Michaels' home to get his side of things, but his wife Linda said he was not available.

After my subsequent story ran on March 15, a Thursday, Al's agent, Art Kaminsky, called me that day to inform me Al was upset, particularly since I had used his daughter's name. Kaminsky told me Al may never talk to me again.

Several months later, Norma and I were out to dinner with Olympic filmmaker Bud Greenspan and his partner Nancy Beffa at Morton's in Beverly Hills. When we sat down, I noticed Al and Linda were at the next table with Al's best friend, Alex Wallau and his wife Martha. Wallau, among other things, was ABC's boxing commentator at the time. In 2000, he became the president of ABC.

When I went over to say hello to Alex, Al never looked up, so I quietly returned to my table.

The feud with Al, if it could be called that, ended maybe a year or two later. A mutual friend, Terry Jastrow, former ABC golf producer and later the president of Jack Nicklaus Productions, invited me to play golf with him and Al at the Bel-Air Country Club, and from my vantage point all was good after that.

One time when I was Al's guest at Bel-Air – I believe it was 2005 – our foursome included Grant Tinker, the producer and TV executive who was married to Mary Tyler Moore from 1962 to 1981, and James Dolan, the notorious owner of the New York Knicks.

Al had me ride with Dolan, whom he introduced simply as Jim. Midway through the round Dolan mentioned his father was billionaire and Cablevision founder Chuck Dolan. Now I knew my cart mate was the guy always getting blasted in the New York Post.

There was a frightening moment that day for me when I almost killed Grant Tinker. After I duffed my drive into the rough on the left side of the fourth fairway, Tinker, driving the other cart, had gone ahead at least 75 yards. He and Michaels were on the right side of the fairway, so I aimed my shot down the left side. I hit it clean, right into a tree trunk, and the ball ricocheted hard across the fairway on the fly and hit the other cart inches below where Tinker was sitting.

I hollered out an apology. "My fault, Larry," Tinker hollered back. "I shouldn't have been up this far."

After the round, I was surprised when Dolan, out of the blue, asked me why I was wearing a DirecTV cap. "DirecTV is our competitor," he said sternly.

"Sorry," I said. "I just grabbed a cap off the shelf in my closet."

The last time I saw Al Michaels was in June 2017 at a Los Angeles Sports and Entertainment Commission "All-Access" fundraising event at the L.A. Coliseum. Kathy Schloessman, the classy LASEC president, had invited me.

"Your name just came up earlier today," Michaels said when he saw me. "Alex Wallau was asking me about you."

I am sure the topic was not that night at Morton's when I got snubbed.

I often heard complaints about Michaels' ego. But a reasonable amount of ego can serve as a driving force to succeed. And there is no argument about Michaels' success as a play-by-play announcer.

Bob Costas was another nationally known broadcaster whom I viewed as having a fair-sized ego. I never had a dust-up with Costas, but I did have an interesting encounter with him in the early 2000s.

Costas called out of the blue and said, "Larry, I'm coming to L.A. and staying at the Beverly Wilshire. Can you meet me for dinner tomorrow night?"

I of course said yes and envisioned a pleasant dinner in the hotel's main upscale dining room. But Costas told me to meet him in the hotel coffee shop. That should have been a hint of what was to come.

Costas, who was waiting for me when I arrived, offered a friendly greeting. But after we ordered, the conversation took a different tone as he proceeded to recite every negative thing that I had ever written about him. I was blown away. I had no memory of about half of what he mentioned. And I have a good memory, as this book can attest.

"How can you remember all that?" I asked.

"I don't want you to think I am obsessed; it is just that I have a very good memory," he said.

"I know I also wrote positive things about you too," I said.

"Yeah, I remember those too," he said as he proceeded to rattle them off.

Costas then said, "I just want to make sure you don't have anything personal against me."

"Of course not," I said.

I then stroked him a little about being brilliant, which he had just confirmed by displaying his photographic memory. If he were a local sports anchor who read my column religiously, I could have understood him remembering all the negative mentions. But he was a national announcer who lived in New York.

I do not think I crossed paths with Costas again until 2016, when he was interviewed by Roy Firestone at a West Coast Sports Association dinner at the Biltmore Hotel. He greeted me and my wife warmly and posed for a photo with us. He also showed off that memory of his by asking in detail about our daughter Jill, whom I think he met only once. But he knew she went to UCLA and was interested in getting into broadcasting.

"How does he know so much about Jill?" my wife asked.

"Photographic memory," I said.

I often saw Costas during Television Critics Association media tours. The 1989 TCA summer tour was held at what was then the Ritz-Carlton Hotel in Pasadena. It became the Langham in 2007.

The day of an NBC Sports session, I noticed Costas standing off to the side with a young man as I pulled up in my car to the hotel valet parking. Costas saw me and waved.

After I got out of my car, I went over to say hello.

"Good to see you," Costas said. "Larry, say hello to Jerry Seinfeld. Jerry, this is Larry Stewart, the TV sports columnist for the L.A. Times."

"Jerry, nice meeting you," I said.

"Likewise," Seinfeld said.

Costas then added, "Jerry has a new show on NBC this fall; it is going to be a big hit."

Costas called that one right.

Chapter 14: Going Back to My Youth

By now you've gotten a taste of the sometimes-glamorous life that my dream job afforded me and may have wondered how I got there. I've alluded to my early years as a shy farm boy, but there's a lot more to it. My hometown is less than 200 miles north of Los Angeles, but worlds apart from the big city.

My older brother John and I were born in Visalia, the county seat for Tulare County, even though the family home was 35 miles away in Porterville. Our mother Greta worked as an X-ray technician in a lab across the street from that town's Kaweah-Delta Hospital.

I was 2 when our family moved to our Lindsay property located three miles west of town. Our home was a two-story stucco box, built by our father Howard. He was a tree surgeon, specializing in budding and grafting orange and olive trees, and a licensed contractor.

I was fortunate that my father, mainly self-taught, learned those crafts. His father, like Frank Gifford's, worked in the oil fields. That is what brought my father's family to the San Joaquin Valley from Southern California in the early 1920s, when my father was barely a teenager. Had he followed his father and become an oil-field worker, I might have also had a nomadic childhood.

Our Lindsay house was not much, but at least I had a place to call home. The lone bathroom consisted of a toilet and a shower. Nothing else. We washed our hands in the kitchen sink. Upstairs was all one room until our father added a separate bedroom for my brother and me when we were maybe 7 and 8.

I once asked my father about the size and the layout of that house. He said it was difficult getting material after the war. I think that was an excuse. My father was extremely frugal. That was a trait that indirectly led to me becoming a sports fan at the age of 9. It happened because my father refused to spend money on any farm equipment. He instead hired a man named Leonard Weiss to do the disking and plowing in our 20-acre orchard.

On a Saturday in the fall of 1955, I was with my mother when she stopped at the Weiss household to pay a bill. As Mrs. Weiss talked with my mother, she suggested I go into the living room and watch the baseball game that was on TV. It was Game 4 of the 1955 World Series between the Brooklyn Dodgers and New York Yankees. This was my first glimpse of a sports event on TV, and I was immediately captivated.

When it was time to leave, I resisted. Since we did not yet have a TV set at our house, Mrs. Weiss suggested that I come back on my bicycle and watch the rest of the game. Once we got home, I pedaled my bike as fast as I could to cover the one-mile distance back to the Weiss' house.

I do not remember much about that game except that the Brooklyn Dodgers won, and that I decided Duke Snider was my favorite player. Through research, I learned the Dodgers won, 8-6, and Snider had a three-run homer and six RBIs. I also learned that Snider hit two homers in Game 5, a 5-3 victory for the Dodgers, who won the Series with a 2-0 victory in Game 7.

It was Game 4 that turned me into a sports fan, the only one in my family.

Coincidentally, the losing pitcher in Game 4 was Don Larsen, who gave up five earned runs in four innings. He had better luck against the Dodgers a year later, pitching his legendary no-hitter in Game 5 of the 1956 World Series.

In 1982, at a TV show taping, I stood between Larsen and Hall of Famer Warren Spahn at a green room bar. As 83-year-old Leo Durocher, serving as the bartender, told stories about former New York Yankee teammate Babe Ruth, Spahn leaned over toward me and said, "This is amazing, isn't it?" It was.

After brutal winter freezes ruined several of our orange crops, my father decided to sell the 20-acre property west of Lindsay and purchase a 20-acre wheat field located three miles east of the tiny town of Strathmore, where nighttime temperatures were a bit higher. That was mainly because the wheat fields that dominated the area absorbed sunlight during the day.

But once farmers like my father started disking in the wheat to plant citrus trees, nighttime temperatures were no different than those west of Lindsay. What was needed was at least one wind machine plus smudge pots to combat the cold, but that required money my father did not want to spend. Nor did he have the property leveled to avoid low spots that flooded during wet winters.

There were also droughts and insect infestations to contend with. The result was we were often broke. I remember one time in eighth grade I wanted to attend a Strathmore High basketball game against rival Lindsay and had the 25 cents to cover admission. My father said he could not afford the gas to take me.

The good thing about the move to Strathmore was a much better house. Our mother insisted on it. It took a year-and-a-half – and an $11,000 bank loan – for my father and hired-hand Harry Turner, with help from my brother and me, to build the concrete brick house. It had two bathrooms, three bedrooms, a dining room, and a living room with a large picture window that our mother demanded. The windows in the Lindsay house were not much bigger than a ship's portals.

My father built an adjacent shop for all his tools and junk. The hope was that the shop would lessen the number of arguments my parents had. My father was a hoarder. My mother, a neat freak, could not help but try and straighten up the shop, and that inevitably led to intense arguments.

The house had a spare bedroom which also served as a den and TV room. Our small black-and-white TV set got only one channel, the NBC affiliate in Fresno.

I recall watching a weekend game during the 1958 NBA Finals between the Boston Celtics and St. Louis Hawks. I was awed by Boston Garden's parquet floor, even in black and white. My mother poked her head in to see what I was watching and informed me that one of the Celtic players was from Porterville. That player was Bill Sharman, who would become one of my closest and dearest friends.

My father Howard was a good, hard-working, religious man. He was involved with the Presbyterian Church in Lindsay, singing in the choir and volunteering his carpentry services whenever they were needed. Sunday school for me and my brother was a requirement.

My father did not drink, smoke, or cuss. He did have a temper, though. When he was mad, he would yell, "What in the Sam Hill!" Sam Hill was not a particular person. That was a popular saying back then because hill sounded like hell.

My father was not a sports fan. He watched only one sports event per year – the Rose Bowl game. As a child, he lived in San Gabriel and had attended the Rose Parade with his family. That spurred his interest in the Rose Bowl game.

What my father loved was fishing and hunting, and he was sure he could pass that love on to his two sons. But neither stuck with me. We went deep-sea fishing in 16-foot rented boats powered by a 5-horsepower motor.

Once we got lost in the fog and had to guess which way the shore was. Several times the motor would not start, and we would be stranded at sea until we could find someone to tow us. One time when the motor would not start, we were near shore and drifting toward a cluster of giant rocks with waves crashing against them. I was scared to death, but the motor started just in the nick of time.

The first time I went deer hunting, at age 12, we got snowed in, 16 miles from civilization. There were four of us, including an elderly friend, Leonard Weisenberger. We made it back to our base camp in Balch Park, located northwest of Springville, but we nearly froze to death. At least Mr. Weisenberger and I were on horseback. My father and brother had to walk out.

My father built a gun closet, but instead of having it in his shop it was in the bedroom I shared with my brother. One time my brother had a friend over for an overnight stay. The friend was fiddling around with a 12-gauge shotgun late at night when it went off. Ever hear a shotgun go off in a house? Trust me, it is loud!

Farm work was something else that never grabbed me. My father loved farming and farm work. My brother liked farm work okay, but his true love was trucking. For many years he was the No. 1 driver for Hannah Trucking, a large company based in the Visalia suburb of Ivanhoe. He also became prominent in the world of restored antique trucks and tractors and has numerous trophies to show for it.

One negative about farm work was having to endure terrible weather. The summers were brutally hot and the winters, particularly on nights when we teenagers lit smudge pots to protect orange crops, were freezing cold. Lighting smudge pots, or smudging, as it was called, was an accepted excuse to get out of school.

An added element in the winter was fog so thick that visibility was nearly zero. I recall driving in it one night as a teenager and having no idea where I was. I had to open the car door to see the road below. I creeped along until finally coming to a landmark I recognized.

As a youth, it seemed I was almost always working. I cannot recall any stretch during my youth when I did not work, either for my father for no pay or for someone else for usually a dollar an hour, or sometimes $1.25 an hour.

My first job, when I was maybe 5 years old, was hoeing furrows. Leonard Weiss, with tractor and plow, made furrows for irrigation in our orchard. Those furrows needed to be connected by short, hand-made furrows to the small cement weirs that distributed the water. It was an easy job, but not for a 5-year-old.

I remember once getting stuck in the mud. I couldn't move. I cried and screamed as loud as I could. My father found me and pulled me out of the mud, but when my galoshes stayed put, I screamed some more.

When our father was building the Strathmore house in the mid-1950s, he was recruited into a three-way partnership of a citrus nursery, where young trees are grown before being transplanted to a field. In this partnership, two businessmen, Jim Volpe and Fred Adams, put up the money and my father provided his skills as a tree surgeon. I imagine my father also told his new partners he had two sons who work for free.

Young citrus trees, called seedlings, do not produce fruit. They need to be budded over to a fruit-producing variety. My father and hired-hand Harry Turner did the budding. My brother and I did other jobs, such as weeding, irrigating, and suckering, which involves clipping off unwanted growth called suckers.

When the budded trees were mature enough to be sold, they were dug up by hand and burlap was wrapped around the ball of dirt covering the roots. They were then transported to an open field. This was a tedious process before the partners bought what was called a "balling machine." This motorized contraption, which was shipped from Wisconsin, was about nine feet tall. My brother and I became proficient at operating it, him up above and me down below. The balling machine sped up the process at least 10-fold.

There was also work to be done on our parent's property. After the wheat was replaced by young orange and tangerine trees, we initially had to water them individually by hand with a hose after first building a basin with a hoe around each tree. After our father eventually splurged on sprinklers, the hoses needed to be moved, or pulled, in the morning and in the evening. We called this job "pulling hoses."

The one job we did not do was picking oranges. The packing houses supplied crews of mostly Mexican workers who handled that.

When we got caught up with work in the nursery and our orchard, we sought out jobs that paid. My main outside employer was Bud Wyatt, the father of my best friend in high school, Hal Wyatt.

Bud, a well-known farmer, employed quite a few of us teenagers at various times. Two of my coworkers were Albert Fogata and Kenny Federighi, two of the best athletes in my class. Albert, as a sophomore, was a star running back on a league championship team.

We stayed in touch, and when Albert, who later went by Al, was stricken with cancer in 2003, I had hopes of playing a role in saving him. I got him admitted to the City of Hope through my neighbor, Dr. David Snyder, a Harvard Medical School educated hematologist at the internationally famous cancer facility in Duarte. Unfortunately, by then the cancer was too far gone, and Albert Fogata, the toughest kid in my class, passed away.

Although my brother and I initially did not get paid for the work we did in the nursery, the two partners, prodded by our mother, eventually agreed to pay us $1.25 an hour.

The worst job I ever had – I forget the employer – was suckering lemon trees. Peter, Paul and Mary told us in the old folk song, "Lemon tree very pretty and the lemon flower is sweet, but the fruit of the poor lemon is impossible to eat." But the thorns were the worst part. After a day of suckering lemon trees, my hands would be bloodied and badly scratched.

I complain about the jobs I had as a youth, but they also provided me with a work ethic and an appreciation for the career I had as an adult. When I would be at, say, a Super Bowl and hear writers complain about the accommodations or the free buffet, I would think that they had no idea how good they had it.

Chapter 15: Career Spans Eight Decades

My mother Greta was trained as an X-ray technician, but writing was her first love, even though English was not her first language. She was a German Jewish refugee, who at age 25 in 1938 was sent out of Germany to the U.S. by her father. Her younger brother, Harry Alexander, joined the British Army and came to the U.S. five years later, settling in Chicago.

Uncle Harry traveled the world as an ambassador for International Harvester. I was close with Uncle Harry and remain close with his daughter Carol Eggerding. Her family includes husband John, daughters Alissa Bowman and Amy Chheda, their spouses, and four grandchildren. They all live in the Charlotte, N.C., area.

My mother, after initially landing in New York, gradually made her way across the country. While working at a tuberculosis hospital in the Central California foothill community of Springville, she met my father.

My parents were total opposites. In the history of marriage, there likely was never a couple more opposite. My father went hunting and fishing and slept in sleeping bags, sometimes on the side of a highway. My mother attended the opera in San Francisco and stayed at the St. Francis, or a hotel of that stature. We rarely, if ever, took a vacation involving the entire family.

My mother was an outgoing socialite. My father was quiet, unless the topic was something that interested him. I think I got a little bit of both parents in me. The writing side came from my mother, the work ethic from my father.

In the mid-50s my mother landed a job writing for the weekly Lindsay Gazette. After we moved to the Strathmore house, she became a correspondent for the Fresno Bee. For 27 years, maybe more, she covered the Lindsay-Strathmore area, plus handled agricultural news for all of Tulare County.

That job fed into her need for attention. She often said, "I'm known wherever I go." There was some truth to that. When I was growing up, I continually heard: "Oh, are you Greta's son?"

The Fresno Bee did a feature story on me in 1990. The writer, George Hostetter, was from Lindsay and knew my mother. The headline on his story read: *Greta's Son Makes a Name for Himself as a Sports Columnist.*

When I was in eighth grade in 1959, the Strathmore High student who served as the school's sports correspondent for the Bee was not available to call in the results of a basketball game. My mother recruited me for the job.

My son-in-law Courtney Sanford pointed out that if I say my newspaper career started in 1959, I could say it spanned *eight decades* since I am still doing freelance work, mainly for the Southern California News Group, which consists of 11 suburban newspapers.

I must admit, eight decades sounds impressive. But I can't be that old, can I?

I became Strathmore High's full-time Fresno Bee sports correspondent as a freshman in the fall of 1960, and I soon was also writing byline stories for the Strathmore Sentinel, a four-page supplement put out by the Lindsay Gazette. I continued in those roles throughout high school. Being a conscientious correspondent for the Bee led to me working part-time in the Bee sports department during college, and that led to everything else.

A key thing for me was setting a life's goal at an early age. It gave me direction and, somewhat, kept me out of trouble. I was in college in the mid-60s when the drug culture was coming to the forefront. Not that I was perfect – I twice got busted for drinking beer as a minor while in high school – but I stayed away from drugs. I did not want anything jeopardizing my career plans.

I remember writing a what-I-want-to-do paper in the eighth grade, stating my goal was to be an L.A. Times sportswriter. In signing my high school yearbook my senior year, my friend Gary Ishida and several others mentioned that someday I would be sports editor of the L.A. Times. At least I got close to that.

After first becoming a sports fan – mainly a Brooklyn Dodger fan – at age 9 during the 1955 World Series, my affection for the Dodgers intensified when the team moved to Los Angeles in 1958. I could now listen to Dodger broadcasts on powerful 50,000-watt radio station KFI. Like so many young fans back then, I often had my large, boxy transistor radio next to my ear in bed at night while listening to Vin Scully. I would have never envisioned even meeting Scully, let alone developing a long, personal relationship with him.

My passion for sports helped me through some difficult times in sixth, seventh and eighth grades. I know, those years are tough for most. But they were particularly tough for me. With the move to the Strathmore area, I had switched schools and found making friends difficult. I was the smallest kid in my class, wore braces and ugly headgear, I was insecure and quiet, got bullied, and was usually one of the last kids to get picked for any team.

A low point came in seventh grade when, during PE one day, my favorite teacher, Mrs. Norma Richardson, with the best of intentions, decided to make me one of the basketball captains. The other captain was Richard Staton, the class's best basketball player. In threatening tones, at least three bullies ordered me not to pick them. Mrs. Richardson saw what was going on and sent the bullies to the principal's office. That just made things even worse.

There were many days when I dreaded going to school.

A big turning point in my life occurred the week before I entered high school. I was looking forward to going out for football even though I weighed only 102 pounds. I had played Little League tackle football in Lindsay and was eager to again strap on a helmet and shoulder pads.

My friend Bobby Vollmer and his older brother Chuck were on their way to pick me up for the first day of football practice when my mother suggested I become the Bee correspondent for Strathmore High sports. She said I would make 25 cents per column inch, meaning a four-inch story paid a whole dollar. I was sold.

When Chuck Vollmer pulled into our gravel driveway in his souped-up 1950 Chevy, I came out of the house and told Chuck and Bobby to go ahead. "I'm not going out for football," I said. "I've got other plans."

I approached my job as a Bee correspondent with uncertainty. At the start of Strathmore's first home game, with clipboard in hand, I walked out onto the field near the Strathmore bench. When Coach Jim Brinkman saw me, he screamed, "What do you think you are doing? You can't be out here."

When I explained I was reporting for the Bee, he let me stay on the sideline.

To report on the game, I called the Bee, collect. When I saw the story the next day, I realized I needed to spell out names phonetically. Among the typos was Strathmore running back Ronnie Jones appearing as Bonnie Jones.

Early the next week my mother informed me that she had arranged for me to do a full write-up on that first home game for the next edition of the Strathmore Sentinel, which came out every Friday. Using my play-by-play notes, I wrote out my first-ever game story in long hand. When I saw it in print, there was the byline: By LARRY STEWART. I was barely 14 when I got that first byline.

My story was good enough to get me hired. This job paid $2 per story. Since I also did stories on the B games, I made $4 a week during football season and as much as $12 a week during basketball season with three teams (C, B, and varsity) playing twice a week. I did even better than that during spring sports.

Working for both the Bee and the Sentinel provided me with lunch money and then some. Five lunch tokens for the school cafeteria cost a dollar. Occasionally I splurged and walked across the street for a burger and a coke at the appropriately named Dinky Diner.

Throughout high school, I was on the sideline for every Strathmore football game, home and away. I also attended every basketball game, every baseball game, and every track meet. I traveled with the teams and felt like I belonged. The only sport I played was basketball, as a member of the C and B class teams.

I was a conscientious correspondent and reporter, taking tedious notes and compiling statistics. If need be, I would go to the opposing team's sideline to get first names, team records and any other needed information. I only reported on home games for the Bee. Coach Brinkman gave me a key to the school office, enabling me to call the Bee right after every game.

My love of sports grew in high school. It helped that Strathmore High, despite its size, did well in sports during my years there. Two coaches were mainly responsible for that. One was Jim Brinkman, who came to Strathmore from North Dakota. The other was Don Kavadas, who also came from North Dakota. Under Coach Brinkman, the football team won league championships my freshman and sophomore years. Coach Kavadas built Strathmore into a small school powerhouse in track and his varsity basketball team won a league title my senior year.

Prior to my freshman year, there were six boys on Strathmore's track team. By my sophomore year, there were 85. Coach Kavadas even had me try out for the track team. He liked my shotput form when I was using a softball inside the school gym. But after he saw my form with an eight-pound shot in my hand, he said, "Well, how about being our scorekeeper?" I accepted his offer.

That was not such a bad gig. The track scorekeeper for Tulare Western High was a cutie and she was my date for my junior year prom. At first the girl turned me down, explaining her parents were orthodox Jews and she could not date a boy who is not Jewish. I said, "Well, I've got good news for you."

When I told her my mother was a Jewish German refugee, that worked. The girl's parents gave her the okay. This was how I learned that having a Jewish mother made me Jewish, even though I was raised Presbyterian and to this day know little about the Jewish religion. The only Jewish people I knew growing up were the Friedmans in Woodlake. The family consisted of two daughters, Keren and Ednah. I reconnected with Keren in 2018 after her photo ran in the L.A. Times with a story about a synagogue in Visalia.

Strathmore High football fell on hard times in the 1970s, '80 and early '90s. There was an 0-32 losing streak, and one season varsity football was dropped.

The creation of a Pop Warner League in the late '80s started a comeback that culminated in 2017 with a lower division state championship and a 16-0 record. I'll come back to this improbable story in this book's final chapter.

A big plus about high school for me was the recognition and respect I got from my sports reporting. I was already seeing the benefit of a byline. I was not just another obscure face on campus. I was more self-confident, and more easily made friends.

As for school, my grades my freshman and senior years met the standard set by California Scholastic Federation, better known as CSF. At Strathmore High, if you made the CSF list, you were rewarded with a bus trip to L.A. or San Francisco.

A trip to L.A. my freshman year included a tour of the L.A. Times Building. As I walked around the building at First and Spring, I fantasized about working there.

After high school, my plan was to attend College of the Sequoias, the junior college in Visalia known as COS, then transfer to Fresno State or maybe Cal or UCLA. But those plans changed after my one and only meeting with my counselor, Charles Solbach. He wanted me to go straight to Fresno State. When I said I could not afford to live away from home, he suggested applying for a scholarship. That was great advice. I ended up getting a $350 scholarship, which meant Fresno State, here I come.

Chapter 16: Off to College

I was stunned when I was notified about the $350 scholarship. I was also stunned to hear from Mary Howard, a member of the Presbyterian Church choir, that my father had mentioned the scholarship at choir practice. "I think he is very proud of you," Mary Howard told me.

I did not think he was even aware that I got a scholarship.

It came from the McMahan Furniture Co., which had stores throughout the San Joaquin Valley. I was one of 15 recipients in 1964. Back then, $350 was a lot of money. I made only about $300 working in the hot sun that summer.

But the key thing about getting that scholarship was it landed me at Fresno State instead of COS. That was a blessing because as an incoming freshman I was hired to work part-time in the Fresno Bee sports department as a prep writer, which meant I would be covering high school sports.

Not only did that job lead to almost everything else that happened in my life, it also paid well. I started off at $3.25 an hour, more than triple what I made doing farm labor.

That money kept me in school since I was getting zero financial support from my parents. The scholarship covered only tuition and books for two years. My Bee paychecks and previous savings paid for everything else. My freshman year, I lived in an off-campus two-bedroom apartment. My share of the rent was $25 a month.

My first week of classes at Fresno State, I returned to my apartment on a Thursday night. There was a note on the door from the apartment manager saying to come see him. We did not have a phone. My mother had called the manager's office and left a message that I had been hired by the Bee. There was no information other than to report to work the next night. No time was given.

My roommate and high school friend, Don Tsuboi, dropped me off at the downtown Bee building around 5 p.m. Don was headed home to be with his girlfriend, Pat Glover, whom he would later marry.

A security guard sent me up to the sports department on the third floor. I sat around until another Fresno State student, Tom Bronzini, arrived around 9. He explained the drill. We would take calls from correspondents, then later write up the games. Other writers would be coming in from games they were covering to help with the calls. There were five or six of us so-called prep writers. One was Doug Krikorian. "Doug is a little different," Bronzini warned.

My first night at the Bee was about to wrap up around 3 a.m. It was an afternoon paper except on Sundays, which meant the Saturday paper did not go to press until the next morning. It was delivered to homes through the San Joaquin Valley in the afternoon.

I had no idea how I was going to get back to my apartment adjacent to the Fresno State campus. Finally, as everyone was packing up to leave, I built up the nerve to say, "I need a ride back to my apartment." There was silence. Finally, Krikorian, who was in the fourth of the five years it took him to graduate at Fresno State, said, "I will give you a ride if you give me a buck for gas."

Krikorian, an avid weightlifter, was an intimidating figure. When he first returned from the game he was covering, he walked over to my desk, and in a tough voice while flexing his muscles and offering a weak handshake, asked, "Hey buddy, what's your name? My name is Doug."

Now this guy was going to give me a ride home. On our way out of the Bee building, we stopped at a men's room. When I was washing my hands, I looked in the mirror over the wash basin and saw Doug standing behind me. He was flexing his biceps. "Hey buddy, these are 17-inch arms," he proclaimed. "Feel them."

I reluctantly felt one of his arms.

"What size are your arms?" he asked.

I was taken aback. I had never measured my arms or even thought about it.

We made it out of the building and into Doug's VW bug. Doug was now not as intimidating. And, yes, I gave him a dollar. He deserved it. He had driven about 30 miles out of his way, since he was living at his parents' house in Fowler, located south of Fresno. Fresno State is in the northeast part of Fresno.

My new job meant I was going to need a car. My mother had promised to help me buy a car if I got good grades my senior year. I did, but she instead spent $1,500 on a grand piano, even though she did not play. It was just for show.

"It was too good of a deal to pass up," she explained.

I never had my own car in high school. Instead, my brother and I pooled our money to fix up his '57 Chevy. It was candy-apple red with chrome rims, a converted on-the-floor gear shift, a souped-up 283 cubic-inch engine, and tuck-n-roll interior. We went to Tijuana to get the tuck-n-roll. My brother and I had to share a car because our father said, "We are not having four cars in this family."

I had good access to the '57 Chevy my senior year because by then my brother was already driving truck full time. But I was headed to college with no car. "It's fashionable for college students to not have a car," my mother said.

But now I needed a car to get to and from work, and out to games I would be covering. My mother drove up from Strathmore and took me to a dealership in Porterville, where the best I could do was a red 1960 Ford Falcon Ranchero for $900.

The next week I was assigned to cover a game at Washington Union High, located in Easton just west of Fresno. That meant I would get a byline in the Bee.

The day after the game, I was so excited about seeing my byline that I drove to the Bee building to get the paper hot off the press at 11 a.m. I opened the Sports section, and there it was – my name in the paper I grew up reading. I placed the paper beside me in my Falcon Ranchero so that I could continually look at my byline as I drove home to Strathmore. I was more excited by that byline than any I would ever get in my career.

No byline in the Herald Examiner, the L.A. Times or any newspaper that subscribed to the Times wire service could match it. Nor could the byline I got for a Pat Riley feature in Sport magazine, nor any of several bylines in the Sporting News. I got a byline in the New York Times in 1976 when I covered a Rangers-Kings game as a freelancer. In 2012, I got a byline in USA Today. In semi-retirement, I still get bylines in the 11 suburban L.A. papers that make up the Southern California News Group.

But it was that first byline in the Fresno Bee in September of 1964 that topped them all.

High school was easy for me, but I soon learned that I had to really study in college. My first college exam was in a psychology class. I failed the test but rebounded and got a B in the class.

In a speech class, I faltered so much that the professor sent me to the school's speech specialist. The specialist told me I sounded fine. I explained I get nervous in front of a group and told him about an experience I had in eighth grade. I had memorized the Gettysburg Address backwards and forwards, but when I got up in front of the class to recite it, I could not get past "Four score and seven years ago." The teacher, Mrs. Richardson, called me back to the front of the class twice more before giving up.

As an adult, I got over my nervousness and did a lot of speaking engagements. When I was with the Times, the newspaper had a speakers' bureau run by Carla Hall, who told me I was her go-to guy in Sports because I rarely said no.

Since there was a time in my life where I could not get up and make a speech, I relished the speaking opportunities. I have done at least a hundred of them at schools, service clubs and so forth. I once got a $500 appearance fee and a nice bottle of wine for making a speech. If only my college speech professor could have seen me then.

But I bombed once in the mid-70s when I was at the Herald Examiner. It was at a roast for Rams Coach Chuck Knox at the Beverly Hilton. Preceding me at the podium was Jim Murray, who opened with, "Damn, I thought this was for Chuck Noll." The reference to the Pittsburgh Steelers coach brought roars of laughter.

Knox was known for his conservative play calling. His nickname was Ground Chuck. I started off my brief speech by saying, "I should open by sending Lawrence McCutcheon off right tackle." Ram safety Dave Elmendorf, who was sitting right below me, turned around and gave me a thumbs up. As for the crowd reaction, the only thing I heard was, "Speak up, we can't hear you."

Now rattled, I got off stage as quickly as I could.

After my freshman year at Fresno State, I lined up a summer job at the Porterville Recorder. The pay was $65 for a six-day work week. Some workdays began at 6:30 a.m. and ended after I covered a city council meeting or something else at night.

One week, when there was a tri-state regional Babe Ruth League tournament in Porterville, my schedule was crazy. I would roll out of bed at my parents' house at 4:30 a.m. to pull hoses for an hour in the dark. Then it was off to the paper to write up the games I had covered the previous night. I would then work all day, return home in the evening to again pull hoses and eat before heading to the ballpark to cover Babe Ruth League games well into the night. Somehow, I survived the week.

One thing I remember about the Recorder was the process for making a long-distance call. I had to take a permission slip into the publisher's office, get it signed, and then have the secretary make the call and transfer it to my desk. This was a small-town paper. But the Recorder job was beneficial. I did a bit of everything that summer.

My first feature story was about a Porterville man who had sent vegetables from his garden to President Lyndon Johnson and got a thank-you note from the White House. The man was a tough interview; he did not have much to say.

My editor, Bob Moyle, read my first story draft, handed it back to me and said, "Why don't you take another shot at this?" I did a second interview and rewrote the story. This time, it got approved.

Moyle helped me a lot that summer. He continually gave me guidance, and on my final day he handed me a written critique of my work. He pointed out many of the mistakes I had made, including missing deadline for a Saturday paper that went to press at noon. But he also offered praise and encouragement.

A highlight for me that summer was getting to meet Bob Mathias, the two-time Olympic decathlon champion from Tulare. Mathias came into the Recorder office because he was campaigning for a seat in the U.S. House of Representatives. He won the election and served four terms.

Many years later, in 2007, when I was at that Paralysis Project fundraiser, I asked Mathias to pose for the photo shown here with me and Porterville's Bill Sharman, left. My plan was to facetiously call the photo "Three Tulare County Legends." But the photographer taking the photo also asked John Wooden to get in the shot as well. I didn't want to tell the Coach he did not qualify for this photo, so he is in it too. No complaints here. It is one of my favorite photos. I call it "Three Tulare County Legends, Plus One."

While at the Recorder, I met an intern working at the chamber of commerce and we started dating. She owned two thoroughbred horses, bred for leisure riding. She suggested going on a night-time ride, and that is when I learned first-hand that thoroughbreds spook easily. We were riding along what we thought were deserted railroad tracks when suddenly a freight train came around the bend. My horse took off, running full speed for about two miles as I pulled hard on the reins. After running across a two-lane highway, the horse reached its stable. Fortunately, the stable gate was open, and I survived.

Back at school, the Bee job continued to go well. There were times I worked three or four nights a week. I recall once getting a $77 check, which more than covered rent, groceries, and beer for a month.

One of my coworkers was Danny Robinson, who for three years was the starting Fresno State quarterback. He would cover a high school football game on Friday night, then play in a college game on Saturday night. Robinson broke most of the school passing records that stood until the arrival of such quarterbacks as Jeff Tedford, Trent Dilfer and brothers David and Derek Carr.

Robinson had a unique writing style. He would follow a theme throughout his game stories. For example, if he chose electricity as his theme, his story would include words such as jolted, stunned, electrified, shocked, lit up, and bolted.

Then there was Doug Krikorian. He would labor at his desk with an open thesaurus next to his typewriter as he wrote up the game he covered. As the rest of us took calls, Doug's phone never rang. I asked him about that many years later. He confessed he put a thick black pencil under the receiver on the phone at his desk. To Doug, his byline story was the only one that mattered.

When I was a sophomore at Fresno State, Bee sports editor Ed Krane offered me two tickets to the East-West Shrine Game on Dec. 31, 1965, at Kezar Stadium in San Francisco.

I accepted the tickets because I wanted to see Heisman Trophy winner Mike Garrett of USC in person. He was that year's big attraction as a member of the West all-star team.

I decided to invite my father to go to the game with me even though he knew little about football. Before accepting my invitation, he asked if he could take some of his tangerines into the stadium to give to people in the stands.

"I guess so," I said.

Our Strathmore orchard included five acres of tangerines, and my father was proud of them.

It was cold in San Francisco the day of the game, so we both wore heavy coats. After we parked, we stuffed our deep coat pockets with tangerines. After we got to our end zone seats, we handed out the tangerines to people around us.

When my father explained he grew these tangerines himself, our new-found friends told him how good they were. After that, it did not matter how the game went, he was glad he came.

As for me, I can still vividly recall being in awe as I watched the great Mike Garrett, No. 20, jog onto the field for the first play from scrimmage. It was his time to shine in the Shrine. He was in the spotlight. Many years later, he put me in a spotlight.

I would first get to know Mike Garrett when he dabbled in broadcasting. After he became USC's athletic director, he selected me to serve on the committee that picked USC Hall of Famers. My Times colleague Mal Florence, a Trojan through and through, was also on the committee and, tongue in cheek, would say, "How did a guy from Fresno State end up on this committee?"

I grew closer to Mike when our wives bonded while the four of us awaited delivery of our valet-parked cars at a charity event. Our wives had similar careers. "We're still talking about you two," Mike said the next time I saw him.

In February of 2005, I ran into Mike and his wife Suzanne at a restaurant in Pasadena. I had just read that USC had filled an opening on its football schedule with Fresno State. "You could draw 100,000 people from the Valley for that game if there was room in the Coliseum," I said. Mike was aware I went to Fresno State.

"We should honor you at halftime at that game," he said. I thought, "What for?" I figured he was just being nice. But he was not kidding. It really happened.

It was Nov. 19, 2005, when I was honored on the Coliseum field. This was at the height of USC football. The Trojans, coached by Pete Carroll, were the defending national champions and ranked No. 1 in the country.

The attendance that night was 92,000. The ceremony took place on the 20-yard line on the west end of the Coliseum. It lasted about 30 seconds because the Fresno State band rushed onto the field, forcing us to get out of the way.

The PA announcer read off a glowing bio and Garrett, in what was supposed to be a surprise, presented me with a USC jacket. I knew about the jacket because a Visalia friend, Chris Young, had read an item in the Fresno Bee and called me.

After returning to my seat, I said to our daughter Jill, a 2000 UCLA grad: "You want this jacket?" Her answer: "Get that thing away from me."

USC traditionally honors a few alums at halftime each season. I was told that I likely was the only alum from an opponent's school to ever be a USC halftime honoree.

The ceremony was supposed to be shown on Fox Sports West during the second half. Before the game, announcers Barry Tompkins and Petros Papadakis told me they already knew about the halftime ceremony. But nothing worked out. No cameraman was on hand to shoot it and the announcers did not mention it because the game became much tighter than anyone could have anticipated. USC, led by Reggie Bush, had to rally in the fourth quarter to win, 50-42. The Trojans were trailing, 42-41, with less than 10 minutes to play.

I was bummed the ceremony did not make the game telecast, but I told myself that this was a huge honor, something I will always remember, and that I should not let anything detract from that. It was really a mind-blowing experience.

Papadakis later apologized for not being able to mention my big moment. I told him it was okay. I couldn't be upset with Petros. My family loves him, particularly my son-in-law Courtney, who listens to Petros and Matt "Money" Smith on sports talk AM 570 every weekday.

Also, as a family, about once a year we would all make the trek to San Pedro to enjoy a night of frivolity at the Papadakis restaurant. Petros and his father John would never fail to have us laughing hysterically with their antics.

During my junior year at Fresno State, I had my first connection to Jim Murray. It happened because of an interesting assignment from a journalism professor. We students were to pick a prominent newspaper columnist, write to them, and then write a report on the columnist, whether we got a response or not. We had all semester to complete the project.

The letter was a key part of the assignment. If it was well written enough to entice the columnist to write back, we were almost guaranteed an A. I selected Jim Murray. It took a while, but about mid-semester I received a fat envelope from Murray. It was filled with material. And I got an A in the class.

Not long after going to work for the Herald Examiner I met Murray when I just happened to sit next to him at a press function. I told him about what he did for me as a college student and thanked him once more.

"I did that?" Murray said. "I usually don't do students' homework for them."

It was a good retort. Murray was almost as witty in person as he was in print. And always humble.

For 20 years, I was proud to be Jim Murray's colleague – and his friend.

After my junior year of college, I did a summer internship at the Tulare Advance-Register. My job in Porterville was not an official college internship. I learned the Tulare job paid $85 a week with Wednesdays off, plus I got four units of credit toward graduation and an easy A. I was ecstatic!

The sports editor in Tulare was Doug Krikorian, who by then had graduated from Fresno State. I often slept on the couch in his apartment that summer. Doug had befriended Alex Szacala, who owned the only gym in Tulare. Alex let us work out there for free. A typical night would be pigging out at Sir George's Smorgasbord and then working out at the gym. I put on 27 pounds in three months. My arm size – yes, I measured – went from 11 inches to nearly 14. When

I went back to school, ready to show off my new physique, I mainly heard: "Boy, how did you get so fat over the summer?"

I only weighed 157. I would love to be at that weight now.

Another thing I recall of my summer in Tulare was teaming up with Krikorian in covering a two-county high school all-star game played in Visalia. He did the game story, and I did the sidebar. It was a preview of things to come. From 1974-78, the two of us covered the Los Angeles Rams for the L.A. Herald Examiner, with Doug doing the game stories and me doing the sidebars.

Doug left the Tulare Advance-Register at the same time I did, but not on his own accord. When the editor handed Doug a press release to rewrite, Doug tossed it into a large trash can. When the editor told him to retrieve it, Doug, in a fit of temper, picked up the trash can and dumped everything in it on the floor right near the editor's desk.

That was Doug's last day on the job.

He went to L.A. after that and eventually got a job at the Herald Examiner in April of 1968. A nasty union strike and subsequent lockout by management in December of 1967 created a lot of job openings at the paper. By the start of the 1968-69 NBA season, Doug was the Laker beat writer, a coveted position.

Without Doug I would have never gotten hired by the Herald Examiner in November of 1969. I have always been indebted for that.

Before the start of my senior year at Fresno State, I bought a 1965 Ford Fairlane. I had it barely more than a month before it got totaled. I got rear-ended by a teenager who was drag racing on Fresno's Shaw Avenue. Incredibly, the police report said I was partially to blame because I switched lanes in front of the drag racer.

I was the sports editor of the school newspaper, the Daily Collegian, during the first semester of my senior year. I had a stipend that paid for two road trips. My first planned road trip was to a Fresno State football game against Cal Poly at San Luis Obispo on Oct. 16, 1965. But now I had a problem: no car.

My mother arranged for me to borrow a car through the same Porterville dealership where I bought my Falcon Ranchero. This was also a terrible car. On the way home, the fuel pump went out and for most of the trip from San Luis Obispo to Porterville I drove 15 miles an hour.

Obviously, I was not going to buy that car. My mother had another idea. She gave me her Falcon four-door sedan and bought herself a new car.

I enjoyed being sports editor of the Daily Collegian. I had the freedom to write on whatever I chose, and I had a certain amount of stature on campus.

I began writing for the Daily Collegian as a sophomore. One of my stories that year involved a longtime assistant football coach, in a fit of temper, using the N-word in a hotel suite after a loss at Hawaii. A young black running back was in the suite and heard the coach, which led to a threatened boycott by all black athletes at the school.

I got a tip and was working on the story in the college newspaper office when Bruce Farris, the longtime Fresno State beat writer for the Bee, got ahold of me by phone. He tried to talk me out of writing the story, saying it might cost the coach his job.

Although a bit intimated, I finished writing the story anyway and went to press with it. The coach met with the black athletes, apologized, and there was no boycott. I believe my story led to the apology that prevented the boycott. Good thing, too. A boycott would have been devastating to an outstanding basketball team, which on Dec. 17, 1965, almost beat Texas Western, losing 75-73 at El Paso.

Four months later, on March 19, 1966, Texas Western won the national championship by beating a Kentucky team that featured Pat Riley and Louie Dampier, 72-65. That Texas Western team featured an all-black starting lineup, a first for an NCAA title game. Texas Western later became Texas El Paso.

When I was the Daily Collegian sports editor my senior year, I got in trouble with the Fresno State cheer squad. I criticized the head cheerleader for choosing to honor a groundskeeper at halftime of a game. The groundskeeper paled in comparison to the honoree the previous season – Joe Dale Sr. of Dale Brothers Coffee, a huge supporter of Fresno State athletics for many years.

The cheerleading squad showed up in the school newspaper office and chastised me for being so cruel to the groundskeeper. I was outnumbered but held my own. The groundskeeper was honored, but it was a toned-down ceremony.

After one semester, I was no longer the sports editor but continued to write for the Daily Collegian as mainly a news and feature reporter. One story that stands out is one I worked on with classmates Dottie Petrick and Mike Lassiter. The three of us, on an expense account, made a trip to the Bay Area to report on the Vietnam War riots at San Francisco State.

The story won a statewide award at a college journalism convention in San Diego, and I was the one who accepted the award from L.A. Mayor Sam Yorty and actress Elke Sommer. I got a kiss on the cheek from Elke.

Dottie Petrick ended up marrying Tom Bronzini, and last I checked they had been married 54 years. Tom worked at the L.A. Times on the Metro and entertainment desks for 37 years.

As college graduation neared, one of my journalism professors, Art Margosian, asked me about my plans. I said I hoped to get a full-time job in the Bee sports department, but if not, I would return to the Tulare Advance-Register, where I had a standing job offer.

A few days later Margosian informed me he had called the editor of the Advance-Register to place an intern there. When the editor said they did not have room for an intern because I was coming back as a full-time staff member, Margosian told the editor I was going to the Bee. But that was not true.

When I called the Advance-Register editor to straighten things out, the editor told me, "If you would rather work for the Bee, we no longer want you here." This was the same editor who had fired Doug Krikorian.

It was now a week before I was to graduate, and I did not have a job.

I scrambled and landed a job as sports editor of the Visalia Times-Delta. But the next day the publisher called to let me know that Mike Novin, previously the sports editor, was returning to that job after getting a degree at Fresno State.

The publisher then added, "We do have an opening for farm editor."

Not what I was looking for, but I needed a job. I thus became the farm editor of the Visalia-Times Delta.

Chapter 17: My Time in Visalia

In Visalia, farm editor ranked over sports editor. For one thing, at that time Cesar Chavez's movement to unionize farm workers was big news – and controversial – throughout the Valley.

But I was not just the farm editor at the Times-Delta. I was the No. 2 sportswriter, a general assignment reporter, police beat reporter, staff photographer at one point, and eventually the assistant editor of the paper.

In the summer of 1968, when Richard Nixon was running for president, I teamed up with my mother and we interviewed his 78-year-old aunt, Jane Beeson, at her home outside of Strathmore. As a 12-year-old in 1925, Nixon moved in with his aunt to take piano lessons. He attended seventh grade at one of the two elementary schools in the Strathmore district, Sunnyside, located a couple of miles west of town.

My mother wrote a story for the Bee, I wrote one for the Times-Delta.

My most memorable Times-Delta sports story was on a football player from Lindsay, Bill Baird. He was the starting free safety for the New York Jets, who, behind Joe Namath, upset the Baltimore Colts in the 1969 Super Bowl.

Baird had been one of my little league football coaches in Lindsay when I was a 90-pound center. His younger brother Bob was also one of my coaches.

In 1956, Baird was the starting quarterback for Lindsay High's league championship team. The star running back was Claude Turner, son of Harry Turner, my father's hired hand. Harry took me to quite a few Lindsay High games, and when Bill Baird and Claude Turner went on to COS in Visalia, Harry took me to those games too. Claude

Turner then starred at Cal Poly San Luis Obispo, where one of his teammates was John Madden.

The first of the many times I interviewed Madden on the phone, I told him my connection to Claude Turner. "You must be from Lindsay," Madden said. I told him I lived in Lindsay through the fifth grade, then moved to Strathmore.

I think I lost him when I mentioned Strathmore. But he was familiar with Porterville because the junior college there was a league rival when Madden was coaching at Hancock College in Santa Maria.

Bill Baird went from COS to San Francisco State, which was where the Baltimore Colts trained back then. Colts Coach Weeb Ewbank, watching a San Francisco State practice, noticed Baird, and later invited him to the Colts' training camp. Baird made it to the final cuts. After Ewbank became coach of the Jets in 1963, he signed Baird, and this time he made the team and became a starter.

For my story on Baird, I interviewed his COS coach, went to his parents' home in Lindsay to interview them, and I also talked to some of Baird's former high school and junior college teammates. I then went to the editor to explain I needed to call the Miami hotel where the Jets were staying to interview Baird.

Sid Hosking, the editor, said, "Can you do the story without making that long-distance call?"

I liked Sid a lot, as did everyone at the paper. But his suggestion about the long-distance call was a reminder that, as was the case with the Porterville Recorder, I was still in the minor leagues of the newspaper business.

The Bee ran a feature story on Bill Baird by Bruce Farris the same day my feature ran in the Times-Delta. The Bee story had a couple of quotes from Baird, but I thought my story had more and better background information.

In July of 1969, Laker legend Jerry West came to Visalia to put on a basketball clinic at COS. NBA players did such things back then. In this case, West also got a minimal fee from Sunkist, which sponsored the clinic. I spent about 15 minutes interviewing West after the clinic and did a nice column on him for the Times-Delta.

You will read in the next chapter about a memorable night I gave West a ride across town not long after I left Visalia and went to work for the Herald Examiner. In later years, West became a friend and helped me out immensely with various charitable ventures. Philanthropy is a major part of Jerry West.

In August of 2019, when I was on the board of the Southern California Sports Broadcasters, he came through when I asked him to

be the featured speaker at an SCSB luncheon at Lakeside Golf Club. I introduced West, and SCSB executive director Martin Leon, shown in the adjoining photo, added a few heartfelt words about West being his all-time sports idol. Jerry, as he usually does, dazzled the audience with a riveting, heartfelt speech about his difficult childhood.

Another person I interviewed while in Visalia was Yogi Berra, who was then a coach for the New York Mets. He came to town during a West Coast swing to scout the Visalia Mets, a Class-A farm team, and I talked to him before a game.

I thought I might get some good lines out of him, maybe even a Yogism or two. But no such luck. When I asked him his impression of Visalia, he said: "I don't know. I just stayed around the pool at the motel this afternoon." The rest of the interview did not go much better.

Norma and I got a chance to talk to Yogi in 2004 when we were at the Baseball Hall of Fame, but I did not mention our Visalia connection. I had even forgotten about that story until I recently found a clipping in a scrapbook.

Since Visalia was about a 35-minute commute from my parents' house east of Strathmore, most nights I stayed in Mike Novin's Visalia apartment, sleeping on his couch. Living in the same apartment building was a young woman I befriended named Melinda, whose boyfriend was Dennis Gilbert, the center fielder for the minor league Visalia Mets.

Gilbert's roommate was shortstop Tim Foli, from Notre Dame High School in Sherman Oaks. Foli hit over .300 in 1969, his one season in Visalia. He would end up spending 15 seasons with seven major league teams. Foli's girlfriend came up from Southern California to Visalia to be with Foli, and she stayed with Melinda for several weeks. Foli, a cocky sort, treated her terribly. I recall her often being in tears as Melinda and I would attempt to console her.

Many years later I asked Dennis whatever became of Foli's girlfriend. I was stunned when Dennis told me that she was Bill Walton's ex-wife and the mother of his four sons.

I got to know Walton when he first got into broadcasting. His first-ever interview with a newspaper reporter was with me, and he opened up about overcoming his stuttering problem at age 28.

In 2004, Norma and I were invited dinner guests at Walton's home in San Diego. Bill's mother was there along with one of Bill's four sons, and of course Bill's lovely wife Lori was there.

At one point, I decided to tell the story of how I knew Bill's ex-wife. When I finished, you could have heard a pin drop. No one said a word. It was an awkward moment. Even Bill was at a loss for words, as hard as that is to believe.

We had a wonderful evening, but later my wife said, "Why in the world would you bring up Bill's ex-wife?"

I explained that I wanted to see the reaction. And I did. There was no reaction.

Chapter 18: L.A., Here I Come

In early October of 1969, when I was still at the Times-Delta, I called into a meeting with editor Sid Hosking and recently named publisher J.C. Hickman. I worried I might have messed up. But it was the opposite. I was being promoted to assistant editor. I got a whopping $10 raise, upping my weekly salary to $125. A story announcing the promotion, along with a photo, ran on Page One.

My mother was thrilled. It gave her something to brag about to her friends. But I soon learned that while the title was good, the job was not. I had to be at work at 5:30 a.m. to fill up the inside pages with AP wire stories. Staff generated stories were later handled by Hosking.

My new job meant I was no longer a reporter. No more going out on stories, no sports columns with my mug shot, no bylines of any kind, just early morning hours and grunt work. And the work schedule put a crimp in my social life, which was at an all-time high. I was now driving a 1969 Chevelle Super Sport, which helped.

Sometime in November, unbeknownst to me, Doug Krikorian called my parents' house and told my mother there was a job opening in the sports department at the Herald Examiner.

My mother, without consulting with me, said something like, "Larry just got a big promotion at the Times-Delta, and he is very happy there."

But Doug never told sports editor Bud Furillo about his conversation with my mother.

One evening around 6 p.m., Furillo instructed Mitch Chortkoff, one of the Herald's more prominent sportswriters, to call

"Krikorian's guy" Larry Stewart at the Visalia Times-Delta and offer him a job.

At small papers like the Times-Delta, the switchboard operator goes home at 5 p.m. When Chortkoff called, the only phone that rang was in the advertising department at the other end of the building from my work area.

Here is another case of fate being kind to me.

After my shift had ended that day, I invited a young woman who worked in advertising to have drinks at the Vintage Press across the street. Around 6 p.m. we both returned to the office before calling it a day. A few minutes later, my friend from advertising walked from her department over to the editorial department, located at the other end of the building. Fortunately, I was still there.

"There is a call for you from Mitch Chortkoff of the L.A. Herald Examiner," my friend said. I was familiar with Chortkoff's byline. In those days, L.A.'s two newspapers were available at Visalia newsstands. I hustled over to advertising, picked up the phone and said, "This is Larry Stewart."

"Bud Furillo wants to hire you," were Chortkoff's first words.

If I had missed that call, I probably would have never left Visalia.

Taking the L.A. job was a no-brainer. It was Los Angeles, the big time. Plus, it was so foggy that winter in Visalia that I had not seen the sun in 29 straight days.

I was officially hired by the Herald Examiner after doing a job interview with managing editor Don Goodenow. My salary was $147 a week, a bump up from the $125 I was making at the Times-Delta. But I would be low man on the totem pole, working a 6 p.m.- to-2 a.m. shift on the night sports desk.

Doug Krikorian said I could live with him in his two-bedroom apartment for $75 a month. It was in Downey, not far from the Herald Examiner building at 11th and Broadway in downtown Los Angeles. Doug's last roommate, Bert Kincaid, had moved out.

I started at the Herald Examiner on Dec. 1, 1969. The day before, I came into the office to meet with Furillo, who informed me I would be working six nights a week, with Tuesdays off. That sounded brutal, even though Furillo said that working six nights a week meant overtime pay.

After my brief session with Furillo, several of the staff members took me out for a steak dinner at the Original Pantry at Ninth and Figueroa (which is still there, incidentally). After dinner, we walked two blocks to the Gala Cellar, a popular hangout for sportswriters and sports celebrities. I would spend many an evening at the Gala Cellar in later years.

I was pretty jacked up about meeting guys I had been reading for years, people such as Allan Malamud, Steve Bisheff, Jim Perry, and Chortkoff.

Three weeks into my tenure, on a day when Perry was in charge, he assigned me to cover a Knicks-Lakers game at the Forum because Krikorian, the beat writer, was ill. West scored 29 of his 40 points in the second half, making 11 of his last 13 shots, in a 114-106 Laker victory. West's performance should have been the lead, but it got buried in the middle of my story.

I think Furillo was out of town, so I avoided getting chewed out.

The night desk crew back then consisted of two people – Leo Noonan and me. My job involved editing stories, writing headlines, putting together sports roundups, reading proofs, and assisting in the composing room where the sports section was assembled.

Furillo had told me that the most important part of my job was making sure there were no typos in either his column or Melvin Durslag's column. With only a two-man desk crew, the job was brutal with no breaks. I did not have time to pour over proofs, so I would miss typos. Furillo would call to scream at me the next night. Furillo's column was called "The Steam Room," and his nickname was the Steamer. I can vouch that the Steamer was a screamer.

Getting screamed at by Furillo was not my only problem. I was far away from home and friends and my work schedule ruled out any kind of social life.

There was another side of Furillo. He had his moments of kindness. The first week in March of 1970, after I had been at the Herald for two months, Furillo, who felt sorry for me, gave me two tickets to a UCLA-USC basketball game to be played Saturday night, March 7, at the Sports Arena.

"Get a date," he instructed.

That presented a problem. The only female I knew in L.A. was a UCLA student, Pam Bradley, whom I had dated when we both worked at the Times-Delta. At the time, she was a COS student but had since transferred to UCLA.

I called her in her dorm room and got turned down. I then made the mistake of suggesting that someone in her dorm might be interested.

"Are you asking me to set you up?" she asked. Well, yeah.

She called the next day. She had found me a date. "She loves sports and is looking forward to the game; you'll like her," Pam assured me.

It turned out that I had gotten scammed by Pam. My date was not a UCLA student, nor a sports fan and did not even have a good personality. She had no personality. She lived in Glendale, did not know we were going to a basketball game and was unaware that USC had upset No. 1-ranked UCLA by one point, 87-86, the night before at Pauley Pavilion. There was a long stretch of silence as we headed to the Sports Arena.

After arriving there and finding our seats, I learned we were sitting right in front of Jerry West and Laker publicity director Jim Brochu. Next to us were Doug Krikorian, who snickered when he saw my date, and Herald Examiner colleague Barbra Zuanich.

Krikorian, as the Laker beat writer, knew West and Brochu and had already learned they had a predicament. They had come in West's Lincoln Continental, which had broken down about a mile from the Sports Arena, and they needed a ride to Brochu's car, which was across town at the King's X bar in Inglewood.

Doug could not accommodate them because he and Zuanich were in her Corvette. After I and my date arrived, Doug pointed at me and said, "Larry will give you a ride."

After learning about the situation, I said, "Sure. I have plenty of room."

After the game, which UCLA won, 91-78, West and Brochu climbed into the back seat of my two-door Chevelle Super Sport. My date sat up front. Here I was, a wet-behind-the-ears 23-year-old, and Jerry West was sitting in the back seat of my car.

"You've heard of Jerry West?" I said to my date as we left the Sports Arena. After getting no response, I added: "He plays for the Lakers."

She shook her head no, then said, "I have heard of Wilt Chamberlain."

That drew a laugh from West. I remember thinking, what a waste. This normally would have been a great way to impress a date.

When we arrived at the King's X, West said, "Can I buy you guys a drink?"

My date said to me, "I don't drink, I just want to go home."

"I'm sorry, we're going inside," I said. "You can have a Coke."

On the trip back to Glendale, not a word was said.

As for the person who set me up – literally – she ended up marrying a reporter we both worked with at the Times-Delta, Earl Wallace. Pamela Wallace, as she became known, and Earl Wallace became screenwriters. They, along with William Kelly, won the Academy Award for best screenplay for the 1985 movie "Witness," starring Harrison Ford. The story was Pam's.

I wish Pam had been able to witness how my date went. It was like she had called Central Casting and asked for the name of someone who could play the role of a bad blind date. I guess I will never know the backstory.

As for Earl Wallace, we once hooked up for drinks in Hollywood and, by chance, again in 1989 in Reno at a private party following a Michael Nunn-Iran Barkley fight. I was nearby on a family vacation at Lake Tahoe and drove to Reno. Wallace spotted me at the party, and we had a nice chat. We discovered boxing promoter Dan Goossen, who managed Nunn, was a mutual friend. Sadly, Dan Goossen died from liver cancer in 2014 at age 64. Earl Wallace died of unreported causes in 2018. I believe he was 73 or 74.

One quick Dan Goossen story. Sometime in the mid-90s, he invited me to a New Year's Eve party at his house. I was working a night desk shift, so I told Dan I would stop by. I arrived around 11:30 and discovered the attendees were mostly Goossen family members and their significant others. The only other male there without a mate was actor Gene Hackman. When midnight struck, the two of us were talking. Everyone else was kissing. I looked at Hackman and he looked at me. We both shrugged, then shook hands.

After living in Downey with Krikorian for three months, I moved into a three-bedroom townhouse near LAX with two guys from Fresno State. One was John Pollock, and the other, Skip Seebeck, was a fraternity brother of John's. One plus of the move was the number of flight attendants living in our apartment building.

Krikorian was a good friend but not a good roommate. He had some weird habits. While reading a newspaper, he would crumble up the pages and throw them on the floor. Our apartment was filled with crumbled-up newspapers and dirty laundry everywhere. I did my best to clean but could not keep up.

One day I was with Doug's best friend and one of his former roommates, Tom Hodges, and we bought a bunch of posters designed to make teenagers clean their rooms, make their bed, put the cap back on the toothpaste and so forth. Tom and I put the posters all over the Downey apartment. About a week later, I asked Doug if he had noticed the posters. He looked around and said, "Oh, yeah." Obviously, they did not have much of an impact.

To Doug's credit, our friendship survived. We had great times together, particularly during the four years, 1974-78, when we traveled with the Los Angeles Rams. And, apparently, his living habits improved over time.

Krikorian lives with his longtime companion, former Olympic swimmer Kathy Heddy Drum, in a beautiful home in the fashionable Naples neighborhood of Long Beach.

Doug spent 22 years at the Herald Examiner until it folded in 1989, then was the lead sports columnist for the Long Beach Press-Telegram for 22 years. He also became a well-known radio personality after teaming up with longtime sports talk show host Joe McDonnell in 1992, first at KMPC 710 and later at several other L.A. radio stations. Their show was called "The McDonnell Douglas Show." Former Herald staffer turned boxing publicist John Beyrooty came up with the name.

I used to get lots of mentions on L.A. sports talk shows, often in unflattering ways. The talk show guys may have thought that goading me into a feud would be one way to get their name in print.

In 1997, 39 members of the Heavens Gate religious cult were found dead in 39 beds after committing suicide in Rancho Santa Fe. Two radio sports talk show hosts working a late-night shift named me as a person they wished would have been in a 40th bed. Amazingly, their listeners agreed, even though I doubt they even knew who I was.

Krikorian, on the air, tabbed me "The Icon of American Journalism." After a while, I was simply "The Icon." People used to ask me, "Is he praising you or ripping you?" I would usually say, "It's just Doug being Doug."

Truth be told, it was a rip. But amazingly, there were people who thought Doug was being serious, or at least somewhat serious.

When I was at a Fresno State journalism department reunion around 1990, an alum who was a Times photographer told a group of professors, "Larry Stewart is big in L.A.; he is always getting ripped on the radio." Ah, my claim to fame.

Chapter 19: Early Years at the Herald

During my first week at the Herald Examiner, one night I picked up the phone and heard, "This is Bill Sharman from the L.A. Stars. I'm calling to see if you got our box score and to give you details of tonight's game."

This was not a PR person; this was a coach, a famous coach, who was calling in the results. It was not that long ago I was taking calls like this from high school prep correspondents at the Fresno Bee. Now it was a legend, and one from Porterville, no less. Bill was a 1944 graduate of Porterville High.

Sharman had to call the Times and the Herald Examiner after every game. Neither paper had assigned a beat writer to the Stars of the American Basketball Association, better known as the ABA. Can you imagine Pat Riley or Phil Jackson calling newspapers after Laker games?

Once Sharman identified himself, I was a bit tongue-tied but managed: "This is a real honor for me. I'm from Strathmore."

"Strathmore, that's amazing," he said. He asked me my name and then said, "Hopefully you can come to one of our games so that I can meet you."

I eventually did get to a game later in the season, a playoff game in Anaheim, as I recall, and that was where I first met Bill Sharman. He became coach of the Lakers the next season. He became the team's general manager in 1976 and later team president.

When I made a road trip with the Lakers for a playoff game in Chicago in 1973, Bill, then the coach, called me "Strathmore," even though no one knew what that meant.

Whenever I would see Bill at the Forum, I would always get a warm greeting. In 1996, at a golf tournament at Griffith Park honoring Dan Hafner, a longtime Times sportswriter who died of cancer, Bill and I shared a golf cart. That solidified our friendship.

After that, Bill and I regularly talked on the phone and played golf together several times a month. There was no agenda with Bill. We just liked each other. He invited me to Porterville when the basketball gymnasium at Porterville High was named after him. He invited me again when he was just being honored.

Several times we made the trip to Porterville to play in a charity golf tournament and would play a practice round the day before the tournament. During one practice round, I chipped in for a birdie on a par-3 and later holed out a sand wedge for another birdie. Strictly lucky shots.

That day Charles Whisnand, the sports editor of the Porterville Recorder, interviewed Bill for a story and Bill told Charles what I had done. My feat got played up in the ensuing feature story and I thought people who knew me from high school would wonder, "Is this the same Larry Stewart?"

Bill was more than just a basketball Hall of Famer – both as a player and a coach. He was a great all-around athlete. He starred in baseball at USC and was drafted by the Brooklyn Dodgers. Stanford recruited him as a quarterback, and he would have gone there had the school allowed him to also play baseball.

On one Saturday in high school, he was the winning pitcher in a baseball game, won a key tennis match and won three events in a track meet. I believe the events were the shot put, the high hurdles and the 100-yard dash. He was a county Class B shot put champion and never lost a tennis match until, at the age of 16, he was beaten in the final of a national competition in Kalamazoo, Mich.

Through it all, Bill was extremely humble. The only time I saw a hint of ego was when Randy Harvey, who was a columnist for several years beginning in 1996, listed some of the greatest all-around athletes to come out of California and did not mention Bill Sharman. Bill called me to complain and even mailed me some clippings and other material, which was unnecessary. I already knew everything.

When I called Randy to make a case for Bill, I was cut off. "Bill Sharman was not an athlete; he was just a shooter," Randy said. End of discussion.

Many years later Keith Jackson asked me to invite Bill, then in his mid-80s, to join us for a round of golf at L.A. Country Club. Our fourth was a young man Keith invited. After Bill left, the young man asked about him. "Bill Sharman," Keith said, "may have been the best all-around athlete ever to come out of California."

That made me think back to what Randy Harvey said about Sharman being just a shooter and not discussing the topic any further. It also made me remember that there was no arguing with Harvey. He was always right.

When Times columnist Helene Elliot complained to me about a particular editor who was driving both of us nuts, I asked, "Have you talked to Randy?"

"I did, and it did not do any good," Helene said.

I decided to try, and as feared, it was a waste of time. "The final product is all that matters," Randy said.

When Harvey first got a column, it ran in space previously occupied by Allan Malamud's popular Notes on the Scorecard column and, for a few months, the Newswire. (Malamed came to the Times after the Herald folded in 1989.) Harvey's column was not well received by a number of staff members. Pete Thomas called it "Notes on a Borecard" and Tim Kawakami tabbed it "Snoozewire."

My friendship with Sharman led to him giving me a scoop on how a decision he made in 1979 changed the course of NBA history. He waited more than 20 years to go public with this story.

Prior to the 1979 NBA draft, Rod Thorn, the general manager of the Chicago Bulls, called Sharman, the GM of the Lakers. The Bulls had the No. 1 pick among Eastern Conference teams and the Lakers, because of compensation for Gail Goodrich signing with the New Orleans Jazz three years earlier, had the No. 1 pick among Western Conference teams. A coin flip would determine whether the Bulls or Lakers would have the first pick in the upcoming draft.

The Lakers had the rights to call the coin flip. But Thorn asked Sharman if he could make the call. The Bulls, as a promotion, wanted the team's fans to determine whether to pick heads or tails. Sharman said yes to Thorn's request before realizing he probably should have consulted with the new owner, Jerry Buss, who had just acquired the Lakers from Jack Kent Cooke.

Thorn picked heads and the coin came up tails. The Lakers picked Magic Johnson. Then the Bulls picked UCLA's David Greenwood.

"In any coin flip, I always picked heads," Sharman told me. "I would have in this case too had I not given Rod Thorn permission to make the call."

Sharman rightly pointed out that if the Bulls had gotten Magic in 1979, then they certainly would not have been in position to draft Michael Jordan as the third pick in 1984. And, indeed, that would have impacted the history of the NBA.

In 2004, Sharman was inducted into the Basketball Hall of Fame in Springfield, Mass., as a coach. He had been inducted as a player in 1976.

Dwyre was aware of how well I knew Sharman, so he assigned me to do a profile.

In interviewing Bill, I asked when he first realized he was good at sports. He said it was when he played marbles in grade school. In the game of marbles, whenever you knock an opponent's marble out of a circle, you get to keep the marble. Bill said he had coffee cans full of marbles in his bedroom at home, which he kept hidden from mother. "She would have made me give them back," he said.

One time I visited John Wooden at his condo in Encino with Carl Bolt, a starter with Bill Russell on the great University of San Francisco basketball teams that won 60 games in a row and back-to-back national championships in the mid-1950s. Sharman was driving up from his home in Palos Verdes to join us.

Wooden and I had a mutual friend named Denny Ryan. I said to Coach, "Bill Sharman and Denny Ryan are the two nicest guys in the world." Said Wooden: "I'd agree with that assessment."

Sharman damaged his vocal cords while coaching the Lakers during the 1971-72 championship season and had difficulty speaking the rest of his life. The voice problems cut his coaching career short, so owner Jerry Buss made him general manager of the Lakers, a position he held from 1976-82. When he was promoted to team president, Jerry West succeeded him as general manager. The two of them built the Showtime Lakers.

When Sharman retired in 1991 at age 65, Buss kept Sharman on the payroll for the rest of his life as a special consultant.

Bill Sharman died Oct. 25, 2013, at age 87.

I often sat with Bill at Laker games. His Staples Center mid-court seats were in row 11. Marge Hearn's seats were a couple of rows behind Bill's. One time when Marge was by herself, I sat with her and that was when we planned our failed scheme to get Chick to announce his retirement.

When Sharman was inducted into the Basketball Hall of Fame as a coach in 2004, I made the trip to Springfield, Mass., on my own. One highlight of many during that trip was getting to meet Bob Cousy, Sharman's old backcourt mate with the Boston Celtics. In the above photo, that is Cousy, left, with Bill and me.

A few months later, I organized a surprise party for Bill on his birthday, May 25, at Phil Trani's restaurant. Don Kramer, a water boy for USC when Sharman played there, helped organize the party, and Phil Trani made it a reality.

Almost 200 people showed up and others, such as Cousy and Goodrich, sent emails that I read at the party. I also read a letter from President George W. Bush, which I had requested with help from my friend and former White House speechwriter Curt Smith, an author of 17 books, including several on baseball announcers. The beautifully written letter from President Bush arrived on my fax machine at home on the night of the party, just as Norma and I were about to leave. A note stated that the original signed copy would be mailed.

After the original letter arrived, I had it framed and set up a dinner date with Bill and his wife Joyce to give it to them. They had a present for me, too – a framed autographed photo of Bill and I together. I have it displayed in a prominent spot in my home office. The inscription in silver ink reads: *"To Larry, Sincere best wishes to a great writer and a great friend! Bill Sharman."*

One of my favorite anecdotes of all time is about getting my shoes shined in downtown L.A. while sitting with Pat Riley, then a player for the Lakers.

I mentioned earlier that I made a trip with the Lakers to Chicago in 1973. It was Game 6 of a playoff series against the Bulls. I filled in for Laker beat writer Mitch Chortkoff, who missed the game because of a Jewish holiday.

Furillo, who did the game stories for playoff games, never thought there would be a Game 6, so when he told me I would be the sidebar guy, he added, "Don't start packing."

But after the Bulls won two games in a row against the defending NBA champion Lakers to force a Game 6, I started packing. I went out and bought some new clothes. This was a big deal – my first road trip with a professional team.

The day the team would leave, I was scheduled to work a morning desk shift. When I got to work, I noticed my shoes were a mess. I asked a security guard at the Herald Examiner Building if there was a shoeshine stand nearby. The security guard told me there was one a few blocks over on San Pedro Street.

I found the two-seat stand and was getting my shoes shined when Riley came and sat down next to me. I was sure it was Riley because of his long hair and prominent mustache. I waited a minute or two and then meekly said, "I'm Larry Stewart from the Herald and I am going to be on the trip to Chicago with you."

Riley gave me a strange look. I did not say anything else.

That afternoon, after I got on the commercial flight to Chicago (the Lakers flew commercial back then), Riley gave me a nod, but no words were exchanged.

Now, fast forward 12 years to 1985 and the NBA Finals between the Lakers and Boston Celtics. The Lakers won the title in Game 6, breaking the Lakers' longtime dreaded Celtic curse.

But the Lakers lost Game 4 at the Forum in Inglewood, 107-105, on Dennis Johnson's last-second shot. I was with the Times by then and at that game. Afterwards, I was in the Forum Press Lounge talking with two friends, Bob Steiner, Laker owner Jerry Buss' head of publicity, and Susan Stratton, the executive producer of Laker telecasts on KHJ Channel 9 (the station became KCAL in 1989).

Riley, who was now the most famous coach in the NBA, walked in and came over to us. Steiner said, "Pat, you know Larry Stewart from the Times, don't you?"

What came next was a stunner. "Yeah, sure," Riley said, then turning to me, added: "Larry, I haven't seen you since we got our shoes shined together." I was more than stunned, I was blown away.

Riley stepped down as the Lakers' coach after they were eliminated from the 1990 NBA playoffs, 4 games to 1, by the Phoenix Suns in the Western Conference semifinals. Riley's agent, Ed Hookstratten, was already in talks with NBC about a commentating job for his client. Riley was hired on June 19, 1990, but not as a game commentator as expected. He was named pregame show host.

Riley spent only one season with NBC before returning to coaching – first with the New York Knicks for four seasons and then becoming president and coach of the Miami Heat.

When NBC hired Riley, the network wanted to play it up big. In somewhat of a precursor to Zoom, the press conference in New York was televised on closed circuit TV. To participate, reporters had to go to an NBC affiliate where they could watch the proceedings and then buzz in if they had a question. I went to the NBC studios in Burbank to participate in the press conference.

My ensuing news story ran on Page One of Sports, followed the next day by a column in which I included the shoeshine story. That prompted a call from Terry O'Neil, the executive producer of NBC Sports who hired Riley.

"I loved that item about you and Pat getting your shoes shined together and him remembering it 12 years later," O'Neil said. "Pat is brilliant and has a phenomenal memory. That's one reason we hired him and made him the pregame show host."

My relationship with Riley grew that year. I interviewed him several times, including once for an in-depth freelance story for Sport magazine.

In 2013, following the public memorial for Jerry Buss, my wife Norma and I spent quite a bit of time talking with Riley and his wife Chris at a private reception. Pat and I reminisced about the shoeshine story and told it to others who were there. I think Pat enjoyed telling it as much as I did.

I finally asked a question that had been on my mind for years: "What were you doing on San Pedro Street that day?" It is sort of a seedy area.

"That's the garment district and I had two tailored suits to pick up before going to the airport," he said.

Apparently, Pat Riley was already a clothes horse.

Riley and I got our shoes shined together in April of 1973, when my situation at the Herald was much improved. My first two years at the Herald Examiner were tough. I'd never had to deal with anyone like Furillo before. He was a bully, and at times I seemed to be his favorite target. I dreaded those 6 p.m. calls from him. On most nights, he would first chew out Leo Noonan, then me for various mistakes in the paper.

Working night shifts with almost no weekend nights off and zero social life, I was as miserable as I had ever been as an adult. But I promised myself that I would gut it out for three years, then decide what to do.

There were good aspects of my job, which, besides working the night desk, also involved covering high school sports. I handled the City Section and Steve Brand the CIF Southern Section.

I got my first byline in the Herald Examiner on Dec. 7, 1969, after I covered a Saturday afternoon football playoff game between Gardena High and L.A. High at East L.A. College. Gardena, the eventual city champion, won, 28-16, but much of my game story focused on a 196-pound defensive lineman named Calvin Peterson, who went on to star as a UCLA linebacker. He played for the Dallas Cowboys when they lost to Pittsburgh in Super Bowl X in 1976.

Allan Malamud put considerable effort into editing my story and improving it. Furillo called me the next day and raved about the job I did. "You are good enough to cover anything," he said. "You won't be on the prep beat long."

The honeymoon did not last long. I was in hot water the next time I missed a typo in one of Bud's "Steam Room" columns.

The biggest upset in sports that I was ever involved with took place toward the end of the 1970 high school football season. Furillo assigned me and a photographer to go out and do a feature story on L.A. Wilson High. The coach, Vic Cuccia, was Italian, like Furillo. Cuccia's team was averaging 61 points a game. The next opponent was Franklin High and Wilson needed only to score 22 points in its next two games to set a new City scoring record. I wrote that it was a foregone conclusion that Wilson would set the record against Franklin.

I asked Furillo if I should cover the game. He said no. "It's going to be a blowout anyway," he said. "And besides, Cuccia will call you with the details."

Cuccia always called in after his games. But on this night, he did not. Nor could I reach him at home. I finally got a hold of Franklin Coach Richard Whitney at home and got the shocking news. Wilson not only lost; it was a shutout. The banner headline over my story read: *It's True: Franklin 9, Wilson 0.*

"We put your story up in the locker room for all our kids to see," the Franklin coach told me. "They were primed about what they read about Wilson and went out and proved it wasn't true."

The next year on the prep beat, 1971, I got to know San Fernando High's Anthony Davis, who often ran from his quarterback position. I went to a practice to interview him and when I asked him for his home phone number, he asked me for my work and home numbers. We talked regularly throughout that season.

The Herald Examiner was his family's paper. One time no one called in the San Fernando game, and he called the next week to find out what happened. I explained that someone needs to call. After the next game he called. He said he had four carries for more than 200 yards, all in the first half. He scored on every carry and sat out the second half. Normally, I might have found that hard to believe, but this was Anthony Davis.

Davis led San Fernando over Granada Hills, 40-15, in the regular season. But when the same two teams met again for the L.A. City championship, Granada Hills, led by quarterback Dana Potter, prevailed, 38-28. Just before the game ended, distraught San Fernando players instigated a fight that ended up involving fans from the stands and drew more than 50 LAPD officers to the site.

My relationship with Anthony Davis remained solid, and he was my source when I broke a story that he and Allen Carter of Bonita High would be joining top recruits Pat Haden and John McKay Jr. of Bishop Amat at USC in the fall.

A month or so after A.D. committed to USC, I heard on a Saturday he might instead go to Valley State, which in 1972 would become Cal State Northridge.

The next day, I was at Dodger Stadium and was headed to the field during batting practice when someone called out my name. It was A.D., sitting in seats right behind home plate. I walked over to him and said, "What is this I hear? Are you considering going to Valley State instead of USC?"

The man sitting next to A.D. asked, "Who is this guy?"

A.D. introduced me. As I recall, the man was either the Valley State head coach or an assistant. It was an awkward moment, so I continued onto the field, using my press pass to get past security. I figured I could always call A.D. later. But A.D. talked his way past security and was soon standing next to me. Again, I asked him about the Valley State rumor. He expressed concern about competing with Carter for a starting spot as a running back at USC. Carter, as a junior, was the state high school 100-yard dash champion.

I said, "You have talked to me about being the best college football player in the country. You go to Valley State, and no one will ever hear about you again."

I do not know if I had any influence over A.D., but he did end up going to USC, much to the chagrin of Notre Dame. He scored six touchdowns against Notre Dame as a sophomore and the banner headline in the Times read: "Davis! Davis! Davis! Davis! Davis! Davis!" A.D. scored four more touchdowns against Notre Dame as a senior in an all-time classic 55-24 USC victory in which the Trojans, with Pat Haden at quarterback, rallied from a 24-0 deficit.

By the summer of 1971, my roommate Skip Seebeck had moved back home to Clarksburg, located near Sacramento. He would soon meet and eventually marry Lois Johnson. John Pollock and I moved to an apartment in Inglewood, and soon another Fresno State grad, Jim "Tippy" Tudman, a fraternity brother of Pollock's, was sleeping on our couch after landing a job with United Airlines.

Eventually, the three of us – Pollock, Tippy and I – moved to a three-bedroom apartment a block off the beach in Venice. Herald Examiner colleague and friend Jim Perry lived nearby in a beachfront apartment.

Perry and I talked about making a concerted effort to find girlfriends. He said I needed to talk to Furillo about getting Friday and Saturday nights off. As I recall, I think Perry talked to Furillo for me, and succeeded.

When Perry made a trip with the Dodgers, Steve Garvey told him that a new place downtown, Casey's Bar, was a good place to meet women. When Perry and I went there to check it out, an attractive blond waited on us. When we left, I told Jim that she liked him and insisted he go back and get her phone number. He eventually did and that waitress, Cathy, would become Perry's wife. They were married until Cathy's death from cancer in 2019.

After Perry began dating Cathy, Casey's Bar became a regular hangout for Jim, me and often Herald Examiner horse racing writer and handicapper Gordon Jones. One night we got to talking to some girls who invited us to a party that one of them was having at her apartment in Marina Del Rey in a few weeks.

Early one Friday evening in mid-August of 1971, Perry walked over to my apartment to remind me that the Marina party was the next night. He and Cathy had other plans, but he insisted that I should go.

"You know how you made me go back and get Cathy's number?" Perry said. "I got a feeling if you go to this party, you're going to meet someone."

I scoffed at that idea. I had totally forgotten about the party. And I told Perry that I had no idea where this party would be taking place. Perry said he had the address and insisted we go in his MG and look for it. When we found the apartment and knocked, a young lady came to the door. "It is my roommate's party," she told us. "There will be a lot of single women here."

The next night, I told my roommates, John Pollock and Tippy Tudman, about the party but they wanted to go to the Oar House, a popular Santa Monica bar.

We went there first, then on to the Marina party.

Although Tippy wasn't called Tippy because he easily got tipsy, he was not in good shape by the time we got to the party. When I saw Tippy talking to a short cutie with curly brown hair, I thought I better go over and rescue her.

Truth be told, she caught my eye when I first saw her, and now Tippy was pestering her. I went over to them and succeeded in wresting her away. After first chatting for a while, we went for a nice walk on a picture-perfect night.

I learned her name was Norma and she had come to the party with a friend. I also learned that she had served in the Peace Corps in East Africa (Uganda), had a master's degree in psychiatric social work from Cal and had just started working at Camarillo State Hospital.

I thought we hit it off, although I was initially a little suspect when I asked for her phone number, and she did not know it. It turned out she had just moved into an Oakwood apartment in Woodland Hills and had a new phone.

"My number is listed under my name," she said as she scribbled on a notepad and handed it to me. Now I had her full name: Norma Gerwig.

I am happy to report that Norma and I will be celebrating our 50th wedding anniversary on June 24, 2022.

Fate had once again been kind to me.

A side note here. If you recall, my mother's name was Greta, so movie buffs may wonder if we have a connection to Greta Gerwig, a prominent actress, director, and screenwriter. The answer is yes. Greta Gerwig is our niece. She is the daughter of Gordon Gerwig, Norma's only sibling.

Unfortunately, we do not have a close relationship with Greta and her parents. We have not seen Greta since she was a teenager. I cannot pinpoint a reason for the disconnect. I just know Norma and Gordon were as close as a brother and sister can be, and I was Gordon's best man when he got married to Chris Sauer in 1980. But our relationship gradually changed after the wedding.

Gordon occasionally emails, but we have not seen him or Chris since 2011. It bothers Norma a lot that she does not have a close relationship with her only sibling. We know little about his life and his family's life.

We were somewhat enlightened by the 2017 movie "Lady Bird," which was written and directed by Greta. It was nominated for an Academy Award as best picture, Greta was nominated as best director, and her screenplay was also up for an Oscar. In interviews, Greta said nothing in the somewhat autobiographical movie happened to her, but it still gave us a peek into her family's life.

When Greta was born, I assumed she was named after my mother. Gordon and Chris had stopped in Strathmore on their way home to Sacramento and met my mother and liked her. But when I thanked Gordon for naming their daughter after my mother, he said that was not the case; they just liked the name.

Greta's middle name, Celeste, comes from the wife of Uncle Larry Gerwig, a cantankerous old codger and blatant braggart. He was Norma's father's brother. Celeste and Uncle Larry often had terrible fights. Right in front of us. But Chris always seemed to like those two.

Even though I never cared much for Uncle Larry, for several years I would buy two Rose Bowl tickets and give them to him. He had a streak of attending every Rose Bowl game and I helped him keep it going. When he could not make it to the 1980 game, I sold the tickets and recouped my money.

Two months later, when Gordon and Chris got married in Sacramento, Uncle Larry was there, and he asked me what I did with *his* tickets. When I told him I sold them, he demanded I give him the money. At first I thought he was kidding. He was not and made a scene, continually yelling, "Those were my tickets!"

I saw Gordon somewhat regularly at the Times in the early 1980s. The Sacramento company he worked for, Systems Integrated, Inc. (SII), supplied the paper with an elaborate computer system for writing and editing. The SII computers were called Coyotes. Gordon, who designed the Coyote keyboard, made periodic trips to L.A. and we often met for dinner in the 10th floor cafeteria.

When our daughter Jill, as a member of Arcadia High's "We the People" Constitution team, competed in the state finals in Sacramento, Gordon and Chris came to the state capitol building to watch the proceedings.

It is unfortunate that Jill and her older sister Kelly are not close with their cousin Greta. They have only two first cousins. The other is my brother's son, John Todd Stewart, a concrete contractor in Stockton.

Chapter 20: My Life on Upward Swing

I wanted my first date with Norma Gerwig to be special. A flight attendant friend, Pat Rogers, had told me that she had Glen Campbell's manager on one of her flights and he offered to get her tickets to a "Glen Campbell Show" taping. Pat succeeded in getting me tickets; I succeeded in getting a date with Norma.

The taping took place on a Saturday afternoon. Our seats were at the end of a section of bleachers. At one point I looked to my right and standing a few feet away was Lucille Ball, who was a guest on the show. I tapped Norma on the shoulder and pointed toward Lucy. After the taping, I took Norma out to dinner at the upscale Randy Tar in the Marina. I think she was impressed.

After another date or two, she invited me to come up to Camarillo for lunch. Before we went out to lunch, she showed me around the state hospital. The unit where she worked was like a scene out of "One Flew Over the Cuckoo's Nest." Only in this case all the patients were women.

One woman in a nurse's outfit came into the unit and immediately got another woman in a headlock and took her down. Men in white suits arrived to break up the fight.

"The craziest person was the nurse," I told Norma afterwards.

"Oh, that woman used to be a nurse but is now a patient," she said.

Later came more dates with Norma. My personal life was on an upward swing and so was my professional life.

Yes, Bud Furillo was a complex, moody person who could be intimidating. But as is the case with most people, he had good traits too. For one thing, he was superb at his craft. He could bang out a column, design the next day's paper, edit copy, and handle a multitude of other tasks – all in one shift.

During the evening hours, he would be in constant contact with whoever was in charge at night, putting his imprint on the next day's section.

Another positive about Bud was his generosity. He always picked up meal tabs. He also passed out complimentary sports tickets to everyone on the staff. Comp tickets were plentiful at most major newspapers back then. Also, it was common for pro sports teams to take beat reporters on road trips at no cost.

The reasoning was the teams benefited from the publicity, good or bad.

In the post-Watergate era, newspapers began eliminating comp tickets and paid-for travel. The Times was quicker to act than the Herald and other papers, although my first boss at the Times, Bill Shirley, did not always heed company policies. He made sure everyone else followed those policies, but he did not.

To make it easier to explain my career path in L.A. it might be helpful to learn some newspaper terminology.

Major newspapers have four divisions – editorial, advertising, production, and circulation. Editorial is broken up into various departments, including national news, local news, entertainment, business, and sports.

In the old days, each editorial department had at least one horseshoe desk. Sitting in the slot in the middle was the editor in charge, or slot person. Usually sitting nearby would be a layout person who would *dummy* the section, or, in other words, map out where stories go. The word dummy does not refer to the person. It refers to the dummy paper used to design a section.

The slot person would distribute stories to copy editors who sat around the rim of the horseshoe desk. Copy editors who "worked the rim" were, colloquially, called rim rats. The slot, the layout person and the rim rats collectively were referred to as "the desk." If you were one of them, you were "working the desk."

The horseshoe desks are long gone, but the terminology remains.

The glamor jobs in the newspaper business involve writing, but a lot of brilliant people prefer working the desk – and they often make writers look good.

However, sometimes the desk is where writers end up after messing up.

When I got hired by the Times in 1978, there was a woman on the night desk named Sheila Moran, who came from the family that had owned New York's Moran Towing since 1860. Sheila had the Kings beat before getting assigned to the desk after botching a few assignments. At dinner one night in the Times cafeteria, she told the desk crew that she had not told her father that she was now on the desk. When asked why, she said, "I don't want him to know I'm a failure."

Not long after that, a tour group came through the sports department late in the day after the night desk crew had come in. Someone on the tour asked the slot man, Bob Lochner, "Who are all you people?"

Lochner, known for his dry wit, deadpanned, "We're failures."

When I started on the night desk at the Herald Examiner, Leo Noonan worked the slot on weeknights, and I was the lone rim rat. It was a skeleton crew. The entire place was understaffed.

By contrast, the staff size on the night sports desk at the Times during my tenure there was usually seven or eight on weeknights, and nearly double that on Saturday nights during college football.

After about a year and a half of working together at the Herald, Leo Noonan, who later changed his name to Ari Noonan, went to a daytime shift and I became the slot guy, with Keith "Boomer" Stepro my helper.

One night, the lone working linotype machine broke down. Left with a shortage of type, I filled one page with old engraved photos I found in a drawer. No stories, no captions, nothing but photos and a hand-set headline that read: "The Many Faces of Sports." A photo of the Chicago Bulls mascot was sideways.

Another time I came to work on crutches, having broken a foot the night before while running in a heavy rainstorm from my car to my apartment. The crutches made it difficult getting from the sports department on the second floor down to the composing room on the first floor.

Making matters worse, to my surprise I had a new coworker, Rich Levin, who was new to the newspaper business. He had never worked a desk shift. Rich, who would later become the head spokesman for major league baseball under four commissioners, started at the Herald, at age 29, as a copy boy, an entry level position. Before that, he was driving a beer delivery truck.

Rich was an all-City basketball player at Hamilton High and the City Section's leading scorer who later was a member of John Wooden's first national championship team at UCLA. While in high school, he was a prep correspondent for the old L.A. Examiner and got to know the Examiner's Dave Kirby. In 1972, he contacted Kirby, who was then on the Herald Examiner staff, to inquire about opportunities in sports writing.

Kirby got him the copy boy job, and three months later he was elevated to the night sports desk. Furillo promoted him without inquiring about his background. Rich came into the job with no guidance or training.

Rich became a close friend of mine, but our first night of working together was tough. When I tossed a wire service story over to him and told him the headline size I needed, Rich just sat there for a minute. "I may need some help with this; I've never written a headline before," he finally said.

Somehow, as I hobbled around on crutches and helped Rich as much as I could, we got the paper out that night.

Levin, a quick learner, in no time became a solid writer and reporter. He had been in the sports department less than a year when, in 1973, Furillo assigned him to the Laker beat. Rich replaced Mitch Chortkoff, who had left the Herald to join his friend Steve Bisheff at the San Diego Evening Tribune. Bisheff went there in 1972 and ended up at the Orange County Register in 1982. Chortkoff, after a short stint in San Diego, went to work for the Santa Monica Evening Outlook. Chortkoff covered the Lakers for the Outlook and other media outlets almost up until he died in 2018 at age 78 following a long battle with diabetes.

Levin covered the Lakers through 1980, then his full-time beat became the 1984 Olympic Games. Leading up to the Games, Rich got to know Peter Ueberroth, the chairman of the L.A. Olympic Organizing Committee. After the Games, Ueberroth became the commissioner of major league baseball and brought Rich along to handle MLB public relations, a position he held for 25 years before retiring in 2010.

In late 1972, I went from the night slot to the morning 7 o'clock shift that Leo Noonan had been working. My new shift involved correcting lots of typos in the first edition and updating later editions with breaking news.

Boomer took over the night slot and for a while worked with Rich Levin. In early 1973, Fred Robledo, the sports editor of the Arcadia Tribune, was hired to work with Boomer on the night desk.

Robledo, a lifelong friend, later became the Herald's golf writer. When the paper folded in 1989, Freddy came to the Times to work on the night desk before becoming a respected and popular golf publicist for Brener, Zwikel & Associates.

In June of 1972, I was still working the night desk at the Herald when Norma and I, on the spur of the moment, decided to get married in Las Vegas.

When I told Furillo, he got us a comp room at the Tropicana. I called John Pollock at his parents' home in Salinas and asked him to be my best man. He accepted and offered to pick us up at the Vegas airport. I did not see how that was possible. He had to first drive to L.A. to pick up his girlfriend, Monica Simon, then head for Vegas.

But amazingly, when Norma and I walked out from the baggage area at the Vegas airport, John and Monica were just pulling up to pick us up. It was perfect timing, and a good omen. We got married at the Chapel of the Bells on the Vegas Strip. Above photo shows Norma and me in Vegas.

After we got married, Norma and I moved into an apartment on Zelzah Avenue near Margate Street in Encino. While we lived there, we attended as many UCLA basketball games as possible. This was during the Bill Walton era, and our press seats were center court about eight rows up. Norma and I both admired Walton as a player, not knowing that someday we would be his dinner guests.

Years later, during one of my visits to Coach Wooden's condo on Margate in Encino, I told him that my wife and I had lived at the end of the street. I asked how long he had lived on Margate. He provided the exact date, April 15, 1972.

Explaining we were neighbors, I kiddingly said, "We could have carpooled to games."

I think Wooden thought I was serious. "We could have," he said. "But you would have had to leave early."

In 1973, Norma started looking for a new job.

"Remember that woman on the unit who you thought was a nurse?" Norma said. "She had been a nurse before crossing over to the other side. If I do not get away from Camarillo State Hospital, that could be me."

She landed a job working with young people at Five Acres, an adolescent treatment center in Altadena. After that, we bought our first house, located in the Chapman Woods area in east Pasadena.

When we had a housewarming party, Furillo arranged to have it catered. That was typical Furillo. He did those kinds of things for staff members. When Steve Brand and his wife moved into a new house, Furillo gave them a new bedroom set. And Brand and I were not among his favorites.

I have always believed that it pays to try and be kind to everyone. Here's a good example of that.

One day a security guard at the Herald called the sports department. I was the person who usually answered calls. The guard said a gentleman in the lobby wanted to talk to someone about a sports dinner at the L.A. Athletic Club.

Because of the strike in 1967, non-employees were not allowed in the building. I decided to go downstairs to the lobby and talk to this gentleman, even though I figured he was probably just dropping off a press release.

The man who introduced himself was Denny Ryan, then a stockbroker for PaineWebber. As a member of the L.A. Athletic Club, he had bought a table to entertain clients at a "Sports Night" dinner. He wanted to have a writer from his favorite sports section sit at his table. Since I was the one who came down to see him, he extended the invitation to me.

Denny was such a gracious host at the "Sports Night" dinner that I invited him and his wife Lynn to come to our upcoming housewarming party.

This marked the start of a lifelong friendship. Through Denny, I met Duke Llewellyn, who ran the L.A. Athletic Club, who also became a good friend. When I was at the Times, it was Duke who set it up for the Sports staff to play pickup basketball games there.

Duke was the chairman and co-founder of the L.A. Athletic Club's John Wooden Award. Because of a dispute over rights to the Wooden name in 2005, Wooden became disassociated from the award. But Wooden told me that the dispute in no way dampened his friendship with Duke. Coincidentally, both died about six hours apart on June 4, 2010. Duke was 93, the Coach 99.

Another reason for being kind to everyone is that you never know who you might be talking with. Here is an example that.

I was in Phoenix in 1995 for the NBA All-Star Game and was sitting alone in a hospitality room waiting for a shuttle to the arena when an elderly gentleman sat down next to me. He started making small talk and soon we were having an enjoyable conversation. It was maybe 15 minutes later that we introduced ourselves. That is when I learned I was talking with broadcasting giant Bill MacPhail, a former president of CBS Sports who in 1980 launched CNN Sports. We had talked on the phone but never met. MacPhail's family was baseball royalty during much of the 20th century.

When I was working the day desk shifts at the Herald, I rarely got invited to join the in-group that Furillo took out to breakfast almost every day. I got bypassed so much that sometimes I felt I was back in seventh grade.

However, one afternoon he said, "Call your bride and tell her you are going out with me tonight."

We started out attending a press function in Beverly Hills at a tennis club. The room was full of celebrities. Most of them knew Bud. I recall two who were there – Bill Cosby and Claudine Longet, Andy Williams' ex-wife who in 1976 was charged with shooting her lover, skier Spider Sabich, at his home in Aspen, Colo. She was convicted of negligent homicide and sentenced to 30 days.

From the press function we went to dinner at Dan Tana's on Santa Monica Boulevard, where Bud picked up the dinner tab. Then we went to a screening of the movie "Last Tango in Paris," starring Marlon Brando. I felt like I was on a date.

Chapter 21: New Beats, Plus TV Column

The first thing staff members asked whenever they arrived in the Herald Examiner sports department was, "What kind of mood is Bud in today?"

If he was in a bad mood, look out.

The department's best writer, in the opinion of Furillo and most of the staff, was Allan Malamud. (Sorry Doug.) Before Malamud became known for his "Notes on a Scorecard" column that he did for the Herald and later the Times, he covered boxing and Kings hockey.

On January 17, 1973, a Wednesday, Malamud came into the office the day before leaving for Kingston, Jamaica, to cover a major fight between George Foreman and Joe Frazier taking place the next Monday. It was the fight in which Foreman knocked down Frazier six times in the first two rounds before the fight was stopped. After the first knockdown, Howard Cosell famously told the ABC audience, "Down Goes Frazier, Down Goes Frazier, Down Goes Frazier."

Furillo was already in the office when Malamud arrived, and I was there too, working a morning desk shift. I did not get a chance to tell Malamud that Bud was in a bad mood. Malamud and Furillo, in the middle of the department right in front of me, got into a huge argument after Malamud asked about overtime pay.

"I'll be writing every day, and I have a Kings game tonight," Allan loudly argued.

"Overtime? For being on a week's vacation in Jamaica?" Furillo shot back.

Malamud, not afraid of Furillo, stood his ground and continued to argue until Furillo said, "No overtime, and you're suspended from the Kings beat."

He then turned around toward me. "Stewart, you're covering the Kings," he said emphatically, and apparently without thinking.

The game that night was against the New York Rangers. I had never attended a hockey game, never watched one on TV, and never read a Kings story unless I had to edit it. I knew hardly anything about hockey.

With help from Kings PR man John Wolfe and others, I covered most of the remaining home games and one road game that season. The one road game I covered was in Oakland against the California Golden Seals. Owned by Charlie Finley, the Seals became the Cleveland Barons in 1978 and then folded in 1980.

The Kings-Seals game I covered was the Kings' next to last game of the 1972-73 season, and the Seals' 3-1 victory knocked the Kings out of playoff contention. It marked the fourth year in a row the Kings would not make the playoffs.

I never covered another hockey game for the Herald. However, in 1976, when I was the assistant sports editor, I got a call from the assistant sports editor of the New York Times, whose paper was not traveling with the Rangers. He needed a hockey writer to cover an upcoming Rangers game in L.A. After learning the story didn't need to be filed until the next morning, I volunteered. The pay ($75) was nice and so was getting a byline in the New York Times.

A year or so later, when I was at a Kings game as a spectator at the Forum, I looked up at the scoreboard and saw: "Welcome vet hockey scribe Larry Stewart." I learned PR man

Mike Hope was responsible for that. It made for a good laugh.

In February of 1973, I covered a J.C. Agajanian-promoted event featuring Evel Knievel jumping over 50 cars at the L.A. Coliseum. That is how it was advertised. In truth, they were junked crushed cars stacked on top of each other.

Prior to the event, photographer Jim Ober and I attended a promotional press function where Knievel was going to make a practice run on the wooden ramp that had been built over the seats at the west end of the Coliseum. A sudden rain forced cancellation of the practice run. But then the rain stopped and Evel decided to make the run. "Get your camera ready," he told Ober.

Agajanian tried to stop him. "You're crazy," he said while standing in front of Evel's motorcycle. "You'll ruin this whole promotion if you get injured – or killed."

"Get out of my way!" Evel ordered, and off he went.

He got halfway up the ramp when his wheels started spinning on the wet wood. The bike bounced one way, Evel the other. He then picked himself up, climbed over seats, picked up his motorcycle, maneuvered it back onto the ramp and rode it back down. "How was that?" he asked Ober. "I don't do flips like that every day. I hope you got it." Ober got it.

Then Evel, still on his bike, held up a hand. "Damn," he said. His little finger was sticking out sideways. He popped it back into place as if it were nothing. Just another routine day for Evel Knievel, I assume.

In March of 1973, I began covering USC basketball when Dick Miller, the Angel beat writer, left for spring training. He had been covering the Trojans.

Coach Bob Boyd could not have been nicer to this young reporter.

He remembered that in 1971 I did a feature story on his son, Crescenta Valley basketball star Bill Boyd, when he was close to setting a CIF Southern Section scoring record. When my story ran,

Crescenta Valley was undefeated and so was USC. The headline on this story read: *Boyd Family: They're 34-0.*

Many years later, around 2014, I got reconnected with Bill Boyd and a friendship soon developed. I was able to find a clipping of that story I did in 1971 and I sent him a copy.

Several days after my 75th birthday in July of 2021, when I was still celebrating, Bill Boyd and his wife Susan joined Norma and me and Denny and Lynn Ryan for dinner in Pasadena.

In 1973, when I was covering USC basketball, Bob Boyd tried to get Furillo to send me to New York for an NIT game against Notre Dame on March 17, St. Patrick's Day. Upper management declined to spend the money and Furillo told me to cover the game off TV and arrange for Boyd to call with postgame quotes.

USC lost, 69-65, in a game refereed by Tom Casey, an Irishman, and Steve Lonzo. They called 28 fouls on USC, two on Notre Dame. USC took two free throws, Notre Dame 33. Bill Boyd shot USC's two free throws, making one, with 7:48 left in the game.

The worst thing, though, was a blatant muffed call with 20 seconds left to play and Notre Dame leading 67-65. A rebound went off Notre Dame's John Shumate and out of bounds. No Trojan was anywhere near the ball, as replays confirmed. But Casey ruled that it was Notre Dame's ball. That clinched the win for Notre Dame. CBS commentator Rod Hundley said it was a terrible call.

Over the phone from New York, Boyd told me, "I've never been involved in a game more influenced by officials. Casey had no business being on the court."

Furillo, who had watched the game, called to tell me my story was going across the top of Page One with this headline: *The Great St. Patrick's Day Robbery.*

The next day I was working the slot and was the first to arrive at the office. I was surprised to see all four phone lines were lit up. Every call was about the same thing: The USC-Notre Dame game story. One caller said, "I feel sorry for the writer, Larry Stewart." I explained I was Larry Stewart. "You must feel terrible," the caller said sympathetically.

I had not yet seen the story and was astounded when I did. The lead read:

What ook lace at Mdison front of a national television audience may come to be known as the Great S. P-trick's Dy Robbery.

It got worse after that. The referees' names came out *Tom Csy* and *Stevt Honzo*. And only half of my story made it into print.

Typos can be embarrassing to a writer because you fear the reader will think you are an idiot. This story was an embarrassment to the Herald Examiner.

I learned that a linotype machine used to put my story in type was malfunctioning and, just prior to the deadline, the only other usable linotype machine in the composing room that night also broke down. There was no one there to fix either linotype machine, although I believe a machinist was called in at some point. But the deadline arrived before the machinist arrived.

The shop foreman, who only cared about meeting the deadline, ordered the front page of Sports to go to press. He did not care what the page looked like.

That exemplified the prevailing attitude of the back shop at the Herald back then. Although reporters and editors cared about the product, top management only cared about the financial aspect of the business.

The Herald Examiner publisher was George Hearst. He was the oldest son of Randolph Hearst and grandson to the legendary William Randolph Hearst. George Hearst's lieutenant was George Szushtrum.

In 1977, a Los Angeles Magazine story alleged the two Georges and a prominent lawyer whose name I cannot remember had established a side corporation that bilked the parent Hearst Corporation out of money by fraudulently billing for services either not done, done on the cheap, or done for no reason.

The headline on the magazine article was *The Money-Making Machine.*

Even after I was named assistant sports editor in June of 1974, I had zero dealings with either George Hearst or George Szushtrum. They kept their distance from most people in editorial. But I did become friends with George Hearst's son Steve, who worked at the paper. He would often call late in the day and suggest a drink at Corky's, a dive bar located across the street. I was usually up for that. Steve, who I liked a lot, claimed the magazine article was filled with inaccuracies.

But it was eye-opening to me. The article pointed out that, among other things, this three-man corporation owned the paper's janitorial and carpentry services, and the lunchroom vending machines.

The Venetian blinds in my office were caked with dirt, rest rooms were a mess, and trash was everywhere. Janitors were rarely seen. Carpenters would tear down a wall for no apparent reason, then put up a new wall near where the old one was.

As for the lunchroom vending machines, I now knew why most non-editorial employees were not allowed to leave the building for a meal. That meant they were forced to eat the awful food in the vending machines.

We in Sports managed to avoid the vending machines by having copy boys make food runs for us. Our main guy was John Beyrooty, who was hired because he was Furillo's neighbor in Downey. Bey, as he was known, would bring in burgers from his family's restaurant, or go out and get a bucket of KFC. When Furillo considered promoting Beyrooty into Sports, he questioned a few of us about his writing skills, asking: "What can he do besides make food runs?" I forget who, but someone said, "Isn't that enough?"

Beyrooty ended up becoming a well-known and respected boxing writer, which led to his career as a boxing publicist.

As for Steve Hearst, he became the head of the Hearst Corporation's real estate holdings, which includes the property surrounding Hearst Castle. My friend Michael Young, who lives in Cambria and is the executive director of the Foundation at Hearst Castle, speaks fondly of Steve Hearst.

In 1962, things at the Herald Examiner began to decline after George Hearst made a critical mistake. That year there was a major L.A. newspaper merger. The L.A. Examiner and the Herald Express became the Herald Examiner and the Times merged with the L.A. Mirror. Hearst, as publisher, wanted the afternoon market for the Herald Examiner. That left Times publisher Otis Chandler with the morning market, which was the one he wanted.

The Herald Examiner, which at one time was the largest afternoon paper in the country with a circulation of nearly 750,000, saw readership slowly decline as society's reading habits changed. Morning newspapers thrived, while afternoon newspapers died.

"George bet on the wrong horse," wrote Dennis McDougal, a former Times staff writer and author of the 2002 book, "Privileged Son: Otis Chandler and the Rise and Fall of the L.A. Times."

Then came the strike/lockout of December of 1967, and circulation suddenly dipped to under 400,000. Advertisers with union ties began dropping their accounts. Circulation was around 350,000 when I left in 1978. It was at 240,000 when the Herald Examiner finally folded on Nov. 2, 1989.

The Herald Examiner Building at 11th and Broadway remained intact as an historical landmark. Built in 1914 by William Randolph Hearst, it was designed by architect Julia Morgan, who later designed the world-famous Hearst Castle, located on the Central California coast near San Simeon and Cambria. A six-year, $80 million renovation of the Herald Examiner Building was completed in 2021.

The newspaper merger of 1962, which doomed the Herald, was a boon to the Times. It became one of the top newspapers in the U.S. as circulation steadily increased. In March of 1990, the Times became the largest metropolitan daily in the country. The daily circulation was 1.3 million; Sunday circulation hit 2 million.

However, the Times' print circulation in 2021 was down below 420,000 and it ranked fifth among U.S. daily newspapers. National newspapers USA Today and the Wall Street Journal ranked No. 1 and No. 2 and were the only newspapers with print circulations above one million. The New York Times was No. 3 and the New York Post No. 4, both below 500,000.

After the strike/lockout of 1967, the saving grace for the Herald Examiner was its Sports section. Readers often claimed they bought the paper just for the Sports and threw the rest away. Management acknowledged that in 1977 when Sports became a separate tabloid section. That format lasted only about a year, changing back to a regular-sized section under new management.

I was not the first to write the Herald's Sports on TV column. That person was Harley Tinkham, an outstanding journalist who went to the Times after the strike and, among other things, created the Morning Briefing column. In 1973, Dave Kirby, then the UCLA beat writer, was doing the Herald's Sports on TV column.

For Kirby, an excellent writer, it was a secondary job. His UCLA beat came first. The TV column mainly involved what I call "rewriting the log," just providing details about the events that would be televised over the upcoming weekend.

In April of that year, Kirby left the Herald for a better paying job as director of public relations for Black & Decker. He offered to take me with him for a considerable bump in pay but doing PR for weed whackers did not exactly fit into my career plans.

I do not think I was Furillo's first choice to take over the Sports on TV column. He initially said he would "give me a shot at it," and said I would have to write a trial column.

Furillo offered no direction or advice, but Kirby did. He said the first thing was to call the network West Coast publicists in L.A. who handled sports – Bud Tenerani at NBC, George Vescio at CBS, and David Dyer at ABC – and get on their mailing list. Those three handled sports on a part-time basis only. The full-time sports publicists were in New York, one for each of the three networks.

When I called Tenerani, he did more than just add me to a mailing list. He invited me to lunch at the Carriage House across from NBC in Burbank. After lunch, he gave me a tour of the NBC studios and introduced me around.

That kicked off a friendship that lasted until Bud died in 1996 at age 67 after a battle with leukemia. I missed his funeral because that day I had a column to write. It was a poor excuse. After that I felt so bad that I vowed I would never again let work keep me from attending a close friend's funeral.

On a writing day in May of 2002, there was a funeral in Visalia for my friend and former neighbor Linda Little Wilson. Linda and I called each other brother and sister, and I called her mother, Imogene Little, my second mother. I wrote my column a day ahead of time so I could make it to her funeral.

I knew that the opportunity in 1973 to write the Sports on TV column for the Herald was a big deal, I just did not envision how big.

For my trial column, I decided to see if Chick Hearn outdrew ABC network Laker telecasts when they went head-to-head. Game 6 of the Western Conference semifinal playoff series between the Lakers and Chicago Bulls, the one I saw in person in Chicago, was the most recent Laker game televised by both ABC and L.A. station KTLA Channel 5. I started making phone calls and got resistance. In those days, ratings were not disclosed.

I eventually got the ratings I sought. Channel 5, with Chick and Lynn Shackelford, got an 11 rating. ABC, with Keith Jackson and Bill Russell, got a 9.

That was my lead item, and throughout I had fresh material.

Furillo liked this "trial" column so much, he said, "We're running this."

As noted in Chapter 1, my first column ran on May 4, 1973.

For my second column, I did a phone interview with talkative Bobby Riggs, who provided me with plenty of good material. He was preparing to play Margaret Court on CBS. Riggs easily defeated

Court, which was a prelude to Riggs famously losing to Billie Jean King, 6-4, 6-3, 6-3, on ABC on September 20, 1973.

Furillo soon decided to run my mug shot with the column. The mug shot drove Doug Krikorian nuts. He went to Furillo and demanded, "How can my protégé Larry Stewart have a column with a mug shot, and not me?"

Furillo eventually caved and gave Doug a column. That is how Doug Krikorian became one of L.A.'s more noted sports columnists.

Meanwhile, I was off and running on my amazing journey on the sports broadcasting beat. As sports talk radio began to grow, the

Sports on the Air
By LARRY STEWART

title of my Herald Examiner column was changed to Sports on the Air.

Some of my fondest early-career memories came from attending taping of sports shows such as PBS' "The Way It Was," hosted by Curt Gowdy, and "Sports Challenge," hosted by Dick Enberg. Both shows were taped in Los Angeles during the 1970s, usually five in one day. The studio green rooms for both shows would resemble a Hall of Fame, only with real live people such as Mickey Mantle, Yogi Berra, and Whitey Ford, or Bart Starr, Paul Hornung and Ray Nitschke – and too many others to name here.

After the tapings, it was off to the Beverly Hills Hotel, where the guests stayed and where we gathered for drinks and storytelling in the iconic Polo Lounge. I recall one night sitting with the legendary Bill Veeck, who at various times owned the Cleveland Indians, St. Louis Browns and Chicago White Sox. Veeck, born in 1914, regaled us with stories of baseball's yesteryears.

In 1951, when Veeck owned the Browns, he famously had 3-foot-7 Eddie Gaedel make a plate appearance. Gaedel walked on four consecutive pitches.

Both "The Way It Was" and "Sports Challenge" were produced by Gerry Gross, who paid his guests a $1,000 appearance fee and had trade-off deals that covered airfare and their stay at the Beverly Hills Hotel. The trade-off deals involved free advertising.

In 1982, when I was at the Times, Gross created another show, "The Great Sports Debate," with George Steinbrenner as the host. I was there when the pilot was taped. The debate was, who was better, Joe DiMaggio or Ted Williams?

The panelists were former teammates of DiMaggio and Williams. The judges were me, Herald Examiner columnist Diane K. Shah, and Times columnist Scott Ostler. With Billy Martin on the DiMaggio panel, Ostler was able to interview him together with Steinbrenner, making for an interesting column.

It was at this taping where I stood at the green room bar between Warren Spahn and Don Larson and listened to bartender Leo Durocher tell stories.

Despite being able to lure great talent, Gross ran into financial trouble and the pilot was never aired. I later learned from Enberg that Gross owed a lot of people money, including Enberg and Merlin Olsen. I was saddened to hear that. Gerry Gross, besides introducing me to sports legends, had offered encouragement and guidance early in my career when I was at the Herald Examiner.

I got to know Curt Gowdy when he was the host of "The Way It Was." I once gave him a ride from Hollywood to LAX and we got a chance to talk. We became closer after I interviewed him in the press box at Dodger Stadium in 1975. (See cover photo.)

Gowdy liked my ensuing column, and we later discussed writing a book together, following him through 1975.

That year his assignments included the Rose Bowl, the Super Bowl, the NCAA Final Four, the Saturday baseball game of the week, the World Series and Sunday NFL football. His idea was to look back, in separate chapters, at each event. He had been keeping notes. There would also be chapters on "The Way It Was" and the outdoor sports show he hosted, "American Sportsman."

Little, Brown and Company, a major publisher, offered us a deal that included a $10,000 advance. Gowdy implied I could use the advance to cover my expenses. My yearly salary was not much more than that.

We planned to have our first long interview session in Buffalo when the Rams played the Bills in a Saturday night exhibition game. I went there with the Rams, and he was there to call the game for NBC. We set aside that Saturday. He cleared his schedule, and I did not have a schedule to clear.

I showed up for breakfast in the hotel where we were both staying and saw that Curt was already there. He was wearing a neck brace, which was not a good sign. He told me it was a nerve problem. He also said that after this season he was being replaced by Joe Garagiola as NBC's lead play-by-play announcer on baseball.

"We better put this project on hold," he said.

I knew that meant it was dead.

Gowdy told me, off the record, that he thought Garagiola used his ties as a spokesman for Chrysler Motors to undercut him. Chrysler was a sponsor of NBC's baseball coverage.

The book deal falling through maybe was for the best. At this stage of my career, I probably was not ready to write a book, particularly one for a major publisher.

When I first started writing the TV column, I was still working morning and weekend desk shifts but also getting more writing assignments. I twice covered Thursday night fight cards at the Olympic Auditorium in 1974.

Prior to the first one, early in the year, publicist Van Barbieri told me I would be paid $50 for doing an on-air interview between rounds with legendary ring announcer Jimmy Lennon Sr. It would be part of the TV coverage on Channel 13.

The night of the fight, Barbieri said Lennon and I would be promoting next week's main event. I told Barbieri I was hardly qualified to do that. He in turn handed me a script he had typed up and told me I had to follow it.

I deviated a little from the script during the interview, which threw Lennon off stride. Somehow, we got through it.

That was my one and only contact with Jimmy Lennon Sr. But 10 years later, in May of 1984, a strange thing happened when Lennon, at a Sugar Ray Leonard-Kevin Howard fight, was introducing dignitaries at ringside. He introduced HBO's esteemed boxing commentator Larry Merchant as Larry Stewart.

A few years later, when there was a group of us having lunch with Merchant, I asked him if he remembered Lennon's faux pas. He did. "I asked Jimmy how he came up with Larry Stewart," Merchant said. "He said he had just seen you."

That was not true. Maybe he meant he had just seen my column, possibly on his flight to the fight in Worcester, Mass.

The second time I covered fights at the Olympic in 1974, Jim Healy, who did the blow-by-blow for the Channel 13 telecasts, was scheduled to interview me on air. Again, I was handed a script. I knew Healy, so I asked him if we had to follow the script. He said, "No, we'll just wing it."

This was the Thursday night after one of the biggest fights ever in L.A. had taken place Saturday night, May 24, 1974, at the Sports Arena. Bobby Chacon had stunned Danny "Little Red" Lopez with a ninth-round knockout before a nearly full house of 16,027 fans at the Sports Arena. Another 2,671 watched on closed circuit TV at the Olympic.

During my interview with Healy, according to the script, I was supposed to hold up a photo of that fight while Healy explained that the first 1,500 fans in the door at the Olympic the next Thursday night would be handed a print. Since Healy had told me we did not have to follow the script, I was unaware of my expected duties and did not hold up the photo.

"Aileen spent $1,500 getting all those prints made up, and I hear she is pissed," Healy said on the phone the next day. "But don't you worry about it. I'll take the blame."

I never heard anything further, and I still got my $50 for doing the interview.

Healy and I developed a good relationship. I wrote about him often and he gave me lots of mentions on his half-hour radio show. If I went to Santa Anita on a Friday, I knew he would be in the press box. One time I showed up on crutches after twisting an ankle playing pickup basketball, and the next Monday my injury was a bit on his show, sound effects and all. My daughter Jill and I heard it in my car, and we both laughed. Healy could make a twisted ankle humorous.

The photo here, taken in the early 1980s at Santa Anita racetrack, shows Healy with my daughters Jill, left, and Kelly.

When Kelly was 8, she wrote Healy a fan letter in which she cited her favorite soundbite, a Cosell imitator saying, "Jim Healy, you've got a horse(bleep) attitude." Healy read the entire letter on the air, calling it the best fan letter he had ever received.

Some 10 years later, I received a letter from a Healy critic who complained about the language on his show and, amazingly, made note of "a letter from a 8-year-old girl that Healy had the audacity to read on the air."

That may be hard to believe, but trust me, it happened. Or, as Healy would say, "I don't make 'em up, pally."

Jim Healy was one of a kind, never to be copied. The few who tried failed miserably. He created a new lexicon for his listeners and his barbs had many targets, with Tommy Lasorda maybe being at the top of the list. Lasorda certainly provided good material.

In July of 1982, Dodger pitcher Tom Niedenfuer was fined for beaning the San Diego Padres' Joe Lefebvre. The next day, Lefebvre's teammate, Kurt Bevacqua, was quoted in newspapers saying, "The guy who should have been fined was the guy who ordered Niedenfuer to throw at Joe, that fat little Italian."

When Lasorda was asked about Bevacqua's comment, the taped response provided Healy with one of his all-time classics. Here is how it appeared in print: *I have never told a pitcher to throw at a batter. I especially would never have a pitcher throw at a (bleeping) .130 hitter like Lefebvre, or a guy like Bevacqua. Bevacqua could not hit water if he fell out of a (bleeping) boat. I will guarantee you one thing. When I was pitching, if (bleeping) guys like Lefebvre and Bevacqua were in the lineup, I'd send a limo to make sure they made it to the park.*

Healy was on radio in L.A. for 43 years. He died at age 70 on July 22, 1994, which was my 48th birthday. I was on a driving vacation with my family. We had spent time in Arizona and Santa Fe, New Mexico, and were now in Colorado.

Before leaving, I wrote an advance obituary on Healy. I was among only a few people who knew he had liver cancer. The day my obituary was printed, I called the paper to check messages on my work voicemail. One was from Patrick Healy, Jim's son, a longtime Channel 4 news reporter. He had apparently noticed the line in the paper that said I was on vacation.

"Thank you for coming off vacation to write that beautiful obituary on my father," Patrick said in the message he left. I called Patrick after returning home to explain I had done the obituary in advance.

That is often done in the newspaper business. Sometimes, that can be a problem. In 2007, I knew that longtime L.A. sportscaster Stu Nahan was losing his battle with a cancerous form of lymphoma, so I did his obituary in advance.

After I turned it in, the obituary editor came over with a question I could not answer. So, I called Stu. A few minutes later, Bill Dwyre came over to my desk.

"I just got a call from Stu Nahan," Dwyre said. "He sounded upset. He wanted to know if you were writing his obituary." I felt terrible. I called Stu and lied. I told him that, no, I was not writing his obituary. I thought that was the best way to handle it.

After Nahan died on Dec. 26, 2007, a memorial was held in a movie theater in Sherman Oaks. Pat Sajak, who worked with Stu when he was a weatherman at Channel 4, was among those who delivered eulogies.

"When I had an opportunity to host a new game show called 'Wheel of Fortune,' the station wouldn't let me do it," Sajak said. "I had a big decision to make, so I went to Stu for advice. He told me, 'Forget the game show, it probably won't be around for long. But if you stay at Channel 4, you'll always have the weather.' I am glad I didn't take Stu's advice."

Chapter 22: Promotion Was a Shocker

By June of 1974, my situation at the Herald Examiner had continued to improve and was about to get better – way better.

I had moved up from the bottom of the totem pole on a 22-person staff, and often worked weekend slot shifts. Steve Bisheff and Mitch Chortkoff had moved on to San Diego in 1972, Jim Perry had left to become sports information director at USC and veteran Jack Disney, a marvelous newspaper man and person, had hit bottom with a drinking problem and was no longer at the paper.

Disney joined Alcoholics Anonymous, got his life straightened out and came back to the Herald before eventually going on to a great career as a horse racing publicist. Jack died on July 1, 2015, at the age of 80 after a long bout with Chronic Obstructive Pulmonary Disease (COPD). Jack was beloved by many, including me.

On the afternoon of Friday, June 14, 1974, I got a message that Don Goodenow, the managing editor, wanted to see me in his office. I had not had any contact with Goodenow since he interviewed me when I was hired in late 1969.

After I sat down, Goodenow said, "Bud Furillo has been fired. When I talked to him, he said you were in charge over the weekend, so I wanted to let you know."

I was stunned. Naturally, I asked what happened. This was all coming out of left field. Goodenow explained it had to do with the sports talk show Bud began doing earlier that year for radio station KABC.

At lunch that day at a coffee shop, George Szushtrum, the No. 2 man at the paper behind publisher George Hearst, noticed a 4x6-inch little yellow and blue placard on his table. Goodenow showed me the placard. It read: *Listen to Bud Furillo on KABC AM 790. Sponsored by Sears.*

According to Goodenow, Sears had just cancelled a $50,000 advertising account with the Herald. Goodenow also said that when Furillo got the offer from KABC, he convinced the two Georges, Hearst and Szushtrum, that the radio show would be good promotion for paper.

"The way I understand it, Bud would always be identified by the radio station as the sports editor of the Herald Examiner," Goodenow told me. "Nowhere on that placard is the Herald Examiner mentioned."

I learned that Szushstrum called Bud after lunch and told him that he could no longer do the radio show. Bud refused and was thus fired. But Goodenow worked it out so that Bud had until Monday to change his mind. In the meantime, I was in charge.

After I returned to my desk, it was not long before Furillo called.

"By now I suppose Goodenow has told you I was fired this afternoon," he said. "Don't worry. They can't fire me. I am the Herald Examiner." I swear that is what he said. It was déjà vu all over again, as Yogi Berra would say. In my first face-to-face meeting with Cosell, he emphatically told me, "I am 'Monday Night Football'."

Furillo did have a Cosell-sized ego. Well, maybe not quite, but close. Furillo ended the conversation by saying, "I will be back by Monday, guaranteed."

According to Andy Furillo, Bud's son who wrote a 2016 biography on his father, Bud was making $345 a week from the Herald and $800 a week from the radio station. Over that weekend, he talked to George Hearst, who offered him a $25 raise, which Bud turned down.

The next Monday, June 17, Goodenow again called me into his office.

"Bud was offered a raise to stay, but he was told he still had to give up the radio show," Goodenow said. "He refused. Bud is now officially fired. He was instructed to turn in his security badge."

Goodenow added, "We are giving you the title of assistant sports editor as we conduct a search for a new sports editor. In the meantime, you are in charge."

Wow, here I was, only 27 and running a major newspaper's sports department. It was surreal.

About a month later, following my recommendation, Malamud was named sports editor. My feeling was that Malamud, not adept at details, was respected by the staff and could make major decisions such as what we cover and who covers it. I was already handling such things as the work schedule, story assignments, daytime editing, and approving expense accounts. I was the one who had to tell Krikorian he could not put all his personal calls on his expense account.

Dummying, or laying out, the sports section had been a Furillo strong suit. Now either Boomer, the night slot person, or I would handle that.

The day Malamud was named sports editor, there was a short story in the paper about our promotions along with a photo of the two of us.

I was not surprised to see in Andy Furillo's book that his father was making only $345 a week as the Herald Examiner sports editor.

Herald management did not throw around the big bucks, even though George Hearst later in life was known for his philanthropy and generosity. When he died in 2012 at age 84, his net worth was estimated at $1.9 billion.

When I was named assistant sports editor, my raise was all of $13 a week. But money was not the important thing, at least not at the time. I was thrilled with my new position.

There were some small congratulatory parties, and one big one, thrown by longtime Dodger beat writer and columnist Bob

Hunter. It took place at Bill Bailey's Irish pub in the Valley and was attended by many of the biggest names in the L.A. sports scene.

At the party, I paused to look around at all the legends. This was another pinch-me moment. One of the highlights was Allan and I posing with John Wooden and Bob Boyd in what might have been the

only time those rival coaches were photographed together.

Wooden spent most of the night at a table talking baseball, his favorite sport, with the legendary New York Yankee Lefty Gomez.

A caricature drawing of Malamud and me by the great newspaper cartoonist Karl Hubenthal adorned the room. I took it home but stupidly never had it framed. I stored it in our garage, and it eventually rotted away.

Chapter 23: The Best Years of My Career

My four years as the Herald-Examiner's assistant sports editor were incredible; the best four years of my career. I was working my tail off but enjoying it. I was pretty much the boss. Furillo was a hands-on boss; Malamud was quite the opposite. I thought Malamud and I made a good team. I handled routine details; he had final say on major issues and the coverage of major events.

One such event was the 1975 trade that brought Kareem Abdul-Jabbar to the Lakers. This was one of the biggest stories in the history of L.A. sports. The Lakers acquired Kareem from the Milwaukee Bucks in exchange for center Elmore Smith, guard Brian Winters, and rookies Dave Meyers and Junior Bridgeman.

The trade was announced at a 10 a.m. news conference on Monday, June 16. Despite Laker owner Jack Kent Cooke's effort to keep it a secret, word leaked out that Jabbar was coming to the Lakers. Cooke had called a meeting the previous Friday afternoon involving top personnel from both the Lakers and Kings. Cooke owned both teams along with the Forum. He also owned the Washington Redskins (now the Washington Football Team.)

In the 2006 book, "Bob Miller's Tales from the Los Angeles Kings," Cooke is quoted as telling the group, "We are going to have a press conference Monday morning here at the Forum, and it will be the greatest sports press conference in history. If any of this happens to leak out before Monday, you are all fired."

The morning of the press conference, Miller had just settled into his office when Cooke came in and said, "Bob, let's rehearse the press conference."

And they did – twice – with emcee Chick Hearn practicing his announcement as the organist played "Lakers March," and the spotlight operator beamed his light on the black curtains through which Jabbar would enter.

Now, nothing could go wrong, right? Not exactly.

At the real press conference, Chick announced: "Ladies and gentlemen, introducing the newest Los Angeles Laker, the most dominant player in the NBA, Kareem Abdul-Jabbar." But Jabbar did not come through the curtains. An awkward moment of silence followed as reporters and others at the press conference started laughing. Miller thought, "We are all going to be fired."

Chick again made the announcement. This time, two hands appeared. Slowly the curtains opened. Out stepped a security guard. More laughter. Jabbar, who was waiting in a locker room, had gone to the bathroom and did not hear the announcement. Eventually, he appeared – and the Lakers' future was now secure.

Laker beat writer Rich Levin, columnists Melvin Durslag and Doug Kirkorian, at least two other staff members, including me, covered the Jabbar trade.

Malamud, meanwhile, had an exclusive about the Kings close to a record-setting $300,000 deal with hockey great Marcel Dionne.

When it came time to dummy the next day's sports section, I had the Jabbar trade at the top of Page One and Malamud's Dionne scoop toward the bottom. But Malamud wanted his story to get equal play with the Jabbar story. Malamud, the boss, got his way. Our Page One banner headline covered both stories.

The next day, Cooke called Levin to congratulate our staff for its coverage of both the Jabbar trade and Malamud's Dionne exclusive. I think Cooke may have been Malamud's source, either directly or indirectly. Otherwise, I think Cooke might have been upset that news of the pending Dionne deal had leaked out.

"I loved the fact that the Dionne story got equal play with the Jabbar story," Cooke told Levin, showing that he knew newspaper lingo. The inner workings of the business fascinated him, so much so that in 1985 he bought the Los Angeles Daily News for $176 million. He owned the paper until his death in 1998.

Cooke's reaction to the play of the two stories was also evidence that Cooke, a Canadian, preferred hockey to basketball.

"I want to invite you and whoever did the Page One layout to come to the Forum for lunch tomorrow," Cooke told Levin.

Rich, unaware of Malamud's influence on the play of the Dionne story, told Cooke I did the layout, which was technically true. I told Malamud about Cooke's invitation and suggested he come too, but he said he could not make it. I am not sure what the reason was. Malamud did not pass up many lunch invitations.

The next day Rich and I met at the Forum and were escorted to a back room. Cooke soon arrived. "Would you gentlemen mind terribly if my coach with the Redskins, George Allen, joined us?" he asked. No, we did not mind.

After Allen arrived, a waiter brought the four of us our lunches – hamburger steak with peas and cooked carrots. I think we had iced tea to drink.

A few weeks earlier, I had lunch with Gene Autry at his radio station, KMPC. We ate in an exclusive upstairs dining room where a waiter in a tuxedo brought us a full menu and took drink orders.

The lunch with Cooke was a far cry from that.

Throughout the lunch, George Allen seemed intimidated by Cooke, whom he called Mr. Cooke, and was relatively quiet. About an hour and a half into our lunch, Allen said, "Mr. Cooke, would you excuse me. My son Bruce is waiting for me in the car in the parking lot and I want to go out and tell him to come in and maybe get a Coke in the Forum Club."

"My goodness, George, bring that poor boy in here," Cooke said. "Why in the world would you leave him in the car?"

"I didn't think we would be this long, and I didn't want to intrude on your planned lunch," Allen said before leaving and returning with Bruce, who was 20 at the time. Bruce Allen would years later serve as general manager of the Tampa Bay Buccaneers and then GM and president of the Redskins.

Bruce Allen's name was in the national news in October of 2021 as the person on the receiving end of many of the emails that led to Jon Gruden resigning as coach of the Las Vegas Raiders.

As for that 1975 lunch at the Forum, it lasted until about 3 p.m. as Cooke regaled us with stories and showed off what he believed was an impressive vocabulary. After the lunch, Rich and I were leaving the building when we heard this over the Forum intercom: "Will Rich Levin and Larry Stewart please report to Mr. Cooke's office?"

He wanted to have our pictures taken. "I just thought of this," Cooke said. "I'm going to put framed photos of media members in the Press Lounge. You two will be the first."

Soon photos adorned the walls of the Press Lounge, where us media guys hung out after Laker and Kings games. Oftentimes, Chick Hearn would tend bar.

In 1979, Jerry Buss bought the Forum, along with the Lakers and Kings, and soon celebrities and hangers-on were also allowed in the Press Lounge. The place became more crowded, but it was still a good place to hang out.

During our lunch with Cooke, Rich and I learned that before making the Jabbar deal the Lakers had considered a trade involving Bill Walton of the Portland Trailblazers. That one involved the Lakers giving up two players instead of four. I think with that deal the Lakers could keep blue-chip rookies Meyers and Bridgman.

Cooke, off the record, said he met with General Manager Pete Newell, Coach Bill Sharman, and Chick Hearn, who besides being the play-by-player announcer was, at the time, also the assistant GM. They took a vote. Newell and Sharman liked the Walton deal. He was younger than Jabbar and the Lakers could keep Meyers and Bridgeman, they reasoned.

Then Cooke voted. He preferred the deal for Jabbar.

When Chick voted, he sided with Cooke, or Mr. Cooke, as Chick and everyone else at the Forum called their boss.

Years later, when I asked Sharman about that meeting, he said, "Chick had told me he liked the Walton deal. But he changed his mind once he learned how Cooke was voting. I don't think he wanted to go against Mr. Cooke."

It turned out the right trade was made. Jabbar played 20 seasons. He, Magic Johnson, and James Worthy were the backbone of the Showtime Lakers. Walton led the Trail Blazers to an NBA title in 1977 and was named MVP the next season, but broken bones in his feet dampened much of the rest of his 10-season career.

Chapter 24: Traveling with the Rams

When I first set a goal of being a big-city sportswriter, my dream was to travel with a major league baseball team. That goal changed over time. I could see the baseball beat was a grind and involved a lot of high-pressure deadline writing.

To me, traveling with a professional football team seemed more desirable, what with weekend trips and daytime games. In the fall of 1974, after discussing it with Malamud, I became the Ram sidebar writer for the Herald. That meant I would join Krikorian, the main beat writer, on all road trips.

Krikorian and I and beat writers from suburban papers traveled on the Ram charter flights, while Bob Oates and any sidebar writer from the Times (often it was Skip Bayless) traveled at their paper's expense. The Times, a hugely profitable enterprise, was out in front of other papers in this regard. However, Oates still got perks.

My wife and I became friends with him and his wife Marnie after I went to the Times. We had them over for dinner at our house a couple of times. When we were all attending an event on the westside, Bob and Marnie invited us for drinks at their house in Baldwin Hills. After we arrived, Bob brought out a cardboard box full of the tiny liquor bottles that are distributed on airplanes.

"Pick out whatever you want," he said.

It was obvious Oates had collected these little bottles while traveling for the Times. During most of Oates' era, Times reporters flew first class. Oates was with the Times 1968 to '95. He died in 2009 at the age 93.

Even though Krikorian and I traveled at the Rams' expense, we were never told what to write, or not write. PR man Jerry Wilcox might suggest a feature story but suggest was all he would do.

The only complaint I knew about came from Jack Teele, the Ram's vice president in charge of finance. I heard it second hand from Krikorian.

In 1974, when the Rams were in Atlanta, Joe Hendrickson of the Pasadena Star-News told me that Pepper Rodgers, the former UCLA coach who was then at Georgia Tech, had invited the L.A. writers on the trip to that Saturday's game against Navy. Hendrickson and I and Rich Roberts, then with the Long Beach Press-Telegram, went to the game and sat in the press box.

Afterwards, we went down to the locker room to see Pepper. "You guys are coming with me and my wife," he said.

He took us to one party after another. And talked and talked.

After the three of us all wrote feature stories on Pepper for our respective papers, Teele told Krikorian, "We don't bring writers on the road with us to have them write stories on Pepper Rodgers."

In 1977, the Rams were 7-3 going into a game at Cleveland. The team had already won four consecutive NFC West division titles and would win a fifth this season, finishing 10-4. But all five seasons under Coach Chuck Knox, the Rams lost in the playoffs, twice in the first round. The Rams lost three times in the NFC championship game, once to Dallas and twice to the Minnesota Vikings.

The Rams' playoff record under Knox displeased owner Carroll Rosenbloom, as did Knox's conservative play calling. Knox's nickname was Ground Chuck because of his penchant for the ground game.

Rosenbloom had Krikorian's ear and voiced his displeasure to Doug throughout the '77 season. The week of the Cleveland game, Rosenbloom, after asking not to be quoted directly, told Doug he was going to fire Knox if the Rams again lost in the playoffs.

Since Doug had an impeccable source for a banner-headline story, we decided to run the story in the Sunday paper to get maximum readership. The first edition of the Sunday paper came out on Saturdays.

The Rams were leaving for Cleveland that Saturday, Nov. 26, a day later than normal because of freezing weather in Ohio. Doug called me that Saturday morning to say he was too sick to make the trip. That meant I would be making the trip by myself and writing both the game story and the sidebar.

I knew the real reason Krikorian did not want to make the trip. He did not want to have to face Knox.

When I got on the plane headed for Cleveland, I saw Knox and general manager Don Klosterman sitting together in the first row. I could not help but notice that Knox was holding the early Sunday edition of the Herald Examiner.

Once we got in the air, Klosterman came back to where I was seated. "We need to switch places," Klosterman said. "Chuck wants to talk to you."

I knew what Knox wanted to talk about. I spent pretty much the rest of the flight listening and consoling Knox. There was not much I could say. It was tough because I liked Chuck as a person.

Knox started off by saying everything was "off the record."

I have never liked that term because off the record it is so ambiguous. It can mean, "You can use this information but don't quote me." It can mean, "You can use this information as background for a story down the road." It can mean, "Don't ever use anything I am telling you."

In this case, Knox meant, "Don't ever use anything I am telling you."

I guess I can use it now since so many years have passed, and Rosenbloom and Knox are no longer with us.

Knox was more upset with Rosenbloom than he was with Krikorian. Knox felt, and rightfully so, that the Rams owner should have called him in for a private meeting, not gone to Krikorian with his complaints. Knox knew Rosenbloom was Doug's source for the story, even though I refused to confirm it.

"I was blindsided by this story," Knox told me.

I think more than anything, Chuck needed someone to talk to, and I was glad to accommodate, although I recall that it was an awkward situation.

I eventually went back to my original seat before we reached Cleveland. There was snow on the ground when our plane landed. The temperature at game time the next day was 9 degrees, and there were no heaters where I was sitting in the press box in the old Memorial Stadium.

After the Rams won, 9-0, I wrote the game story *and* a sidebar on the flight back to L.A. I also had to type up the game statistics, something I always did. The sidebar was on player reaction to playing in such cold weather. It was tough for them, but I think it was worse for us writers sitting in a freezing press box.

The Rams again lost in the first round of the playoffs that season, this time to the Minnesota Vikings, 14-7. Before Rosenbloom could fire him, Knox left the Rams in January after being hired as coach of the Buffalo Bills.

It was not always friendly skies on the United charter flights.

My first trip with the Rams was a memorable one. It was to New England for the Rams' third game of the 1974 season after two home victories. On the flight there, we landed in Boston. Someone in the Ram organization decided that after the game, which turned out to be a 20-14 loss, we would head south to Providence, R.I., for the return flight. The idea was that this way we would avoid the traffic headed north to Boston from the Patriots' stadium in Foxboro.

When we got to Providence and its small airport, there was a problem. The airport's only truck that pushes planes away from the gate had broken down.

"We can put everyone up for the night and get you off first thing in the morning," a young United employee told Rosenbloom.

I just happened to be standing right next to Rosenbloom and this poor young man. I heard the conversation perfectly.

"We just lost a very important game we shouldn't have lost," Rosenbloom responded. "If my team is not on the practice field tomorrow morning at 9 a.m., I'm going to buy United Airlines and you are the first person I'm going to fire." The young man walked away and soon came back with a new plan.

"We'll have a commuter flight from New York up here in an hour," he said. "That plane will take you back to JFK and you will be on your way from there."

All the equipment and suitcases had been loaded on the charter flight in Providence before it was known there was a problem. Now, everything would have to be unloaded from one plane and put on another. Then it would have to be done all over again at JFK.

At JFK, Krikorian had time to dictate at least a partial game story. Soon we were on our way from New York to L.A., about nine hours behind schedule. After five hours in the air, we started descending into what we thought was LAX. The captain came on the intercom with this bit of news.

"We know it has been a long day, but unfortunately we have some bad news," the captain said. "LAX is fogged in and we have to land in Ontario (located 30 miles east of L.A.)"

We touched down at 3:30 a.m. When everyone stood up, anxious to get off the plane, the captain said, "More bad news. There is no one here to push the stairs so we can get off the plane. A call has been made and someone is on the way. Also, three buses have been ordered and they will transport you to your cars at LAX."

The captain turned off the jet engines and soon the plane was like a sauna. Finally, someone arrived and pushed the portable stairs up to the plane. It was around 6 a.m. when we got to our cars. I volunteered to take the stories Doug and I typed on the plane to the office in downtown L.A. on my way home to Pasadena.

There was another trip a year or two later when we had to land in Ontario. This time, the stairs were in place and the buses were there. But there was still another problem. The bus that Doug and I were on going to LAX had a fan belt break, and the driver pulled into a service station in Alhambra.

Doug and I decided to get off the bus and call our wives. Doug's then-wife Melita was spending the weekend with Norma. They drove to Alhambra and picked us up. We retrieved our cars from LAX either later that day or the next day.

In 1975, the Rams won a Monday night game in Philadelphia. The plan was to fly home after the game, but we got word LAX was fogged in, so we would spend the night in Philadelphia. Rookies were sent on beer runs, and the parties were on. The Rams had beaten the Eagles, 42-3, and Fred Dryer and Isiah Robertson had scored on intercepted passes. There was a lot to celebrate.

When I checked out the next morning from our Marriott Hotel, the couple in front of me was complaining loudly about how the partying kept them up all night. "We are never staying in a Marriott again," the wife proclaimed.

Two players overslept and missed all three buses headed to the Philadelphia airport. One of the players was All-Pro guard Tom Mack. I ran into Tom not long after that at Phil Trani's restaurant and asked what happened.

"I didn't get my wake-up call," Mack said. "I had to get back to L.A. on my own. But the worst part was explaining what happened to my wife."

Despite some problems during the four seasons I traveled with the Rams, the trips for the most part were great. And easy. No ticket windows, a wagon to place our suitcases, easy access to the plane, and three buses waiting for us on tarmacs wherever we landed. Suitcases were transported to our hotels, and we either picked them up in the lobby or they were delivered to our rooms.

Players and writers did not hang out together much. There were some exceptions. I recall one Saturday afternoon in 1977, tight end Charle Young, from Fresno's Edison High and USC, spotted Doug and I in the hotel lobby. "Where you guys going?" Charle asked. When we told him that we were going to a movie, he asked if he could join us. That was cool. Young was a Fresno legend as the San Joaquin Valley player of the year in both football and basketball.

At some point during games, Krikorian and I would discuss who would write what. For example, when the Rams played host to the Atlanta Falcons on Dec. 11, 1976, it was likely going to be the final game at the Coliseum for the great Merlin Olsen, who was at the end of his 15-year Hall of Fame career. The Rams won, 59-0, so Krikorian's angle was the proficiency of the Ram offense. Olsen was my sidebar, complete with a layout of photos, all taken by Jim Roark.

Sometimes, our game plans were not set. After the Rams defeated the Seattle Seahawks, 45-6, on Oct. 31, 1976, I went into the locker room with no idea of what to write. But then I spotted Ron Jaworski, the Rams' third string quarterback behind James Harris and Pat Haden, and noticed he appeared upset as he took off his uniform.

Chuck Knox had used every player on the roster except Jaworski. After I approached him, he implied he wanted to be traded. "I plan to talk with Chuck this week," he said. "I want to know where I stand. If the Rams do not want me, I'll find someone who does."

Jaworski was traded to Philadelphia for Charle Young that spring. Jaworski and the Eagles were a good mix. In 1980, he led the Eagles to the Super Bowl, where they lost to the Oakland Raiders, 27-10. That season "Jaws," as he became known, was the UPI NFL Player of the Year.

Many years later, during Jaws' stellar career as a broadcaster, I ran into him while visiting ESPN in Bristol, Conn. "Do you remember that story I wrote after you didn't get into that game against Seattle?" I asked. "Of course," he said. "It helped me get to Philadelphia and then eventually end up here."

Another example of the power of the press.

The last Ram game of the 1977 season was in Washington, D.C. The day before the game, Krikorian and I decided we would get up early and visit the sights. We invited the Press-Telegram's Rich Roberts to join us. It turned out to be one of the best days during my four years of Ram trips. (I didn't know it at the time, but this would be my last trip with the Rams.)

Krikorian, Roberts and I saw as much of Washington as we could in one day. When we visited the Capitol Building, we found our way to the office of California Senator S.I. Hayakawa. Since it was a Saturday, he was not there. But an aide was, and he showed us around and answered all our questions.

The next day in the Robert F. Kennedy Stadium press box, Don Klosterman brought around Ethel Kennedy and introduced her to us reporters.

In 1984, I met Courtney Kennedy, one of Bobby and Ethel Kennedy's 11 children, when I was on a dinner cruise around the Marina Del Rey marina, a media event arranged by ABC as part of its massive promotion of the 1984 Los Angeles Olympics.

USA Today's Rudy Martzke and I were chatting on the upper deck of the dinner cruise yacht when ABC's Jeff Ruhe and his wife approached us. Ruhe was the coordinating producer of the L.A. Games and Rudy had arranged to interview him. When the two of them stepped away, I began chatting with Ruhe's wife, whom I had not met before.

She was a good conversationalist, although she seemed reluctant to talk much about herself. Maybe 10 minutes into our conversation, after I told her I worked at the Herald Examiner prior to the Times, she said, "My cousin worked at the Herald, on the news side," she said.

Naturally, I asked, "What's your cousin's name?"

"Bobby Shriver."

"Bobby Shriver?" I repeated. "Are you a Kennedy?"

She smiled and admitted she was.

I told her that I had met her mother through Don Klosterman at the Redskins game in 1977.

"Don Klosterman is our family's best friend," Courtney said.

I would see Courtney again, on Jan 12, 2000. It was at the wake for Klosterman in the Bel-Air Country Club. She remembered me but seemed more subdued than she was 16 years earlier.

However, she gave me her phone number and address in Bethesda, Md., and invited me and my wife to visit sometime.

Courtney divorced Ruhe in 1990 and married Paul Michael Hill in 1993.

Hill, who was not at the wake, had become globally known for being wrongly imprisoned for 15 years after he was coerced into confessing that he was involved in several bombings on behalf of the Irish Revolutionary Army (IRA).

Courtney married Hill aboard a yacht on the Aegean Sea. Klosterman had told me that he walked Courtney down the aisle. Courtney and Hill, after moving to Ireland, were legally separated in 2006. I was saddened to read that their daughter Saoirse died at the age of 22 of an accidental drug overdose in 2019 at the Kennedy compound in Hyannis Port on Cape Cod.

Of all the people I met during my career, Don Klosterman was the most amazing.

An All-American quarterback at Loyola Marymount and a backup on a Ram team that featured Norm Van Brocklin and Bob Waterfield, Klosterman spent nearly a year in a hospital after a skiing accident in Alberta, Canada on St. Patrick's Day in 1957.

He underwent eight surgeries and was told he would never walk again.

Within a year, he was walking with a cane. He was a member of the Bel-Air Country Club and, despite little use of his legs, could hit a golf ball farther than I could on two good legs. Playing with him was always a blast.

In Chapter 32, I have more on my relationship with Klosterman and the memorable Super Bowl Week in New Orleans in 1990 when we stayed at the same hotel. When he died at age 70 in 2000 after a heart attack, I wrote his obituary and covered his funeral.

Chapter 25: Rick Monday's Heroics and Steve Garvey Jr. High

One of the more memorable days I had while working a desk shift at the Herald Examiner was Sunday, April 25, 1976. I was in the slot when photographer Jim Roark came in from an afternoon game between the Dodgers and Chicago Cubs at Dodger Stadium.

"I think I've got a good picture," Roark told me.

He went on to explain that in the fourth inning two guys jumped out of the stands in left field and were trying to burn an American flag when Rick Monday, then the Cubs' center fielder, sprinted over and grabbed the flag.

"I'll see what I have when I get in the dark room," Roark said.

Roark came back maybe 20 minutes later and casually laid the black-and-white photo on my desk. "What do you think?" he asked.

"Are you kidding me?" I exclaimed, "That is going on the cover!"

For about a year, the Herald Examiner's sports section was published as a tabloid to make it stand out. The idea was to highlight the paper's best section. When new management came in, the thinking was why make it easy to pull out the sports section and throw the rest of the paper away. Sports eventually went back to a regular-size format.

After I saw Roark's photo, I called Tom Singer, who was covering the game. I told him about the photo and said, "That's your main story." The game, which the Dodgers won, 5-4, in 10 innings, was secondary.

The Herald's cover headline the next day read: "Cub Snuffs Stadium Protest." The photo caption read: "A Run for Old Glory."

We had the photo and the story; the Times had only a note.

The two perpetrators were a father and his 11-year-old son from Missouri protesting the treatment of Native Americans. They had doused the flag with lighter fluid, but it was in Monday's hands

before they could put a match to it. Monday, a 1962 graduate of Santa Monica High, became a Dodger in January of 1977 via a five-player trade that involved Bill Buckner going to the Cubs. Monday retired as a player in 1984 and became a full-time Dodger broadcaster following the death of Don Drysdale in 1993.

I need to slip in a note here. Don Drysdale ranks up there among my all-time favorite people. His widow, Ann Meyers Drysdale, does too. Writing Don's obituary was a hard one to do.

Roark's photo of Monday saving the flag was nominated for a Pulitzer Prize.

Another person who immediately recognized the importance of Monday's heroics was Fred Claire, then the Dodgers' vice president in charge of marketing. He was sitting next to Jeff Fellenzer, a USC student who was running the Dodger Stadium message board. Claire told Fellenzer to put this on the message board: "Rick Monday . . . you made a great play."

And Jim Roark took a great photo.

His credit line always read James Roark, but everyone called him Jim. He was a tremendous sports photographer, maybe the best I was ever around. I rewarded him by arranging for him to go on at least part of the ABC junket to Montreal prior to the 1976 Olympics.

He provided a great photo layout to go with my story after we both got back to L.A.

My first time dealing with Roark was in 1970 or '71 when he was assigned to the L.A. City high school track and field meet, which I was covering.

He was very raw at the time. He told me he knew nothing about sports and asked what he should shoot. I said to make sure to get a photo of a particular 880-yard runner. Roark got a photo of the runner all right, but he took it at the 440-yard mark, the halfway point, when the runner was trailing. He had nothing of the runner winning the race at the finish line.

"Why didn't you take the photo at the end of the race?" I asked.

"I don't know," Roark said. "What difference does it make?"

I was not pleased. But that all changed as Roark's career took an upward turn. Unfortunately, his life took a downward turn after the Herald folded in 1989 as he battled alcoholism and went from job to job. In 1995, after a night shift as a cook in Portland, Roark was mugged and fatally beaten. He was 49.

His obit included this passage: *As chief sports photographer for the Los Angeles Herald Examiner, Mr. Roark took one of the most famous pictures of the post-Vietnam era.*

In March of 1978, when I was still at the Herald, I broke a national story. I should say my mother and I broke a national story.

During a routine call with Mom, she happened to mention that Dodgers' Steve Garvey was coming to Lindsay, the town where I went to school through the fifth grade. Garvey and wife Cyndy were coming there for a ceremony in which Lindsay's junior high school would be christened Steve Garvey Junior High.

I soon realized there was a story here of interest beyond Tulare County. Schools are named after Presidents and war heroes, not baseball players.

When I called my mother back the next morning, I got further details and recruited her to cover Garvey's visit, knowing she could handle the assignment. She got quotes from students, their parents, and members of the Lindsay community, and she also took photographs. I talked on the phone to Garvey, Dodger executives, and the Lindsay school's relatively new principal, Bob Edwards. It was his idea to let the students pick a new name for the school.

Among the names were two Oakland Raider players, but Edwards settled on Garvey because of his then squeaky-clean image. The school library was named after that learned scholar, Tommy Lasorda. A remodeled school counseling center was named after Cyndy Garvey.

The story my mother and I wrote after the christening ceremony had a joint byline and was accompanied by a photo my mother took. It showed Steve and Cyndy standing in front of the school's sign with students lined up behind the sign. There was also an editor's note about my connection to Lindsay and my mother's journalism background.

The story was picked up by national wire services Associated Press and United Press International, and the Sporting News ran it in total, with the joint byline and the same photo.

I found a clipping of our story on Steve Garvey Junior High in a scrapbook. I was pleased to see the Garvey story was balanced with both positive and negative quotes. Here are samples of negative ones:

"Nothing but a publicity stunt," said one parent.

"We're setting ourselves up for ridicule," said another.

"What happens after Garvey retires and is long forgotten about?" asked a prominent member of the community.

After our story ran, Garvey did not complain about the negative quotes. He thanked me for the story and told me how much he enjoyed meeting my mother. He said he planned to visit the school annually and suggested I make a future three-hour trip to Lindsay.

This was long before the Garveys' messy divorce, Cyndy's complaints of Steve's infidelity, and stories of Steve's mishandling of his finances.

Garvey's fall from grace took many by surprise. Jim Murray in 1989 wrote: "Steve Garvey, a womanizer?! St. Steve?! When we called him Father Garvey, we meant the Roman-collar type." Bumper stickers in San Diego, where Garvey had finished his 18-year playing career, read: "Honk if you are carrying Steve Garvey's baby," and "Steve Garvey is not my Padre."

I made the first of my two trips with him in 1980, traveling in a limo with Times colleague Scott Ostler. Sports editor Bill Shirley assigned Ostler to write the story after I suggested it. The always classy Ostler insisted I come with him. Garvey invited Scott and me to ride up to Lindsay with him in a limo. We hooked up with Garvey at the Magic Mountain offramp on the I-5 Freeway.

Several months later, in August of 1980, Steve and Cyndy were the subjects of an in-depth cover story in a national magazine, Inside Sports. The headline on the cover read: TROUBLE IN PARADISE. It was the beginning of the end of a marriage that for years was publicly perceived as perfect.

I made my second trip to Lindsay with Garvey in 1982. This was after Dwyre had become sports editor, so the story was all mine. It was just Garvey and me.

The mode of transportation was a Budweiser motor coach operated by two drivers employed by Anheuser-Busch. The meeting place again was the Magic Mountain offramp. When I got on the bus, I noticed there was Garvey memorabilia everywhere. On the motor coach's couch and elsewhere were trophies, plaques, and framed pictures. A 40x8-foot mural was broken up and strewn on the floor. Garvey and I sat in two comfortable chairs up front.

"There is beer on tap, if you'd like a beer," Garvey said, pointing at a keg.

It was 7 a.m., way too early for a beer.

Garvey explained that he and Cyndy were moving out of their home in Calabasas to a home in Malibu and he was donating the memorabilia to the school. He and Cyndy were separated and in the process of getting a divorce. She was living in New York but had returned for the move and was at his house with their daughters, Trisha, then 7, and Whitney, 5.

When we arrived at the school in Lindsay, Garvey greeted people he had not seen in a year, calling most by name. He hugged the men and kissed the women. One of my mother's prized possessions was a photo of Garvey kissing her during his first visit to Lindsay.

Among the activities during that 1982 visit was an assembly in the school cafeteria, where Garvey raved about the school and its students. He also took questions and, inevitably, there were questions about him and Cyndy.

"Why didn't you bring your wife?" was one of those, and it brought moans of disapproval.

"That's a good question, a very good question," Garvey said. "Cyndy lives in New York now. We're separated but remain good friends."

A while later came this one: "Why did you and Cyndy break up?"

Garvey, again: "That is a good question. Sometimes people just cannot live together. That doesn't mean they don't love each other."

Garvey handled all questions with the deftness of a politician, always saying the right thing. But something unusual kept happening during the assembly. The school secretary, Kathy Kern Smith, came into the cafeteria on three separate occasions to tell Steve he had "an emergency phone call." Each time, Garvey was gone for about 10 minutes before returning unphased.

I knew Kathy from Strathmore High. She was two years ahead of me and the school's head cheerleader as a senior. Before we got back on the Budweiser motor coach, I pulled Kathy aside to ask her about those emergency calls. She said they were from Cyndy – and she was hysterical.

After we pulled away from the school, I informed Steve that I was told those calls were from Cyndy and asked what was going on.

"Just some problems with the movers," he said calmly.

I had time, so I let it go. We chatted informally until we got near Bakersfield.

"Regarding those phone calls from Cyndy, I understand she was very upset," I said. "I was told she was crying."

"There are a lot of emotions in that house," Garvey said, again remaining cool and calm.

We continued to talk almost nonstop until we reached the Magic Mountain off ramp. Before I got off the motor coach, Garvey thanked me and expressed how much he enjoyed our conversation.

My ensuing story ran in the Times on Page One of Sports on Monday, Feb. 22, 1982, and jumped to an inside page. I did not mention Cyndy's phone calls since I did not have any concrete information.

Several months later, I realized I missed what was really going on with those "emergency phone calls" after reading a story in People Magazine. Cyndy, in talking about the day she discovered evidence of her husband's affairs during their marriage, said they were in the process of moving from their Calabasas home to Malibu. "Steve was out of town," Cyndy was quoted as saying.

Yeah, he was with me in Lindsay.

I was amazed when I read the People Magazine story and wondered how in the world did this man manage to act so calmly. Years later, a friend passed along this quote, which originated with John Boggs, Garvey's former agent and business associate: "Garvey's demeanor, regardless of the circumstance, is always as perfect as his hair. Never a hair out of place."

In 2009, Steve Garvey Junior High was converted to a to a K-8 school and in 2011 renamed Reagan Elementary.

After our trip to Lindsay in 1982, whenever I saw Garvey, he was always pleasant. He would greet me warmly and, if Norma was with me, she would get a kiss on the cheek.

In 2013, at my request, Garvey and infield mates Ron Cey and Bill Russell were celebrity guests at a charity golf tournament in Glendora benefiting Sowing Seeds for Life, the local food bank.

Not long after that, I played in Garvey's charity golf tournament at Bighorn Golf Club near Garvey's home in Palm Desert. The celebrity in our foursome was Al Geiberger, Mr. 59. He earned that moniker when, in 1977 at the Danny Thomas Memphis Classic, he became the first person to shoot a 59 in a PGA tournament.

At Bighorn, Geiberger helped my foursome finish third. Our reward was getting to select a memorabilia item. On display was mostly Garvey memorabilia, but I chose a Mike Trout jersey.

"What's the deal with that choice?" Garvey asked me.

I explained I had a friend named Fred Trout who was down on his luck. This jersey, with TROUT on the back, was going to be a gift for my friend.

Chapter 26: My Last Year at the Herald

With the ouster of George Hearst and George Szushtrum, a new regime began arriving at the Herald in 1977. First came publisher Francis Dale, a former Navy commander in World War II, a former part-owner of the Cincinnati Reds, a high-ranking Republican, and a former U.S. ambassador.

He bought a home in the Chapman Woods area of Pasadena, where we lived. The difference was our home was in a modest part of

Chapman Woods. Dale moved into the ritzy area a few blocks south.

In one of my first dealings with Dale, I hit him with a softball question. I asked if the paper might sponsor a softball team. Dale, looking to lift morale, said yes and gave me the okay to buy flashy jerseys with our names on the back.

My idea of forming a softball team came after I did a feature story on a Dodger Stadium pregame appearance by the "Happy Days" softball team, which featured Ron Howard (above), Henry Winkler (below), and other cast members. After my story ran, a "Happy Days" producer called to see if we had a team they could play.

After getting Dale's approval and ordering jerseys with names on the back, I lined up a game against the "Happy Days" cast. It took place at

Balboa Park in the San Fernando Valley. We won, 7-4. The "Happy Days" team was not used to losing. A rematch was lined up, and we won that game too.

We played a few other celebrity teams before we eventually put a notice in the paper stating we would play any organized softball team anywhere.

The Herald Examiner softball team is shown here. Front row: John Beyrooty, Chick Perkins, Larry Allen, Larry Stewart, Fred Robledo, and John Sevano. Second row: Keith "Boomer" Stepro, Bob Keisser, Tom Singer, Jack Disney, Lyle Spencer, Mitch Chortkoff, and our shortstop, who worked in the composing department.

We had a good team. Our record was 9-0 when I got a call from Penthouse Magazine. An editor there asked if we would play against a team of Penthouse Pets. The answer was yes.

We needed a special site for this game, so I called legendary USC baseball coach Rod Dedeaux to see if we could use Dedeaux Field. "You can as long as I get to umpire from behind home plate," Dedeaux said. I took a cue from Dedeaux. I usually played right field, but as team manager I named myself the catcher for this game, even though I am left-handed.

After the game, which we intentionally lost, we all went to the Gala Cellar. While there, Dedeaux had another idea. "Why don't we move this party to my beach house in Malibu?" he suggested. Some of the Penthouse Pets liked that idea, but the majority thought it was a little too late for that.

"Some other time," Dedeaux said.

Whenever I saw Dedeaux after that, he would ask, "When are we having that party with the Penthouse Pets?"

Another game at Dedeaux Field was against the L.A. Kings, which meant we were facing professional athletes who knew how to swing a stick. But we still won in an upset, and one of our stars was center fielder John Beyrooty.

Dedeaux thought I was the centerfielder. Whenever I would see Dedeaux at a function after that, he would say, "Hey, Tiger, how is my centerfielder?" He would proceed to tell people, including some of the biggest names in baseball, such as Commissioner Bowie Kuhn, what a great center fielder I was. People would give me a strange look, but I never bothered to correct Dedeaux.

The softball outings were fun, but things were getting worse at the Herald.

Dale brought in Jim Bellows as editor in early 1978. Bellows had been an associate editor from 1967-74 at the Times, where he oversaw feature sections and created a Sunday magazine called West.

More importantly, Bellows was nationally known for reviving newspapers in trouble. Bellows, 56, hired several editors, including 34-year-old Ted Warmbold as executive editor. Bellows' plan, according to what Warmbold told Malamud and me, was to overhaul the newsroom but leave Sports pretty much alone, except that within six months a top person and lower-level person in our department would be gone. Warmbold's prediction about Sports was right on. On my final day in May of 1978, John Sevano, who had recently been elevated from a copy boy position to cover prep sports, was let go.

Maybe I was supposed to be the top-level guy. Jack Disney, who replaced me as assistant sports editor, soon had his title and his

$50-a-week-raise taken away. Bellows brought in his own guy, Fred Heldman, as the new No. 2 person in Sports. Heldman was soon elevated to sports editor, allowing Malamud to concentrate on his "Notes on a Scorecard" column. Heldman was never popular among the staff and did not last long.

If I indeed was the top-level guy in Sports being targeted, I do not think Bellows had anything against me personally. It was my position. Malamud was a popular and well-known columnist. He was too high profile to target. I was not.

I ran into Bellows a few years later. He was friendly, almost overly friendly, and even mailed me a copy of a manuscript of his memoirs that was eventually published in 2002. The title, "The Last Editor: How I Saved the New York Times, the Washington Post and the Los Angeles Times from Dullness and Complacency," tells you all you need to know.

Prior to the start of the 1978 baseball season, Warmbold called me into his office to let me know that the Herald planned a 40-page tabloid supplement on the Dodgers, and I would be in charge.

One of my duties was to arrange for Tommy Lasorda to speak at a breakfast in front of potential advertisers. Lasorda showed up with shortstop Bill Russell, who many years later became a good friend who helped me a lot with my charity work.

"It was great that you brought Bill Russell with you," I told Tommy at the breakfast in 1978.

"Ropes is like a son to me," Lasorda said, calling Russell the nickname he was given by some veteran players when he first was called up to the Dodgers. The veterans claimed they had to show Russell, from Broken Arrow, Okla., the ropes about being a major league ballplayer.

Lasorda was considered an ambassador for baseball, but most of us on the inside knew he had a mean streak. That mean streak was on full display in a feud he had with Russell later in their lives. Russell, who replaced Lasorda as manager of the Dodgers in 1996, was fired after two and a half seasons. Russell at the time believed that Lasorda had been bad mouthing his managerial skills. Lasorda denied it and never spoke to Russell again.

Russell and I became friends around 2005, when he was working for Big League Dream Sports Parks. I knew Rick Odekirk, whose family created the company. In later years, when I got involved in charity work, Russell always came through whenever I asked him to make an appearance of any kind.

I was quite familiar with the details behind Lasorda's beef with Russell. One time, while sitting with Tommy in the Dodger Stadium press box dining room, I tried smoothing things over.

"You and Bill were like father and son," I told Tommy.

"That is why I will never ever speak to him again." And he didn't, even though many people attempted to patch things up between those two.

That 1978 breakfast spurred on the Herald Examiner advertising department, and soon there were enough ads to make the Dodger supplement a go. It was left to me to generate enough copy to fill it. I busted my butt putting that supplement together. The final two days before it went to press, I worked from 7 a.m. nonstop until midnight both days.

Working day and night became somewhat the norm under the new management. There was another problem as well. Bellows declared that the Herald would no longer allow any employees to accept comp tickets nor allow professional teams or promoters or anyone to pay travel expenses.

It was the right move, but it did nothing for sagging morale.

For me, it meant no more Ram trips. The paper would only pay expenses for the main beat writer, who was Krikorian.

If I was going to stay at the Herald, I needed a pay raise, and I passed that along to Malamud when he called to tell me how much management was pleased with the Dodger supplement. Malamud called back an hour or so later and excitedly announced, "You will have an extra $100 in your next check."

A $100-a-week raise sounded good. Then it hit me.

"Am I getting a raise, or is that a one-time bonus?" I asked.

"A one-time bonus," Malamud said. "But that's good, isn't it?"

No, it was not.

In January of 1978, we bought our house in Arcadia, where Norma and I still live. On March 10, Jill was born, which meant I now had a family of four to support along with paying the mortgage on a new, bigger three-bedroom house. Norma, at this point in her life, was not working.

It all added up. It was time to call Times sports editor Bill Shirley.

Chapter 27: Getting Hired by the Times

The first thing I did was call my friend, track meet promoter Al Franken, who wrote a glowing letter of recommendation to Shirley. The letter even included good things about my wife and her background. Franken also called Chuck Garrity, the Times' highly respected assistant sports editor. Garrity told Franken this was a good time for me to call Shirley. The Times needed help on the sports desk.

When I called Shirley and told him the Times is where I had always wanted to work, one of the first things he said was: "I assume you know how to do layouts." I said I did.

I have always emphasized to young people to become versatile by learning all tasks that are associated with your job. If I had told Shirley that I did not know how to do layouts, I likely would never have been hired.

Shirley explained the Times was starting a San Diego edition and there was an opening for a layout person who would work in the main L.A. office. The way it worked was, the San Diego edition's pages were produced in L.A., then sent via satellite to the Times' Orange County plant in Costa Mesa for printing. Once compiled, the full newspapers were trucked to San Diego County for distribution.

I told Shirley I was interested. I figured I had to get my foot in the door. It did not matter that I was going from the No. 2 position in the Herald sports department to a mid-level job at the Times. I figured the Herald would eventually fold, and I had a family to support.

After everything was finalized, I started at the Times on May 23, 1978.

I got to know Bill Shirley during that ABC junket to Montreal before the 1976 Summer Olympics. ABC took care of all reporters' expenses. I am not sure what kind of deal Shirley had because cost-free junkets were against Times policy.

During the five-day junket, I often sat with Shirley at meals and on buses taking us reporters to various venues. It was not a case of me kissing up to Shirley, it was more the other way around. He was the one taking the initiative, seeking me out and then joining me. I certainly did not mind. I found him to be pleasant company, a far cry from the person who became my boss.

On the junket's final night, during the cocktail hour at a five-star restaurant, Shirley, with a glass of wine in hand, walked over to me. Soon Olympic host Jim McKay joined us. "Gee, I wouldn't know you two worked for competing newspapers," McKay said. "You guys seem to be joined at the hip."

Shirley eased away and sat at a different table that night. But by then it did not matter. The seed had been planted. Had it not been for that junket, Shirley likely would not have hired me two years later.

Shirley and I agreed on a starting weekly salary of $500, but Shirley reneged. I learned when I got my first paycheck that my salary was $450. That was a typical Bill Shirley move. And this one cost me an incalculable amount of money since all my merit and cost-of-living raises at the Times were based on a percentage of my salary. I can only imagine how much it cost me over 30-plus years by starting out at $450 instead of $500. I would need a Caltech math whiz to figure that out.

When I questioned my first paycheck, Shirley said, "You will soon be getting a cost-of-living raise that will get you to $500." The raise, which turned out to be $45, came more than a month later.

Shirley pulled another cheap shot in the process of hiring me. He said I would have to come in for what he called "a mandatory tryout." He did not specify for how many days. I came in on a Saturday and at the end of the shift, Chuck Garrity, who was working the slot, asked me if I was coming back the next day.

"I guess so," I said. "Do I get paid?"

"Of course," Garrity said. "You're working. It will be on your first paycheck."

"Okay," I said. "See you tomorrow."

That first paycheck, with a gross of $450, did not include two days' pay for my tryout. When I mentioned it to Garrity, he told me, "Don't let Shirley get away with that. Go in his office and tell him you were not paid for your tryout."

I followed Garrity's advice, which was a mistake. Shirley told me, "We pay the people we want and sometimes even cover their travel expenses. In your case, you called us, we didn't call you."

Cut off right at the knees.

An anecdote from Garrity provides further insight into Bill Shirley.

A few years before I came to the Times, Shirley invited Chuck to play golf. Before teeing off, Shirley collected money from Garrity for his share of the greens fee. After the round, they had lunch, and Shirley again collected money from Garrity before walking off to supposedly pay the bill.

Garrity later learned from golf writer Shav Glick that the golf and the lunch had been comped. Glick had set it up. Back at the office a few days later, Garrity noticed an expense voucher on Shirley's desk. Shirley had put golf and lunch with assistant sports editor Chuck Garrity on his expense account.

Double dipping is getting something free and then putting it on an expense account. Since Shirley also collected money from Garrity, this was a case of *triple dipping.*

On a more positive note, at least Shirley hired me. No other Herald sports staffer was able to successfully transition to the much larger and more prestigious L.A. Times during the Herald's post-strike era. Shirley generally looked down on the Herald, and I think it infuriated him whenever he heard that the Herald had a better sports section than the Times, which was not an uncommon opinion.

One thing I often heard was that the Herald's sports section was livelier.

I think that was because at the Herald the writers generally had the freedom to decide what to write and their copy was not heavily edited. At the Times, editors who sat behind a desk were more in control of what appeared in the paper.

Particularly unpopular with Times writers back then was assistant sports editor Jack Quigg, who prided himself on not knowing much about sports. He would hand out assignments, often odd ones, and then heavily edit or even rewrite stories after they were turned in. The combination of Shirley and Quigg drove away a lot of good writers.

After Bill Dwyre replaced Shirley as sports editor in 1981, Quigg stuck around for three more years before retiring. Dwyre then brought in Mike Kupper from Milwaukee to replace Quigg, and the atmosphere in the Times sports department, already on an uptick because of Dwyre, improved even more.

At the Herald, it was a two-man desk in Sports during the week and a three- or four-man desk on the weekends. During my tenure at the Times, as noted earlier, the weekday night desk crew was seven or eight and on busy Saturday nights, it was almost double that.

When I started there, I worked off by myself, redoing the L.A. edition of Sports into the San Diego edition of Sports. That involved subbing out L.A. stories and inserting San Diego stories. Making it work was like a jigsaw puzzle and hoping that all the pieces fit.

After a couple of months of working on the San Diego edition, I was stunned when I saw a note from Shirley that everyone got in their mailbox. The note said Reid Grosky had been hired from the New York Times to handle layout duties for the San Diego edition. There was no mention of me.

I went to assistant sports editor Chuck Garrity. "What's going on?" I asked. "Did I mess up? Am I being fired?"

Garrity explained Shirley was maneuvering to make himself look good. Reid Grosky's salary would be coming out of the Orange County/San Diego edition budget. With me moving over to the L.A.

desk, Shirley was gaining an extra copy editor, me, without affecting his budget. I was already on the L.A. payroll. The move was probably a plus for me, but the way Shirley went about it bothered me.

The launch of the San Diego edition came during an era of expansion for the Times. An Orange County edition, complete with a separate sports department, was started in 1968 at a new, modern plant in Costa Mesa. Next came the San Diego edition in 1978, followed by a San Fernando Valley edition in 1990, produced at a modern plant in Chatsworth.

The San Diego edition was the first to go. Its final day of publication was Nov. 6, 1992. After that, Reid Grosky joined the L.A. sports desk.

The Valley edition staff was hit hard when the Times had the first of its many layoffs in 1995, and the Chatsworth facility was closed in 2010.

The Orange County plant closed in 2010.

The Times' circulation peaked at 1,225,189 daily and 1,514,096 Sunday on March 31, 1990, making it the largest metro daily newspaper in the country. Editor-in-chief Shelby Coffee, who had succeeded the legendary Bill Thomas the previous year, gave out coffee cups and T-shirts to commemorate the occasion. I still have my cup and T-shirt, although the shirt is a bit tight these days.

The Times was hit with an advertising slump a year later, marking the start of a downhill spiral that got worse with the onset of the computer age. The worst thing was the loss of classified ads, which meant the loss of a dual revenue stream – the money that the classifieds bought in plus the money paid to buy the paper.

The loss of classified ads also meant a drop in circulation, and ad rates were based on circulation.

Prominent Times sports columnists Bill Plaschke and T.J. Simers both started out working for the San Diego edition.

Plaschke, who was working in Seattle, was hired as the beat writer for the Padres in 1987. He was soon transferred to L.A. and had his own column by 1996. He replaced Jim Murray on Page One after Murray died in 1998.

Simers was hired away from the San Diego Union in 1990 to cover the Chargers for the Times' San Diego edition. He soon was called up to the L.A. office and assigned the national NFL beat. In 2000, he became the Times' Page Two columnist, albeit a controversial one. Readers either loved or hated his bitingly acerbic columns that often were designed to draw more attention to himself than the people he wrote about.

Simers left the Times in 2013 for the Orange County Register but did not last there long. Simers, falsely claiming he was forced out at the Times, sued the newspaper for age discrimination. He won a $7.1 million judgement in 2015, but the judge hearing the case overturned that judgement because Simers was not fired or forced to leave. Simers had the number of columns he wrote reduced, which could be viewed as a demotion. But it was not a termination.

Simers' lawyers appealed the judge's decision, and his case went back to court in 2019. Simers this time won a $15.4 million judgement, but again the judge overturned it, ruling the dollar amount was excessive. That is where it stands as this is being written.

When Simers was the Times' Page Two sports columnist, his desk was close enough to mine that I could easily hear his loud and boisterous phone conversations. He thrived on verbal confrontations. He treated them as a sport.

He usually won, but I witnessed a real beat down by actor James Garner in 2001. It was as if Bret Maverick and Jim Rockford had combined forces.

Hollywood publicist Jim Mahoney called me to ask about Simers. "He's different," I said. Mahoney, who was then the president of the Bel-Air Country Club, said, "I'd like to see for myself. How about you two, and Bill Dwyre, come out to the club for a round of golf?"

I couldn't find a day that worked for all three of us, so it was just T.J. and me. Our fourth was Frank Chirkinian, the longtime golf producer for CBS Sports. After the round, we sat at the "A" table, where there were seven of us, including comedian Bob Newhart. Soon Garner arrived and sat between T.J. and me.

Mahoney first introduced Garner to T.J.

"Are you that guy?" Garner asked. "What is wrong with you? Do you just hate everyone? Have you ever written anything nice about anyone?"

T.J. initially was speechless as Garner hammered away. Finally, T.J. spoke up. "I just try to interject some humor into sports," he said.

Garner responded, "So you think you are a comedy writer, I know comedy writers, and you're no comedy writer." And then he went back on the attack.

It was a one-sided bashing that seemed to last five minutes. When Garner finally eased up, Mahoney said, "I also want you to meet Larry Stewart."

Garner put his arm around my shoulders and said, "I love your column."

It was a sweet moment for me.

To T.J.'s credit, he called me the next day after he had finished writing his column. It was all about his exchange with Garner. Since he was not taking notes, he wanted to check on the accuracy of what took place.

After T.J. read what he had written, I was tempted to ask, "What, no mention that Garner loved my column?" But I resisted.

Garner became one of T.J.'s favorite targets. Garner's real name is Bumgarner, and T.J. had some fun with that.

A few months later, I ran into Garner at an ESPY golf tournament in Simi Valley. He told me he had just been on Jay Leno's show.

"I felt like using the opportunity to really tear into T.J.," he said, "but I knew that would be playing right into his hand. He would have loved getting mentioned on national TV, even if I was ripping him." I told Garner that his thinking was correct.

When Bill Shirley hired me, I pitched the idea of me doing a weekly TV-Radio column. I cited stories the Times underplayed because the paper did not have anyone covering sports broadcasting. One example I used was when Ross Porter, a prominent sports anchor for KNBC Channel 4, was hired as a Dodger announcer in 1977. I did a full column for the Herald, while the Times had one sentence under the heading "Names in the News" in the Newswire column.

Shirley was not swayed. He turned down my pitch. "We don't want to glorify the competition," Shirley, a native of Arkansas, told me in his southern drawl. When I asked about writing feature stories on my own time, Shirley said, "I guess that would be okay, as long as you do them on your own time."

I waited for a hot topic. In July of 1978, a little more than two months after I was hired, I had one that would not only be a good read but would also lend itself to good photos. Shirley, fortunately, agreed.

The story was about "sexploitation" in sportscasting. ABC Sports a few months earlier had hired supermodel Cheryl Tiegs. She looked good in a swimsuit on the cover of Sports Illustrated, but did that qualify her to be a sports announcer?

The trend of hiring beauty queens and models as sportscasters began in 1975 when CBS Sports tabbed former Miss America Phyllis George to work on "The NFL Today." NBC hired blonde bombshell Regina Haskins to work on its NFL pregame show in 1977, then came the hiring of Tiegs. While I was working on my story, CBS hired another beauty queen, Jayne Kennedy, to replace Phyllis George.

When I interviewed Tiegs, a 1965 graduate of Alhambra High School who attended Cal State L.A. for two years, she was pleasant and certainly no airhead. She followed sports and was a fan of Jim Murray. But her sports announcing career did not last long. She appeared on ABC's Kentucky Derby coverage and worked a World Team Tennis All-Star match in Las Vegas with Chris Schenkel and Cliff Drysdale. That may have been all she did. I do not remember anything else.

I also interviewed Phyllis George, Jayne Kennedy, and Regina Haskins, plus Jane Chastain, who became the first female network sportscaster when she was hired by CBS in 1974. Chastain is believed to have been the first female television sportscaster anywhere when she was hired by an Atlanta TV station in 1972.

Andre Kirby, an established ABC sportscaster who at the time was doing some fill-in reporting for KABC-TV after moving to L.A. from Baltimore, told me, "I was a sports broadcaster before I was pretty."

Others I interviewed included network executives such as Don Ohlmeyer, then with NBC, and several prominent male sports broadcasters, including Vin Scully, then working for both CBS and the Dodgers.

Scully, who had worked with George on "Challenge of the Sexes" and "Celebrity Challenge of the Sexes" in 1976 and '77 on CBS, said, "Phyllis knows her strengths and weaknesses. What she does she does very well."

After I turned in my type-written story to Shirley, he did not say anything. Nor did he say anything after it ran on Aug. 3. It appeared, along with six mugshots, on Page One of Sports and jumped twice to inside pages. The main headline read: *Just Another Pretty Face?* A smaller headline under that one, called a deck headline, read: *High TV Ratings Are Now Something Like 36-24-36.*

From 1962 to 2009, the Times, in conjunction with the Washington Post, had a wire service that, at its peak, went to more than 600 newspapers. Many of those papers picked up my story and gave it good play. Around the office, I got a lot of positive reaction, but nothing from Shirley.

During my first year at the Times, I continued to write one or two bylined stories a month on my own time. Most were TV related, but not all of them.

George Allen, beginning his third stint as coach of the Rams, was fired on Sunday, Aug. 13, 1978, after two preseason games. I was working a desk shift when the news broke and got pressed into action. Chuck Garrity, who was working the slot, told me, "Put on your writer's cap and head out to the Rams' training camp."

After interviewing players, I hustled back to the office to bat out a sidebar that went with Ram beat writer Ted Green's main news story.

One night in November of 1978, less than six months after I had been hired by the Times, I got a call from Green. I first met Green in the early 1970s playing pickup basketball at North Hollywood High with other sportswriters. None of us could stand Ted Green. His arrogance was beyond belief.

But when he called me in 1978, he was surprisingly pleasant. Or at least civil.

"I've got great news for you," Green told me. "You are going to get to cover the Stanford-Cal game at Berkeley this weekend. This is the only sports story Otis Chandler reads each year. This could really help your career."

Chandler, the Times publisher, was a Stanford grad.

Green explained he had a college fraternity reunion that weekend. When I asked if Shirley had approved the change, Green assured me he had. But he had not. Shirley was blindsided and visibly upset when I told him about the phone call from Green. Shirley first called Green, then reluctantly gave me the green light.

Green also told me that he had arranged for me to pick up a game credential at the Press Will Call window at Berkeley's Memorial Stadium. But this too was not true.

Since this was going to be my first road trip for the Times, I was impressed when I learned Times reporters flew first class, stayed in any hotel of their choosing and, if so desired, could get up to $500 a day in cash. The cash advance, of course, had to be accounted for. I had no reason to request a cash advance.

The night before leaving for Berkeley, I was working a desk shift when, at halftime of that night's Laker game, we learned no Times reporter was at the Forum. Green was the beat writer for both the Rams and Lakers. Apparently, his fraternity reunion was a two-night affair, and no one was filling in for him.

Chuck Garrity, who was also in charge that night, told me, "Grab a typewriter out of Shirley's office and hot tail it to the Forum. I'll make sure there will be a credential waiting for you."

It was well into the third quarter when I arrived. Using the play-by-play printout distributed to writers, I began writing what is called running matter. It is what writers write during a game to fill out the bottom part of a deadline story. The deadline was 10:30, and it was now close to 10.

I made the deadline while also managing to get all the pertinent details into my story and even a couple of quotes. It was an important game. The Lakers won their 12th straight and Kareem Abdul-Jabbar had 32 points, 23 rebounds, 8 blocks, and 9 assists. Jamaal Wilkes had 23 points.

When I was done and checked in with the office, Garrity said, "Super job! The readers will never know you weren't there for the first half."

The next morning, I was off to Berkeley. When I went to the Press Will Call window, I learned there was no credential for me. Fortunately, I had that day's Times sports section with me, so I showed the person at the Will Call window my byline on the story of the previous night's Laker game. That got me the credential I needed.

In my Stanford-Cal game story, I highlighted Stanford's All-American sophomore running back Darrin Nelson, the star of a 30-10 victory. "Nelson Runs Away with the Big Game," the headline read. He had 177 rushing yards, 36 receiving yards and two touchdowns.

The next Monday, Shirley stopped by my desk. I thought he might have something nice to say about either my Laker game coverage or my story on the Stanford-Cal game. I was wrong.

"How come you covered Friday night's Laker game?" he asked.

After I explained the circumstances, he said, "I guess that is why it wasn't a very good story."

Garrity overheard that comment. "Don't let that bother you," he said after Shirley walked away. "That is just Shirley being Shirley."

Also, when I complained to Shirley that Green had not arranged a credential for me for the Stanford-Cal game, even though he said he had, Shirley did not seem to care. Green apparently could do no wrong in Shirley's eyes.

Coincidentally, I got reconnected with Darrin Nelson 33 years later, in December of 2011, when I was doing some consulting and writing for UC Irvine. Nelson was the senior associate athletic director at UC Irvine, working alongside athletic director Mike Izzi. Those two had also worked together at Stanford. Nelson came south mainly to be closer to his parents in Compton after spending 15 years as an associate athletic director at his alma mater.

I did a profile on Nelson for the UC Irvine website that was accompanied by a photocopy of the Stanford-Cal game story I wrote in 1978.

The topic of writing running matter, which I did when I covered that Laker game that Ted Green missed, reminds me of an anecdote involving Times colleague Mal Florence, a real character who was always quick with the one-liners. When he was the Laker beat writer, he took a young intern with him to a game. While sitting high up in the press area at the Forum, Florence explained how he had to write running matter while the game was going on.

The intern wanted to know how Mal found time to write.

"I just signal down to the coach that I need a timeout," Florence told her.

Bill Sharman was then the coach, and Florence was very aware of his idiosyncrasies. At the opportune time, Mal stood up and signaled timeout – and got lucky. At that moment, Sharman got off the bench and called a timeout.

The next day at the office, the intern, talking to Harley Tinkham, said, "Did you know Mal calls timeouts for the Lakers?"

Tinkham's head hit the desk. "Mal has struck again," he said. Tinkham knew Mal well. They were roommates at USC and lifelong best friends.

Two more Mal Florence anecdotes before I move on. The first one is well-known and often repeated in sports writing lore.

When Bill Shirley was sports editor, the Times' Laker beat writer did not cover all road games. Shirley, a Southerner who did not care much for pro basketball, viewed Laker travel as an unnecessary expense.

During the 1971-72 season, the Lakers, coached by Sharman, went on a 33-game winning streak, the longest win streak by any major U.S. professional team. The Lakers' streak ended in Milwaukee on Jan. 9, 1972, when the Bucks beat them. Kareem Abdul-Jabbar, then with the Bucks, had 39 points and 20 rebounds in a 120-104 victory.

The next morning, Florence got a phone call from Shirley in his hotel room. "Now that the Lakers have lost, you might as well come on home," Shirley said. "The Laker trips have been costing us too much money."

Sixteen of the victories during the streak had come on the road. Three more road games remained on this trip – in Detroit, Cincinnati, and Philadelphia.

Florence reluctantly packed his two suitcases. As he was walking through the hotel lobby, Sharman spotted him. "Where are you going, Mal?" Sharman asked.

"I'm going home," Florence said before adding, "I don't cover losers."

Mal continued walking before eventually turning around and smiling.

Years later, when I asked Sharman about the incident, he said, "It took a moment to sink in. Then I laughed."

My other Mal Florence anecdote also involves Sharman.

In the middle of the NBA Finals in 2002, Mal, Bill and I played golf on the Harding course at Griffith Park. There was a foursome in front of us that we talked with briefly on the first tee. We saw them again at lunch. After Mal left to go to the restroom, one of the guys, noticing Bill had on a Laker shirt, asked for his opinion about that night's game between the Lakers and Indiana Pacers.

Bill, who was friendly with everyone, gave the man an in-depth analysis.

"Wow, you know your stuff," the man said. "Do you work for the Lakers or are you just a fan?"

"I'm just a fan," Bill said modestly.

I decided not to let Bill get away with that and said, "He's not just a fan. He's Bill Sharman."

The guy went nuts. "I can't believe this!" he said. "I'm from Boston and you and Cousy were my all-time favorites."

The man calmed down enough for Bill to say, "And this is Larry Stewart. You read him in the L.A. Times."

Again, the guy went nuts. Well, maybe not nuts. But he explained he is in the film business and never misses my TV sports column. He then called a friend on his cell phone and said, "You're not going to believe this. I'm in the restaurant at Griffith Park and sitting next to Bill Sharman and the sportswriter Larry Stewart."

Meanwhile, Mal had returned from the restroom and witnessed all this. He tapped me on the knee and asked, "What's going on here?"

"This man is just excited to meet Bill and me," I said with a smile.

Replied Mal, "Better not tell him who I am, he'll wet his pants."

Getting back to Ted Green, his Times career eventually imploded.

His troubles started on Sunday, Dec. 28, 1980. As the Ram beat writer, he was covering a playoff game in Dallas. He was no longer also covering the Lakers for the Times, but Shirley had allowed him to take a side job as a Laker commentator for ON TV, an over-the-air pay service that had launched a few years earlier and televised selected home games involving L.A. teams.

The Ram game in Dallas presented a problem. He also had to get to the Laker game at the Forum that night at 6:30. To make it to the Laker game, Green devised a sketchy plan. He would leave the Rams game at the end of the third quarter, fly to LAX, head to the Forum, go into an office there, and call Times sidebar writer Rich Roberts, who would be writing in the Dallas press box. Roberts would provide Green with details of the fourth quarter and a few post-game quotes. He then would write his game story and file it from the Forum.

One problem, though. Green's flight from Dallas got fogged out of LAX and landed in Las Vegas. Now things got difficult. After getting a hold of Roberts, Green's alternate plan was to dictate his story off the top of his head from a pay phone at McCarran Airport.

When Green called the office to dictate, Garrity took the call and could hear slot machines in the background. I was nearby and heard Garrity ask Green, "Where are you calling from?" And then: "What the hell are you doing in Vegas?"

Green was busted. But not fired. Nor was he fired after he refused to do as upper management ordered and give up the ON TV Laker commentating job.

But the Dallas fiasco and other offenses eventually got Green fired in the winter of 1981. By then, he no longer had Bill Shirley in his corner because Dwyre was now the sports editor.

After Green was fired by Dwyre, I think just about everyone in Sports was glad to see him go.

Green unsuccessfully tried sports talk radio before settling in as a sports producer at an independent TV station, KTLA Channel 5. Amazingly, Randy Harvey hired him in 2010 to do some freelance writing for the Times website, but I do not think that job lasted long.

Even though Shirley was not impressed with the job I did filling in for Green, I kept writing on my own. I averaged one or two bylined stories per month.

In April of 1979, cable television was just beginning to get a foothold in sports broadcasting. Cable television had been around for 20 years, but mainly just to provide better reception. In 1975, Home Box Office, which became better known as HBO, began the first pay-cable entertainment channel.

Now cable television was delving into sports programming. People in Los Angeles could watch the Atlanta Braves on Ted Turner's so-called superstation. Originally it was WCTG but soon changed to WTBS to signify Turner Broadcasting System. Also, Chicago Cubs were available on WGN in Chicago.

What did the future hold? Was more sports programming coming? And how much would it cost viewers?

I set out to find out after successfully pitching an in-depth story. I spent nearly a month doing research and making dozens of daytime phone calls from home prior to working night desk shifts.

When I lined up an interview with Turner, I was told I had only 10 minutes. But when I got him on the phone, I think I asked one, maybe two, questions. He talked almost nonstop for about 30 minutes.

While working on the story, I discovered there were plans for a 24-hour sports channel. One channel with nothing but sports? To me, it sounded like a crazy idea. How do you fill 24 hours with nothing but sports programming?

Bill and Scott Rasmussen, a father and son from Hartford, Conn., were the ones behind this crazy plan. After getting a tip about their proposed all-sports channel, I first called Stu Evey of Getty Oil, whose company planned to back this project with a $10 million investment. Through Evey, I was able to contact Bill Rasmussen, who told me this channel would be called the Entertainment and Sports Programming Network, or ESPN for short.

He said they needed the word *entertainment* in the title because at the time they thought they would have to run old movies to fill programming gaps. It turned out they could fill 24 hours with nothing but sports, even though it meant repeating a lot of programming.

Although I had my doubts this thing would ever fly, I decided it would be worth a sidebar. The two stories ran on May 25 of 1979 and dominated that day's Sports section. The main story ran across the top of Page One and jumped to Pages 13 and 14. The sidebar, which ran on Page 13, was one of the first stories ever written about ESPN, certainly the first outside the east coast.

The Page One banner headline read: *CABLE TV: A BONANZA AWAITS THE SPORTS JUNKIE*. The deck headline read: *But It Is a Bonanza That Has a Hitch*.

The hitch was that cable television would not be free. The monthly cable bill could be as much as $9 a month. I know, but this was 1979.

Shirley never said a word about the stories until a few days later, after I turned in an expense account detailing $101 worth of phone calls I made from home. Back then, phone companies charged for each phone call.

Shirley walked over to my desk holding my expense account, which I had left on his desk the previous night.

"We allow you to do these stories on your own, but we can't have you turning in an expense account," he said. "In the future, you have to come into the office to make phone calls on our Watts line. You can't be costing the company any money."

My thought was, "Thanks for the kind words, Mr. Shirley."

In the three years I worked for Shirley, I think the only time he complimented me on anything, albeit indirectly, was for a headline I wrote on the 1980 Boston Marathon in which Rosie Ruiz was the surprise winner until it was determined several days later that she had cheated by not running the full 26.2-mile course.

There were suspicions immediately after the race. My headline, which ran at the top of Page One, read: *Did Rosie Run a Fast One – or Pull One?*

The next day, Shirley said, "The managing editor (George Cotliar) asked me to compliment whoever wrote that headline and I understand it was you."

Shirley then pointed out the headline broke a few stylebook rules.

"We're not supposed to use question marks in headlines, and we're not supposed to use first names," he said. "But in this case, it was okay."

Stylebooks are considered bibles to editors who write them, but I always thought following style was overrated. Readers certainly do not care about style.

The Times stylebook called for spelling out National Collegiate Athletic Assn., the National Basketball Assn., and other such bodies. I and others advocated for using call letters such as the NCAA and the NBA. Eventually, that became the standard.

The New York Times stylebook required that it use Entertainment and Sports Programming Network, not ESPN. The network objected. It wanted to be known by its call letters. But the stuffy New York Times would not budge. So, the name was officially changed to ESPN, Inc. The call letters now mean nothing.

Not long after I got chastised by Shirley for seeking to be reimbursed for making work phone calls from home, I got another gut punch.

John Hall, the Times' Page Three sports columnist, told me upper management wanted a sports TV column and that he told Shirley, "We've got the perfect guy to do it sitting on the desk, Larry Stewart."

Hall quoted Shirley as saying, "Larry Stewart may be good enough to write for the Herald Examiner, but he is not good enough to write for the L.A. Times."

It was a blow, but I understood it. I think Shirley liked me as a person. We got along great during that junket in Montreal prior to the 1976 Summer Olympics, and when I was working a day shift, we had pleasant conversations.

As I mentioned on Page 193, I think what he had against me was that I came from the Herald. He could not fathom that there were people who thought the Herald had the better sports section.

My opinion was that back then the Times' sports section was cleaner, meaning fewer typos, and it was better organized and larger. I think what made the Herald's sports section livelier was that the Herald was a writer's paper, while the Times an editor's paper. Excessive editing tended to water down stories.

After John Hall told me what Shirley had said about me not being good enough to write for the Times, I explored other job opportunities. I first applied for sports editor at the San Gabriel Valley Tribune. But my job interview with an assistant managing editor lasted all of two minutes. The guy was a zero.

Things were totally different when I interviewed for the position of sports editor at the Long Beach Press-Telegram. Managing editor Rich Archbold and everyone there were totally professional. I was there all day and had lunch with outgoing sports editor John Dixon. A week or so later Archbold called to thank me for my time and interest and informed me that staffer Jim McCormack was being elevated to sports editor. That proved to be an excellent decision.

Turns out, things worked out for the best. Less than two years later, Shirley was demoted, and Bill Dwyre was named sports editor.

Chapter 28: Shirley's Demise, My Rise

I was working a Sunday desk shift in June of 1981 and Dave Moylan was in the slot. He handed me a story written by Shirley to edit. The dateline on the story was Geneva, Switzerland. The topic was the International Olympic Committee.

As I recall, much of the story focused on Anita DeFrantz, an Olympic rower at Montreal who had just been awarded the Olympic Order for her contributions to the Olympic movement. It was a glowing story, too glowing.

"This story reads like a payoff piece," I told Moylan, who agreed.

In journalistic terms, a payoff piece is a positive story, often referred to as a puff piece, in which a writer is compensated in some form, often with free travel.

The next day, when I came into the office, Moylan waved me over. "Bill Shirley is no longer the sports editor," he said.

What I heard second hand is that when Shirley informed his boss, editor-in-chief Bill Thomas, about his planned trip to Geneva, Thomas told him he could not go. Shirley in turn decided to take vacation time and go anyway. That meant he would have to pay his own way or go against Times policy and have someone else pay, such as the IOC. One thing for sure, Shirley did not pay his own way.

Shirley was already in hot water. A few months earlier, Times investigative reporter David Shaw was working on a story on Super Bowl ticket scalping. When Shaw grilled travel agent Surl Kim about where he gets tickets for his Super Bowl tour packages, Kim became agitated and told Shaw to look at his paper's sports editor.

Word was that when Shirley was questioned by Bill Thomas about scalping Super Bowl tickets, he came up with a doozy of an excuse. Shirley claimed he provided Kim with Super Bowl tickets in exchange for better deals on travel for Bob Oates and other beat writers who traveled, thus saving the Times money.

Like Bud Furillo at the Herald, Shirley must have felt he was indispensable. Otherwise, why would he have risked his job by taking that trip to Geneva?

But Shirley did not get fired. He only got demoted and ended up with a cushy writing job in which he got to pick his own assignments.

Two months earlier, in March of 1981, assistant sports editor Chuck Garrity left the Times for NFL Properties. Around the same time, John Hall left for the Orange County Register. Shirley was the main reason both men left.

Garrity's replacement was Dwyre, the sports editor of the Milwaukee Journal. He was recommended by Moylan, a former assistant sports editor at the Chicago Tribune who knew Dwyre from Associated Press Sports Editor conventions.

Dwyre, then 42, took the job with the understanding that he would eventually be replacing Shirley. Dwyre figured that would be several years down the road. With the sudden demotion of Shirley, Dwyre's wait was not long. Dwyre went to work at the Times in April of 1981 and was named sports editor in June.

Staff morale improved immensely under Dwyre. One of the first things he did was schedule one-on-one meetings with every staff member. He showed genuine interest in getting to know everyone. He asked all of us how we thought we could improve not only the Times sports section but also our own situations. I of course suggested a TV column. Dwyre said he would consider it.

After serving under Furillo and Shirley, Dwyre was a godsend. No one is perfect, but Dwyre came close during the 25 years he was my boss. He was a genuinely good person, although he despised having a "nice guy" reputation. He could be tough too – when it was warranted.

I now started writing again on my own.

The baseball strike of 1981 had silenced the nation's announcers, so in early July I got a hold of as many as I could to see how they were filling the void. Chicago's Harry Caray, who complained about losing more than $2,000 a week, told me, "I don't think it would be possible for me to get in a welfare line. I haven't missed any alimony payments, and I pay alimony to two ex-wives."

Vin Scully said his wife Sandi gave him a Father's Day card in which she had written: "I love you even though you are unemployed and under foot."

That story got picked up by numerous papers, including the Washington Post.

The week of Sept. 21 of 1981, prior to a game between Oklahoma and USC at the Coliseum, I got a tip from ABC Sports publicist Donn Bernstein.

I first met Bernstein in 1967 when he was sports information director at UC Santa Barbara. I made a road trip there when I was sports editor of the Daily Collegian, the Fresno State school paper. Bernstein treated me royally, as if I were from a major publication.

Bernstein left UCSB when the school dropped football in 1971 and was at the University of Washington for three years before taking the PR job at ABC Sports. In that role, he worked closely with me when I was at the Herald. And he knew that I was hoping to get a TV sports column at the Times.

"I got a good one for you," he bellowed over the phone. Bernstein always bellowed. He had only one voice level – loud. It was part of his charm.

Bernstein told me that since ABC had chosen to televise the upcoming USC-Oklahoma game – No. 1 vs. No. 2 – the network would not be able to televise either the USC-Notre Dame game at South Bend, Ind., on Oct. 24, or the UCLA game at the Coliseum on Nov. 21.

ABC, the only network televising college football, had USC on three times the previous season. That meant, under the NCAA's antiquated restrictions, USC could make only two appearances on ABC in 1981. The Oklahoma game was one of those two.

Beginning in 1982, when a new television deal with ABC and CBS took effect, there were fewer television appearance restrictions. And a Supreme Court case in June of 1984 opened the floodgates. That season, nearly 200 games were televised, up from 89 the previous season.

But in 1981, as hard as it is to fathom now, USC was on national television only three times, and one of those appearances was on NBC from the Fiesta Bowl, where the Trojans lost to Penn State, 26-10. The two ABC appearances were against Oklahoma and UCLA. Notre Dame was having a second down season under Gerry Faust, so its game against USC was scrapped by ABC.

The two USC games ABC chose to televise in 1981, against Oklahoma and UCLA, were both last-second thrillers.

The John Robinson-coached Trojans beat Oklahoma, 28-24, on a touchdown pass from John Mazur to tight end Fred Cornwell on the game's last play. In writing this book, I called my good friend Mike Lamb, who was a sophomore on that USC team. I knew he and Cornwell were close friends.

"That play made Cornwell a legend," Lamb said. "What people forget is that, on the previous play, Mazur passed to a wide-open Marcus Allen in the back of the end zone, but Cornwell, thinking the pass was for him, leaped up and knocked the ball off target. He was almost a goat instead of a hero."

In the ABC-televised game against UCLA on Nov. 21, USC won, 22-21, which kept the Terry Donahue-coached Bruins from going to the Rose Bowl. Heisman Trophy winner Marcus Allen, a senior, ran for 219 yards and two touchdowns, the second one late in the fourth quarter. The game was won when USC's George Achica blocked Norm Johnson's 46-yard field goal attempt.

Lamb told me that assistant coach Marv Goux deserved a lot of credit for that block. "Marv had studied game film and spotted a weak spot in UCLA's field goal formation," Lamb said. "He inserted Achica into the lineup and told him exactly what to do."

I went to Dwyre with Bernstein's tip and several other good items. I knew telling him that ABC likely would not be televising that season's USC-Notre Dame game would get his attention. Dwyre is a 1965 graduate of Notre Dame.

"Write it," Dwyre said.

The by-lined column, which Dwyre referred to as "TV notes," ran on Page One and jumped to Page Eight.

The lead note was of course on the USC football situation. A secondary note   was on a realignment of NFL announcers by CBS. Vin Scully had been working with John Madden and getting rave reviews. But executive producer Terry O'Neill, as he had previously planned to do, in mid-season had moved Hank Stram over with Scully and put Madden together with Pat Summerall, much to Scully's chagrin. "You just get used to somebody and then they split you up," Scully told me. "It's like learning to dance with one partner and then having to change partners."

I also had an item involving a Sugar Ray Leonard-Thomas Hearns pay-per-view fight held the previous Saturday night and how sports anchor Stu Nahan of KNBC had illegally shown highlights that night. He simply taped the fight at home and brought the tape with him to the station.

"I paid my $15 to get the fight," Nahan rationalized. Not sure if there was a penalty or not. Probably some sort of fine.

Dwyre was pleased and gave the go-ahead for more TV notes columns, but for now I would have to write them on my own time.

My second batch of TV notes the following week was sort of a follow-up to the first one. Because ABC chose not to televise the 1981 USC-Notre Dame game, that meant it could only be shown in L.A. on tape delay.

Channel 13 was the regular carrier of delayed USC telecasts, with Mike Walden calling the play by play. But Channel 13 could not televise the game because it had a telethon scheduled for that night.

After Channel 7 got the rights, that station chose to use sports anchor Ted Dawson as the play-by-play announcer instead of Walden. This provided me with some juicy fodder. "I was humiliated," Walden told me. "What an unprofessional way to do things."

Now I was off and rolling, even though I was writing on my own time. But my TV notes ran haphazardly on various days and in various places in the section.

Scott Ostler, an outstanding and clever writer, had taken over the Page Three spot after John Hall left for the Orange County Register in early 1981. His column ran five days a week.

Scott became a good friend and for a brief time lived in Temple City, which is adjacent to Arcadia.

After the 1981 baseball strike ended, Scott was assigned to do a column on fan reaction. He invited me to go bar hopping in the Pasadena-Arcadia area and help him get quotes. After getting thrown out of two places, we ended up at a dive bar on Baldwin Avenue in Arcadia called The Station. Scott got all he needed from customers there, and The Station would become a regular hangout for me.

Ostler and I were teammates on a basketball team in an adult league at Cal State L.A. I am not sure if it was after one of our games or where we were when Scott confided in me that he was planning to ask Dwyre for a raise. He said his salary was $40,000 and that two of our colleagues, Mike Littwin and Alan Greenberg, were telling him he should be making $50,000.

I was skeptical. Those two were envious of Scott being the Page Three columnist, so I wondered if they had Scott's best interests at heart. Scott might have had the same thoughts. He did not want to agitate Dwyre in any way.

"I think I'll give Dwyre the option of giving me a $10,000 raise or having me write only four columns a week," Scott told me.

I knew how that would turn out, but at the time had no idea the impact it would have on me.

A week or so later, I found a note from Dwyre and Jack Quigg in my mailbox that was distributed to everyone. It read: "Beginning next week, Scott Ostler's column will run Monday through Thursday and Larry Stewart's TV notes will run on Page Three on Fridays. Also, Stewart's desk shifts will be reduced to four days a week, with Wednesdays designated as his writing day."

I felt the euphoria in my face as I read the note. Once a week I would be occupying the same space John Hall occupied for years. This was huge. I put the note in my pocket. The next night I went to a Laker game at the Forum. I wanted to spread news of my good fortune. I saw Ostler in the Press Lounge after the game and went over to him. "Have you been in the office?" I asked. He had not.

This was awkward. It was good news for me but not for Scott. I knew he would have preferred getting the $10,000 raise. I still had the note with me, so I showed it to him. He read it, then offered a handshake.

"This is great for you," he said. "Congratulations."

I am sure he meant it.

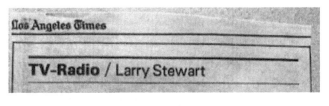

Although Dwyre initially called my column "TV notes" and it had just a regular byline, now that it was on Page Three, it looked like a column.

But for several years, Dwyre continued referring to it as "TV notes." I understood why. There were writers in the department, such as Littwin and Greenberg, who were envious of Ostler's columnist stature. The envy would have been double that if Dwyre called it "Larry Stewart's TV column." To many in the department, I was still just a desk guy.

Don't get me wrong. I liked Littwin and Greenberg. Neither was a Ted Green type. I was sad to hear that Greenberg, who left the

Times in 1985 to become a columnist and beat writer for the Hartford Courant, died of a heart attack in March of 2007 at age 55.

I was not a featured columnist like Murray or Ostler. I wrote a specialty column, and there were a number of those. Most of the beat writers were given specialty columns, whether it be the NFL, the NBA, college football and college basketball, golf, tennis, soccer, motor sports or whatever. Dwyre gave longtime desk hand Bob Cuomo a well-deserved college baseball column.

This was the post Bill Shirley era, and Dwyre was improving morale while at the same time putting out a sports section that met the journalistic standards of a newspaper regarded as one of the best in the world.

I continued to work four nights a week, although there were several years in the 1990s when I was given two writing days per week. The paper was booming, and we had tons of space.

Assistant sports editor Rick Jaffe essentially gave me two connected pages in the middle of the sports section. In technical terms, this is called a double truck. This two-page double truck included my column, one or two photos, the TV-radio sports listings for the entire weekend, a list of TV ratings for past weekend, and another list of guests appearing on upcoming sports programs.

This required additional work, thus the additional writing day. I was pleased with this, but not everyone else was. Colleague Tim Kawakami was working the desk four nights a week and getting only one day to write his boxing column.

"Why does Stewart get two writing days and I get one?" he asked Dwyre, who came back with a perfect retort: "Stewart is a slower writer than you are."

I got this tidbit from Kawakami, who told me he had no rejoinder to Dwyre's retort.

Working the desk was not a bad gig, at least in the old days. It beat suckering lemon trees or pulling sprinklers in the wee hours of the morning

One of my more memorable nights on the desk came on Sept. 26, 1981.

Baseball ruled the sports world during the '60s, and during that time Sandy Koufax, a left-hander like me, became my No. 1 idol. I know I am not alone there.

On this night, Nolan Ryan, in his second season with the Houston Astros and facing the Dodgers, pitched the fifth of his seven no-hitters, breaking the record of four no-hitters that he shared with Koufax.

I was working a rewrite shift. In the slot was Bob Lochner, who came over to me around 8 p.m. He told me that the Times' longtime baseball writer Ross Newhan had been trying to get a hold of Koufax to get a quote about Ryan's record-setting no-hitter.

Lochner, who said Ross and his wife Connie were going out for the evening, asked me to give Koufax a call. Lochner gave me the number Ross had given him.

I called the 805 area-code number which I believe was Paso Robles. There was no answer. (Answering machines were not common until the mid-'80s.)

Twice I tried again. Still no luck. Around 9:45, Lochner suggested I try Koufax one more time. This time, the phone was answered.

"Is this Sandy Koufax?" I asked.

"Yes, who is this?"

"This is Larry Stewart from the L.A. Times."

"What in the world, why are you calling me at this time of night?" an irritated Koufax responded. "What is it you want?"

I apparently awakened a sleeping Koufax. But I pressed on.

"Did you hear about Nolan Ryan's no-hitter?"

"Yes. So, what does that have to do with me?"

This was not going well.

"Well, as you know, you and Ryan shared the record of four no-hitters. We just wanted to get a quote from you about Ryan's accomplishment."

Koufax continued expressing his displeasure in no uncertain terms before eventually calming down and giving me a usable quote. He essentially said he knew that Ryan would someday break the record.

After I hung up, I told Lochner and others on the desk that night about Koufax's reaction.

For years after that, whenever something big would happen, Lochner, or someone else, would invariably say, "Larry, how about giving Koufax a call and get his opinion?"

My friend Pete Bonfils, longtime Dodger batting practice pitcher and baseball memorabilia collector, assured me that Koufax was a sweetheart of a person. Others who knew Koufax well told me the same thing.

Everyone has bad days and bad moments. Trust me, I've had a few.

Chapter 29: The 1984 Olympics

A highlight of my sports writing career came when Los Angeles hosted the 1984 Summer Olympics. The Times, under Dwyre's direction, had a staff of well over 100, including 59 credentialed reporters, working almost nonstop on coverage of those Olympics. Beginning 10 days prior to the opening ceremony, we put out a special 44-page Olympics section for 26 days in a row. During that stretch, we also put out a regular sports section.

I had only one day off during those 26 days, and I used it to take my family to the last day of the track and field competition. I first tried buying tickets through the Times but had better luck as just a regular person.

My workdays went from mid-morning to close to midnight. I watched as much of the TV coverage as possible, wrote TV columns, worked copy editing shifts and was the slot man for the non-Olympics section a few times.

I was among the staff members who literally moved into the nearby New Otani Hotel. My wife and daughters, like many Southern Californians, were out of town for most of the Games. Fearing the terrible traffic jams that never materialized, they spent time at Lake Arrowhead and San Diego.

Dwyre did an unbelievable job piloting the Times through the Olympics and was justifiably honored for it. His awards included National Editor of the Year from the National Press Club in Washington, D.C., and the National Headliner Award from the Press Club of Atlantic City. At the Times annual awards dinner in 1985, he won the paper's top prize, the one for Sustained Excellence. In 1996, he was presented the Associated Press Sports Editors' prestigious Red Smith Award.

The Times was in its heyday in 1984, so Dwyre had total support from management and tremendous resources. To paraphrase what Washington Redskins owner Jack Kent Cooke said about Coach George Allen's budget when he fired him, Dwyre had an unlimited budget and managed to exceed it.

One of my pre-Olympic assignments was to do a feature story on ABC commentator Donna de Varona, a gold medal-winning swimmer at the 1964 Olympics at Tokyo who competed as a 13-year-old at the 1960 Olympics in Rome.

I went to New York to interview her, plus talk with other ABC personnel, and hopefully get a sit-down with Roone Arledge, who at that time was the president of both ABC Sports and the network's news division.

During my time as a TV sports columnist, I made it to New York close to once a year, always flying first class until the Times was sold to the Tribune Co. in 2000. After that, reporters were told to search for the cheapest flights.

During my trip to New York to interview De Varona, I pleaded with ABC Sports publicist Irv Brodsky to set up an interview with Arledge.

"He doesn't have the time," Brodsky insisted.

"Tell him I came from L.A. to talk to him," I suggested.

"No." "Just 10 minutes?" "No." "Five minutes? "No." Two minutes?" "No."

During my nearly 35 years of covering sports broadcasting, I had one-on-one interviews with most top TV executives. But never Arledge. He rarely, if ever, did one-on-one interviews with reporters. I think he was afraid it would be exposed that he was not the genius he was made out to be, that he was just a guy in the right spot at the right time who hired good people.

In 1983, the Los Angeles Chamber of Commerce honored four people at a dinner at the Century Plaza Hotel. The four were Muhammad Ali, Dinah Shore, John Wooden and Arledge.

My wife and I were guests of ABC. Jim Brochu, the former Laker publicist who was now with ABC, wanted us there so I could meet Arledge. At a pre-dinner VIP reception, we were having a nice conversation with Wooden when Brochu came over and said to me, "Come with me, this is a good time for you to meet Roone."

When we got close to Arledge, there were others lined up to meet him. As we stood there, I became irritated. "We left John Wooden for this?" I thought.

Finally, we got to the head of the line. While being introduced, I stuck out my hand. Arledge started to stick out his hand but then raised it and began waving. "Robert, Robert Stack," he called out as he walked away toward the actor, leaving Norma and I just standing there.

Brochu tried to rally. "We caught him at a bad time," he said. "Let's try again."

"No thanks," I said.

A highlight of the 1984 Games was gymnast Mary Lou Retton's gold medal-clinching performance on the vault at UCLA's Pauley Pavilion on Friday, Aug. 3. The 4-foot-9 Retton topped off the night by scoring two perfect 10s on the vault, although she only needed the first one to clinch her victory over Romania's Ecaterina Szabo and become the first U.S. woman gymnast to win an Olympic medal of any kind, let alone a gold for the individual all-around title.

Richard Hoffer wrote the main news story that appeared under a banner headline on Page One of the Olympics section and 26-year-old Rick Reilly wrote a sidebar that appeared under a three-column headline on Page 34.

Hoffer and Reilly were quite a team. Both ended up at Sports Illustrated. Reilly went there in April of 1985 and became the magazine's esteemed back-page columnist. Hoffer followed soon after and became a senior writer in an SI career that spanned 25 years.

Hoffer's Times coverage of Retton's triumph was named Best Reporting Story of the year by the Sporting News. But it was Reilly's sidebar that sticks out.

Reilly found a way to get past security and stand next to Retton's personal coach, Bela Karolyi, who was not allowed on the floor. Only the U.S. coach, Don Peters, was allowed on the floor. Karolyi finagled his way into a photographer's well close to the floor, and Reilly finagled his way to a spot next to him.

ABC had a camera trained on Karolyi and throughout the competition that night Reilly, wearing horn-rim glasses, was continually seen leaning over to listen to what he was saying. Those of us watching in the Times sports department were stunned to see our young colleague.

When Retton stuck her gold medal-clinching vault, Karolyi at first could not immediately get to her. He looked around for somebody to hug. There was Reilly.

Here is how Reilly described what happened next:

"Yawoooo," he bellowed as he put me in a half nelson.

"Gmmphmph!" I said, that being the only literate thing I tend to manage when my lungs have been collapsed.

The next huggable thing Karolyi found was Retton, considerably more deserving and tenfold more huggable.

The Times discouraged reporters who were not columnists from interjecting themselves into stories. In this case, it was justified.

Olympic filmmaker Bud Greenspan also had a camera trained on Karolyi that night, giving Reilly an unexpected significant role in Greenspan's excellent official film of those Olympics, "16 Days of Glory." On camera, Reilly appeared uneasy, like someone who knew he was someplace where he did not belong.

I learned through Greenspan's film that Karolyi had somehow gotten a credential as an equipment handler. Here is what Reilly told me years later about what he did: "I saw where Bela was and thought I had to get down where he was. I turned my credential around and as I approached a security guard I pointed and said, 'I'm trying to get over there.' Amazingly, the security guard let me through."

His sidebar on Retton's big night was among the many well-crafted stories Reilly wrote for the Times. But it was not error-free.

"I could hear everything Bela was yelling at Mary Lou, or at least I thought I could. I wrote he called her 'Little Body,' which made sense to me at the time," Reilly told me. "Two days later someone told me he was yelling, 'Little Buddy'."

In 2012, Dan Guerrero, then UCLA's athletic director, hired me to do a series of 10 stories for the UCLA Athletics website on sports legends who had competed at Pauley Pavilion. Guerrero was looking for ways to promote the $136-million renovation of the arena, which reopened in 2013.

Mary Lou Retton was the topic of one of my stories. I interviewed her on the phone from her home in Houston. She was a great interview and a sweetheart of a person.

I first met Mary Lou in 1995 at a cable television convention in Anaheim. The photo here shows me with her and Joe Namath,

along with Steve Greenberg, left, and Brian Bedol, the creators of the Classic Sports Network. Retton and Namath were there to promote the new channel.

In my interview with Mary Lou in 2012, of course one of my first questions was about her gold-medal-clinching vault. "That vault changed my life," she told me. "One step on the landing, one little mistake and everything would have been different."

She also told me that her father Ronnie was a teammate of Jerry West's at West Virginia. I did some research and found that Ronnie Retton, as a 5-7 senior guard, played in the 1959 NCAA championship game won by Pete Newell's Cal Bears, 71-70. Retton scored two points; West, then a junior, scored 28.

I called West to ask him about Ronnie Retton.

"He was a very active, pesky player," West said. "We were a very quick team and if we got a little sluggish, he would come off the bench and get us going. He was an invaluable player on our team, and a great all-around athlete."

When interviewing Mary Lou, I asked her if she knew who the young man in the horn-rim glasses was standing next to Bela. She did not, so I told her.

"That was Rick Reilly!" she exclaimed. "I never knew that."

Mary Lou and I stayed in touch for a while, emailing back and forth. I sent her the photo of us taken in 1995 that included Joe Namath. She remembered the cable television convention but, understandably, did not remember me.

In 1984, on Wednesday, Aug. 1, two nights before Retton won the all-around individual women's gymnastics title, there was the team competition in which the U.S. finished second to Romania. The silver was the first team Olympic medal of any kind U.S. women gymnasts had won since 1948.

In a subsequent TV column that ran on Friday, Aug. 3, I took commentator Cathy Rigby to task for not only her unabashedly rooting for the U.S but also rooting against Romania. This took place while ABC was receiving global condemnation for its biased coverage.

Appearing in the middle of my column, in what is called a window in newspaper lingo, was a mugshot of Rigby along with, in large bold-face type, this passage from my column: "Worst performance by an ABC commentator so far was turned in by Cathy Rigby Wednesday night on women's gymnastics."

That was a hard hit, particularly on someone I had met in Montreal in 1976 and found to be a delight.

I understood her rooting for the U.S. She had starred in gymnastics for the U.S at the 1968 Olympics. What bothered me more was her rooting against Romania. When Szabo faltered on the balance beam, Rigby said: "A big break there. We may be able to make up some points there."

On Saturday, Aug. 4, the day after the women's all-around competition, I picked up the phone at my desk and heard, "This is Cathy Rigby."

I hated these calls. Throughout my career, I had to deal with people who were unhappy about something I wrote. I always tried my best not to add fuel to the fire. But I was stunned this time. Rigby told me she agreed with the criticism. That rarely, if ever, happened.

"After the compulsories on Monday, the U.S. coach (Don Peters) was furious with me," Rigby said. "He complained that I was rooting for the Romanians. Other people did too. I went the other way and just went too far.

"I realized it later, but you have to understand that for 20 years American gymnastics was my life. And here, finally, we were accomplishing what we had set out to accomplish."

That was winning an Olympic medal in team competition.

As Retton got ready for her all-important vault on the final night, Rigby said on the air, "I hope she has her wings on tonight."

When I told Rigby that sounded like rooting, she replied, "The second I said it I wished I hadn't. I said to myself, 'There you go, doing it again'."

The rest of our conversation was pleasant. When she learned I had two daughters, she offered me tickets to an upcoming performance in Long Beach of her as Peter Pan. I politely declined and thought, "Wow, what a nice person!"

Throughout my career, I saved many of the letters and postcards from readers I received as well as folders full of email printouts. They fill two big drawers in a desk at home. I usually tossed the negative ones, but not all.

A postcard I saved was dated Aug. 3, 1984, the day my rip at Rigby was printed in bold-face type. This communique was succinct.

Listen Asshole,

I'm fed up with your bad-mouthing TV announcers. What happened? Were you turned down for a job at ABC? What or who made you an expert on announcing. I'm a subscriber to the Times and I've seen that crap in your columns quite a bit. Cathy Rigby won her job. What in hell did you ever do, Asshole?

At the 1972 Olympics in Munich, the darling of those Games was Olga Korbut, a 15-year-old pig-tailed gymnast from the Soviet Union. Helping make her a star in the U.S. was ABC commentator Gordon Maddox, an Olympian who had coached gymnastics at Cal State L.A. His genuinely enthusiastic commentary informed viewers that what they were seeing was extraordinary.

In 1991, I interviewed Korbut when she was in Southern California at Dana Point for the taping of a "Greatest Sports Legends" segment.

Most of the interview was conducted through an interpreter, but Olga spoke some English. Five months earlier, she and her husband had moved to the Atlanta area from the republic of Byelorussia. They were married in 1978, one year after retiring from gymnastics.

In my interview, she talked at length about her efforts to help victims of the 1986 Chernobyl disaster. Millions were exposed to radiation after an explosion at a nuclear power plant. Korbut and her husband lived in Minsk, 180 miles northwest of Chernobyl.

She was glad to be in the U.S. In Byelorussia, she was making only 200 rubles ($312) a month as the republic's national gymnastics director, and there were no opportunities to make money off endorsements.

I met Bart Connor, a star for the U.S. men at the '84 Olympics, after he was hired by NBC as a commentator to work alongside Dick Enberg and Retton at the '88 Games at Seoul. In '84, Connor helped the U.S. team shock the world by upsetting heavily favored China with a perfect 10 on the parallel bars. His gold medal in that event was the first gold medal for the U.S. in men's gymnastics in 80 years.

The U.S. win over China was equated to the U.S. hockey team upsetting the Soviet Union in hockey at the '80 Winter Olympics in Lake Placid, N.Y.

I interviewed Connor at his apartment in West L.A. prior to the '88 Games and we stayed in touch until the University of Oklahoma alum moved to Norman, Okla. He began dating Olympic legend Nadia Comaneci in 1990, less than a year after she defected from Romania and they opened a gymnastics academy in Norman. They were married in 1996 in Bucharest on national television.

In 2006, Bart and Nadia were at a Paralysis Project dinner and provided me with a good Morning Briefing item. Bart said when he and Nadia were in Chicago and checked into a hotel, he noticed the desk clerk's name tag said *Nadia*. "That's a nice name," Connor told her. After the young woman said she was named after the famous gymnast, Connor pointed at his wife and said, "This is Nadia." The clerk replied, "Oh, were you named after the gymnast too?"

On the one-year anniversary of the '84 Olympics, the Times put out one more 44-page special section. After that, those who worked on the '84 Olympics coverage were invited to a dinner at the Miramar Hotel in Santa Monica.

At the end of the evening, we each got a decorative cardboard box filled with all 27 of the 44-page special sections. The top of the box featured a color photo of the opening ceremonies under a headline reading OLYMPICS '84. My box remained unopened in our garage for more than 36 years. My wife at times over the years would ask why I was hanging onto it. She had the same question about old scrapbooks in the family room closet.

I would always tell her, "Someday I may write a book."

Chapter 30: Building Relationships

The year 1985 was a good one. I was now entrenched as the Times' TV-Radio sports columnist.

At a Dodger game in the spring of 1985, I ran into Dennis Gilbert, the former centerfielder for the Visalia Mets. I had seen him a few times before and he had told me he had become a successful life insurance agent. Now he told me he had started a sports agent business called the Beverly Hills Sports Council. Dennis was mostly handling the baseball side, with veteran sports agent Mike Trope concentrating on the football side.

Dennis, aware of my Visalia connection, told me that one of their clients was Mike Young, the UCLA wide receiver from Visalia. Dennis said Young, who also played baseball at UCLA, had been drafted by the New York Mets.

"Would you like to meet Mike Young?" Dennis asked. When I said I would, Dennis set a dinner at Pips, then a private dinner club on Robertson in Beverly Hills. Dennis had a membership there.

I had heard from friends back home about Mike Young and Visalia's great Mt. Whitney High football team of 1979. That team went undefeated, won a Valley championship, and was rated as one of the top teams in the history of California high school football.

Young, as a junior, was the star receiver. Lupe Sanchez, who later was a four-year starter at cornerback for UCLA, was the star running back. The offensive line was anchored by Don Mosebar, who went on to star at USC. All three would play in the NFL.

Mike Young, who went by Michael Young after college, chose to pursue football instead of baseball and had a 10-year NFL career that included four seasons with the Rams, four with the Denver

Broncos, one with the Philadelphia Eagles and part of one with the Kansas City Chiefs.

That dinner at Pips, which took place shortly before Young was drafted in the sixth round by the Rams, could not have gone any better. Dennis and Michael became lifelong close friends of mine. One of Michael's UCLA teammates, Terry Moore, who joined us later that evening, also became a good friend. And through Moore, I met Mike Izzi, whom I have mentioned previously. Izzi was a track athlete at UCLA, initially a decathlete before focusing on the javelin.

I helped Izzi land a job at Stanford by recommending him to Gene Washington, an associate athletic director. I had gotten to know Washington, a football standout, when he worked as a sports reporter at Channel 7 in L.A. Izzi spent 16 years in sports administration at Stanford, then 10 years as the athletic director at UC Irvine before becoming the AD at Cal State Northridge in 2018.

Through Dennis, I connected with too many people to mention. His client list included, besides Bonds and Saberhagen, Mike Piazza and many of the biggest names in baseball. Also, through his life insurance business, he had an in with the Hollywood set. Beginning in 2002, he put on an annual gala benefiting baseball scouts. In 2012, backed by investors, he was a finalist to purchase the Dodgers. He and his wife Cindi live in a beautiful home in the exclusive Holmby Hills neighborhood east of UCLA.

As for Michael Young, I ended up becoming a pseudo-member of his amazing Visalia family. Bill and Diane Young, Michael's parents, had three children, Chris, Michelle Barnes, and Michael, in that order. All three are happily married to their high school sweethearts. And everyone in this family, which includes seven grandchildren and various relatives, gets along. I know they get along because I have witnessed it a various family functions.

Chris Young and wife Paula are retired teachers. Michelle works in a law office and her husband Chuck is a prominent Visalia contractor. Michael was a pro football player who became a top marketing and financial executive with the Broncos, the Arena

League Colorado Crush and eventually the Dodgers. He and his wife Jill live in a beautiful home in Cambria on California's central coast.

What stood out to me over the years was how Bill and Diane always treated everyone, and everything, the same. To Bill and Diane, there was no difference between an NFL game involving their younger son, or a volleyball match or a high school JV football game involving a grandchild.

Early on, Bill Young invited me to a family gathering at Camp Nelson, a mountain resort located above Springville. When I asked Bill who else would be there, he said, "Just family members."

"But I'm not a family member," I said.

"We consider you a family member," he said.

That sealed the deal.

Bill and I became golfing buddies. We played all over, from Oceanside to Fresno but mostly in Visalia. We were not good but always had a great time.

Bill died on Nov. 20, 2015, at the age of 83 after a long battle with cancer. There was a huge turnout for his funeral. The next day a small group was invited to dinner at Michelle and Chuck's home. Norma and I were included in that group.

During my career, there was one story, far more than any other, that I wish I would have gotten to write but never did. I had hoped to write about Bob Chandler's successful battle with cancer. I instead wrote his obituary in January of 1995 and covered his funeral.

We had become friends, good friends, after I misquoted him in one of my columns. Yes, you read that correctly.

Before I met him, Chandler was an outstanding wide receiver on John McKay's USC teams. As a junior, he was named the most valuable player of the 1970 Rose Bowl game. While with the Buffalo Bills, he led the NFL in receptions for three seasons (1975-77). He was a key member of the Oakland Raiders when they beat Philadelphia in the 1981 Super Bowl.

Chandler had been one of the best all-around high school athletes ever in Southern California. He was All-CIF in football and basketball and, as one of the nation's leading decathletes, he high jumped 6 feet 7, pole vaulted over 13 feet and put the 12-pound shot 57 feet.

I got to know him after he retired from the L.A. Raiders in 1982 and got into broadcasting. Chandler was working at Channel 7 in 1983 when the station hired another former NFL star, Gene Washington, upping the number of sportscasters on the payroll to seven. A source at the station said Chandler might be the odd man out. I called Chandler at his home in San Marino and then, in my column, I quoted him as saying he would be "disappointed" if he lost his job.

I got a couple of phone messages from him the Friday my column ran, but we did not connect until the following Monday. He complained I misquoted him, that he had never used the word "disappointed." He said what he meant to convey was that the competitor in him would make him fight to keep his job.

I checked my notes. He was right. He never used the word disappointed. I apologized and offered to run a "for the record" correction.

"No need to do that," he said. "I was pretty upset on Friday, but I've calmed down. And it was partially my fault for not making myself clear."

That was refreshing to hear. It planted the seed for a friendship that grew over time. Chandler and Channel 7 did part ways, which led to a better job as the co-host of the "2 On the Town" show on Channel 2. He later became the Raiders' radio commentator.

Bob and I often played golf with Pat Haden. Those two were near scratch golfers and often had a bet going. My goal was to just stay out of their way.

When Michael Young was in his second season with the Rams, I told Bob about my friendship with him.

"I'd like to meet him," Chandler said. "I think I could help him."

I arranged a meeting at a well-known sports hangout, Trani's Majestic restaurant in San Pedro, a precursor to Phil Trani's Long Beach establishment.

After I picked up Chandler at his home in San Marino, he said, "My best friend is in town, and I invited him to join us. I hope that's okay?"

That is how I got to meet another close friend of mine, Leo Hart, a backup quarterback for the Buffalo Bills when Chandler was the team's star receiver. Hart had been an All-American at Duke and he and Chandler initially met at the 1971 East-West Shrine game in San Francisco. Hart was the starting quarterback for the East, Chandler a starting wide receiver for the West. They later roomed together at the Bills' training camp and became best friends.

These days Leo frequently calls to check in. Or I call him. We got together at several Super Bowls and, more recently, in Atlanta where he and his wife Glenda live, then again in California's Napa Valley when they also had a home there.

That night in San Pedro was the start of my friendship with Leo Hart and cemented my friendship with Chandler. I loved hearing Bob's stories, particularly those about his oftentimes rocky relationship with USC Coach John McKay.

Here is one of them. In 1967, when Chandler was on the freshman team (there were freshmen teams back then), McKay thought he was showboating during a no-pads, no-contact practice session with the varsity team during the week of the USC-UCLA game. Chandler, playing defensive back, knocked a pass away from star receiver Earl McCullough two plays in a row.

"McKay was watching from a tower and came scrambling down, ran over and really cussed me out," Chandler told me. "I thought, 'I don't need this.' I walked out of practice, packed up all my stuff in my little MG and planned to leave USC and transfer. But as I was getting in my car, (assistant coach) Marv Goux approached. He said McKay was sorry about what happened at practice and handed me $50 to take my girlfriend at the time out for a nice dinner."

That was probably a petty NCAA violation, but after all this time, who cares?

Added Chandler: "I thought that was a nice gesture and decided to stay at USC. I found out later that McKay never apologized or gave any money to Goux to give to me. Goux did all that on his own."

During the 1994 football season, I got a tip that Chandler had cancer. I think my heart skipped a beat. Not Bob Chandler. He never smoked, was a light drinker and was always a picture of good health and fitness.

I immediately called him, and he confirmed my worst fears. He gave me all the details, saying it was a rare form of lung cancer. He also asked me not to write anything about it. But when I told him I had to write something about why he would be missing Raider broadcasts, he said he would write something out and call me back. When he did, he read me a carefully worded paragraph about how he was going through treatment for cancer.

"When I beat this thing – and I will beat it – then we'll sit down and I'll give you all the details," he told me privately.

Toward the end of the 1994 season, in December, the Raiders were playing a Monday night game in San Diego. I was there and at halftime I went into the visitors' radio booth to say hello to Bob. I was taken aback. He was no longer the handsome man who got women's attention wherever he went.

Bob told me he had just played three rounds of golf at Augusta National, site of the Masters. He went there as a guest of Peter Ueberroth, the mastermind behind the 1984 Summer Olympics in Los Angeles and former baseball commissioner, and Jim Nordstrom, who was then co-chairman of the luxury department store chain that bears his family's name. There was a fourth in the group, but his name escapes me.

During my visit with Chandler in the broadcast booth, he told me he shot a 76 in one of his rounds at Augusta, an astonishing score considering his body had been ravaged by chemotherapy. "I could still kick your (butt)," he said with a smile.

"There is no doubt about that," I replied.

"When am I going to be able to write that story we've talked about?" I asked.

He turned solemn and said, "We're not."

I knew what he meant. I could feel the lump in my throat and the tears in my eyes. I said, "Hey, great seeing you Bob," as I turned and walked out of the booth. I had to leave, or I would have broken down.

That was my last conversation with Bob Chandler. He died about four weeks later, on Jan. 27, 1995, at the age of 45, leaving his wife Marilyn and three children, Marisa, Justin and Emma. The day after Bob died, Marisa got a notice that she had been accepted at Harvard.

Leo Hart delivered the eulogy at the funeral under a huge, filled-to-capacity tent on the grounds of the Rose Hills Mortuary in Whittier. It was during the O.J. Simpson trial, and since Simpson was a teammate at USC and in Buffalo and was a close friend, speculation was that Simpson might show up at the funeral. Judge Lance Ito had declared a recess for the day. There must have been at least a dozen TV satellite trucks parked along the street in front of Rose Hills.

Simpson was a no-show, but much of his defense team was there. So was A.C. Cowlings, who I spotted signing autographs for some kids. I guess that was a nice gesture, but it seemed inappropriate to me.

I wrote Bob Chandler's obituary, and I wrote about his funeral, but I was never able to write the story I so desperately wanted to write – that Bob Chandler, a winner in so many ways, had won his battle against cancer.

In 2010, I wrote a freelance magazine piece about my relationship with Bob Chandler, and a version of it appeared on the USC Athletics website. But it was certainly not the story I wanted to write.

Chapter 31: 1994 Had Its Ups and Downs

The first half of 1994 was okay. The second half was not.

One thing I recall about the early part of 1994 took place on April 6, a Wednesday. I was on a family vacation at our time share in the Palm Springs area. It was my wife's spring break from her job as a special education teacher. We were watching the news and saw a clip of Ram quarterback Jim Everett, during an interview with Jim Rome, knocking over a table and attacking the sportscaster.

Rome kept prodding the quarterback by calling him Chris Evert. He had given Everett that nickname after a phantom sack during the 1989 NFC championship game against the San Francisco 49ers. Everett went down before being touched and was criticized by commentator John Madden during the game and by many others afterwards.

On the 1994 show on ESPN2, Everett warned Rome to quit calling him Chris. "If you call me that one more time, you might want to go to a station break," Everett warned. But Rome did not heed the warning and, many believed, got what he deserved. Everett never punched Rome, just pushed him down before being pulled away.

As I watched the clip, I was glad I was on vacation. This was not something I would enjoy writing about. It would not have been pretty. I agreed with just about everyone else – Rome was the bad guy here.

"Even my grandmother said she would have punched him," Everett told Jay Leno two night later.

My friend and colleague, Chris Dufresne, wrote about the incident, but it was a story that did not go away in a day or two. It was still a hot topic a week later, after I returned from vacation.

When I called Rome, he said, "Larry, I'm glad you called. I want to talk to you, but I want to talk to you in person. I don't want to just talk over the phone."

We met at his studio in Hollywood and went for a late dinner at Miceli's, a popular Italian restaurant. In media interviews the previous week, Rome offered trite and unconvincing excuses for what he did. By now, the 29-year-old feared for his career. I got a full-blown apology. The banner headline on my column published on April 15 read: *Rome Owns Up to Mistake and Has to Live It Down.*

I had an interesting relationship with Rome. He began regularly writing to me and sending me tapes when he was working for a small Santa Barbara radio station, KTMS. I eventually wrote him back. He told me years later that when he saw the letter, he thought it was someone playing a joke on him. No, it was me. I told him about Jim Murray writing to me when I was in college.

I did a phone interview with him when he got hired by XTRA, a powerful all-sports radio station in San Diego. He told me he rented a car to drive to San Diego for his interview, fearing his own car might break down. He was obsessed about getting that job. As Rome grew in stature, there were times I criticized him. That did not go over well. To his listeners, I became Stewey the Clown.

In 1996, I got a call from a young man named Travis Rodgers, who was from Arcadia. I had met Travis through a friend a few years earlier when Travis was a pitcher on the baseball team at UC Santa Barbara.

"Jim Rome is advertising on the air for a producer," Travis told me on the phone. "I faxed in a resume. Do you know Rome well enough to give me a recommendation?"

I told Travis I was not sure a call from me would hold much weight, but I would give it a shot. When I called the home number I had, there was no message on the answering machine. Just a beep.

But I left a message, not sure Rome would get it. But he did, and that call led to Rome hiring Travis as his producer, a job he had for more than 10 years before branching out and starting his own show.

Not long after Travis started working for Rome, the three of us had lunch.

"I had more than 200 applications for that job," Rome said. "After getting your call, I literally dug through a waste basket to find Travis' resume. Without your call, there is no way Travis gets the job."

I think you can see by now that I have had a good life. But I've learned through interviewing rich and famous people, no one has a perfect life.

Mine hit a difficult period in mid-94. I learned while I was on vacation with my family visiting my uncle, Harry Alexander, in Santa Fe, N.M., that my mother, Uncle Harry's sister, was in bad shape.

I guess you could call it a mental breakdown. When we returned from vacation, I drove up to the Visalia area to see what was going on. She had sold the Strathmore property and moved to a nice mobile home trailer park in Exeter after my father died in 1991, one day after that year's Super Bowl.

Now, things were a mess. An unscrupulous couple had taken her in – and taken a considerable amount of her money. She had become addicted to Ativan, a sedative to combat anxiety and depression. Dealing with her was like dealing with a young cocaine addict. With help from my Strathmore neighbor, Imogene Little, we got her away from the couple who had taken her in and taken her money.

But I had my hands full. My brother John, who lives in Visalia, chose not to get involved. I made weekly trips up to Visalia to deal with my mother as she got kicked out of one assisted living place after another. Nobody could handle her.

The next six months were grueling. Stops to visit Bob Saberhagen in Pine Mountain helped, and Bill and Diane Young were lifesavers.

Although I slept in my mother's mobile home in Exeter, the Youngs' house in Visalia was my home away from home. Their daughter Michelle, who works in a law office, lined me up with an attorney to handle some of the legal paperwork.

There was no facility in Visalia that could handle my mother. At the last one we tried, I was told, "You have two weeks to get your mother out of here."

That sounds cruel, but my mother was going around telling visitors – and anyone else who would listen – that she was being beaten. And she continually called 911 or an ombudsman with outlandish stories of abuse. There was no truth to any of them.

I finally moved my mother to a facility near me, the Santa Anita Retirement Center in Temple City. That eliminated the long drives, but more importantly this was a bigger and better place for her. She was my mother, and I wanted the best for her, even though she did not make it easy for me. Quite the opposite.

Until she died in April of 2001 at age 88, I had to check on her daily and frequently take her to doctor's appointments.

She saw a psychiatrist in San Marino for a while, and he diagnosed her as being bi-polar. That was hardly news to me. She always had severe mood swings.

One day we were in the psychiatrist's office waiting to be seen. Another patient, an elderly lady, was also in the waiting room. My mother struck up a conversation.

"Do you know my son?" my mother asked. "He is a famous sportswriter."

There was no reaction from the disinterested woman.

My mother continued anyway. "He is the best son in the world," she said.

Five minutes later, while meeting with the psychiatrist, she told him I was abusing her. "He is the worst son in the world," she told the psychiatrist.

He asked her the reason for that. "He won't let me have a phone," she said.

Phone calls were not the only problem. One time in Visalia she escaped from a hospital where she was receiving psychiatric day treatment and took a cab to her lawyer's office. She paid her cab fare with a check, despite not having money in her account.

The lawyer called our house, but I was in San Diego. This was the same day I was at the Raider-Charger game where Bob Chandler gave me his bad news. Fortunately, my wife spared me the trouble of calling me. It was not until the next day, after I returned home, that I learned about my mother's escapade. The lawyer, unsure what to do, eventually had my mother transported to the assisted living facility where she was then staying – and I got a hefty bill.

Around the same time my mother went off the rails, things at work took a downturn as well. I cannot say one thing was connected to the other, but I began making more mistakes than usual. A new slot person, who had good technical skills but, in my view, lacked people and managerial skills, gave me my first negative performance review. And things with this person went downhill from there.

Assistant sports editor Rick Jaffe suggested the two of us sit down for a meeting. I thought that was a decent idea, but it never happened. It got so bad I had thoughts of leaving the Times. But I got some good advice from a stranger I played golf with one day in Arcadia.

"Leave a job for more money or better conditions," the stranger told me. "But never leave because you are not getting along with a supervisor. Generally, those situations tend to change every three years or so. In a 40-year career, three years is only about seven percent of your career."

I thought about that. I had endured 3½ years of Bud Furillo and three years of Bill Shirley. I could endure this latest rough patch. There were still a lot of positives about my job. And thankfully Bill Dwyre was still my main boss.

Chapter 32: Super Bowls, O.J., and More

During my time as an L.A. sportswriter, I was directly involved in the coverage of eight Super Bowls. I loved Super Bowl weeks.

Before the first Super Bowl at the L.A. Coliseum in 1966, Commissioner Pete Rozelle, a former PR man himself, told his PR staff to spare no expense in entertaining the press. "I want the writers covering the Super Bowl to go back to their papers and tell their editors and colleagues what a great week they had," Rozelle reportedly said.

The 1977 Super Bowl was the first one I covered. The Oakland Raiders defeated the Minnesota Vikings, 32-14, at the Rose Bowl, and I wrote a sidebar for the Herald.

I invited my Strathmore friend Byron Tillery and his wife Janie down for the game. One party we attended that Super Bowl Week was at Chasen's in Beverly Hills. I got to meet one of my idols, country and western singer Charley Pride, and Janie Tillery got hit on by O.J. Simpson.

My next Super Bowl was 1983, when Washington defeated Miami, 27-17, at the Rose Bowl. Leading up to that game, I covered the media days for the Times and filed notes, which are short items.

I had the same assignment in 1987, prior to the New York Giants beating the Denver Broncos, 39-20, at the Rose Bowl. That week I had a memorable interview with Giant second-year cornerback Herb Welch, a 12th round draft pick in 1985 out of UCLA who was now a starter.

Welch, from Downey, arrived at UCLA in 1983 as a walk-on JC transfer from Cerritos College. He told me his big break at UCLA came his junior year when starting cornerback Lupe Sanchez was injured. Welch replaced Sanchez in the starting lineup that season and, with Sanchez graduating and moving on to the NFL with the Pittsburgh Steelers, Welch was a UCLA starter throughout 1984.

I told Welch that Lupe was a friend, as were other UCLA teammates of his. I named Mike Young, Terry Moore, Mike Hartmeier, and Dave Baran.

"How do you know all those guys?" Welch asked.

I explained it was mainly because of my friendship with Young. "Lupe and Mike are from Visalia and I'm originally from that area," I said. "My hometown is southeast of Visalia."

"Lindsay?" Welch said, which surprised me.

"Have you heard of Strathmore?" I asked.

"Sure," he said. "I have relatives in Plainview."

That blew my mind. Plainview is a settlement of some 900 people located three miles west of Strathmore. Welch said his relatives, whom he had not seen in years, were a great uncle and aunt.

Welch then said, "I've got another one. My wife and I live in an apartment building in New Jersey, and we are friends with the couple next door. The wife's parents own the Paul Bunyan Motel in Porterville."

The night before the 1987 Super Bowl, my wife and I attended an NFL Players Association dinner at the Century Plaza. During a VIP pre-dinner reception, CBS' Andy Rooney and his wife Marguerite ended up standing next to us.

My wife, a Rooney fan, struck up a conversation. We discovered Rooney is even more of a curmudgeon in person than he is on the air. Whatever my wife asked, Rooney usually had a pat response: "That's a stupid question."

Mrs. Rooney leaned over to me, pointed to two people wearing Giant jerseys and asked, "Are the Broncos having a separate party somewhere else tonight?"

After I explained this was not a Giants party, her husband snarled, "She never knows where she is. To her, this is just another free meal with free cocktails."

It was an uncomfortable six minutes with Andy Rooney.

Joe Theismann was the quarterback of the Washington Redskins when they beat Miami in the 1983 Super Bowl and when they lost to the Oakland Raiders in the 1984 Super Bowl. Leading up to the 1985 Super Bowl, the Redskins and Theismann lost to Chicago in a divisional playoff game.

ABC had the 1985 Super Bowl. During the 1984 regular season, ratings for "Monday Night Football" dipped. Howard Cosell claimed it was because he was no longer in the booth and O.J. Simpson was.

ABC denied that was the problem, but Roone Arledge decided to spice things up for the Super Bowl and put an active player in the booth and move Simpson to the pregame show. Theismann was his first choice. Had the Redskins made it to the Super Bowl instead of the San Francisco 49ers, the player in the booth would have been Joe Montana.

With the Super Bowl taking place at Stanford Stadium, I convinced Dwyre that a trip to the Bay Area to cover the TV coverage was warranted.

So, you ask, why attend an event to cover the TV coverage?

The answer is access. It allowed me to do in-person interviews with announcers and the production staff, both before and after an event.

Instead of being in a press box during a game, I would be in a production trailer in the TV complex. USA Today's Rudy Martzke would almost always be there too at major events, plus one or two other local TV sports columnists, a couple of network publicists, and maybe a few special guests. I would watch an event on a TV in the trailer and take notes as if I were watching at home. I would then do post-event interviews and file my column from the trailer.

Among the many events I watched in a TV production trailer was Kirk Gibson's home run in the bottom of the ninth inning of Game 1 of the 1988 World Series. At the following year's World Series, when the San Francisco earthquake, measuring a 7.1 on the

Richter scale, hit before the start of Game 3, I was on site in a production trailer. I address that experience in detail in the next chapter.

I was in a production trailer at ABC's prime-time Tiger Woods-David Duval match-play shootout at Lake Sherwood Country Club northwest of L.A. on Monday, Aug. 2, 1999.

Woods wrapped up a victory when Duval, on the par-4 16th hole, hit his ball in between two boulders in the middle of the fairway. That is right, the boulders are in the fairway.

ABC Sports publicist Mark Mandel and I were in a trailer that I was not supposed to be in because we got the live audio feed. That enabled me to hear what the announcers were saying during commercial breaks.

After Duval's unlucky tee shot at the 16th hole, the network went to a commercial break. I could hear course reporter Judy Rankin talking to the announcers in the broadcast booth about those boulders in the middle of the fairway. She said they fell off a truck while the Jack Nicklaus-designed course was being built.

I heard Rankin say, "Workers called Jack to the site and asked him what they should do. Jack said, 'Just leave them there'."

But once back on the air, Rankin, as well as the other announcers working the event, declined to tell that story, apparently to avoid embarrassing Nicklaus.

This was a great item, but Mandel asked me not to use it because it would get him in trouble for having me in this particular trailer. I did not use it in my review in the paper the next day, but I did use it in my column the following Friday, attributing it to talk in the TV complex.

I will switch gears here and discuss the year I covered horse racing. It was a new chapter in my life, and I enjoyed it.

The 2008 Kentucky Derby was among the major races I covered, and the beat allowed me to meet a lot of interesting people. One was John Harris, horse owner, breeder, and agribusiness giant in the San Joaquin Valley. He may be best known as the owner of the

Harris Ranch Inn, an oasis in the middle of nowhere on the I-5 Freeway.

I spent a day with Harris in 2011 when I did a freelance story on him for Thoroughbred Times, a national magazine. I met him at his ranch where he lives in a mini-Hearst Castle about 25 miles east of Fresno on the shoreline of the Kings River. We flew on his single-engine plane to his horse ranch near Harris Ranch Inn. The trip is 25 minutes by air, an hour-and-a-half by car. My brother John was with me, so he volunteered to drive my car from one ranch to the other.

Another time Norma and I were the guests of Harris and his wife Carole. We stayed in the four-bedroom guest house, which features a full-sized swimming pool *inside* the house.

When I first started covering horse racing for the Times, I heard rumblings from veteran racing scribes that I was miscast on the beat. That was true, but I think I made up for that by scrambling for stories. While the veteran beat writers spent time handicapping races and placing bets in the press box, I was always wandering racetracks looking for stories.

One time I was in the Frontrunner, the huge fifth-floor restaurant at Santa Anita, and spotted track owner Frank Stronach. He invited me to join him and his group, which included then-track president Ron Charles. I got a revealing interview, and Charles later told me reporters from other papers complained to him, thinking he had set it up. Charles told them I had just happened by.

No matter what I was covering, I was always on the prowl looking for something different. I learned a lot about going after a story when I was at the Herald Examiner. It was important at that paper because we were always trying to beat the Times. Conversely, the Times, at least under Bill Shirley, regarded the Herald as a non-factor.

My reporting instincts came into play during Super Bowl Week in 1985 after I flew up to San Francisco mid-week to attend an ABC press function. Frank Gifford, Don Meredith, O.J. Simpson, and

Roone Arledge were all made available to reporters, but it was Theismann who drew the biggest crowd.

It was difficult getting anywhere close to him, but it did not really matter. It was doubtful he would have anything provocative to say, and if he did, I knew there would be a quote sheet handed out to all reporters.

Off to the side, I spotted actress Cathy Lee Crosby, with whom Theismann had been romantically linked. There were rumors that Theismann had left his wife of 14 years for Crosby (no relation to Bing Crosby).

I sauntered over and found a chatty Cathy. It helped that she was a native of L.A. and an alum of USC. She said she grew up reading the Times.

She told me that she and Joe were living together on a farm outside Leesburg, Va., and were planning to be married after his divorce was final on March 1. She said they met while at a Special Olympics event in Vermont. "He kept calling me until I finally agreed to go out with him. I love him very much and plan to spend the rest of my life with him."

Things apparently did not go as planned. They never married and their relationship ended in 1991 amid suits and countersuits over money. But in 1985, their relationship was a good story.

When I was done talking to Cathy Lee Crosby, there was another piece of gossip that interested me involving Simpson. At this point in time, I had a good relationship with Simpson, so when I got the opportunity at the ABC press function in San Francisco, I pulled him aside to ask him about the rumor that he was dating Theismann's ex-wife.

"It was in some publication," Simpson told me. "I can't remember which one. I do not even know her name.

"Worse than that was 'Entertainment Tonight' saying I was dating Cathy Lee. Cathy called me and we both tried to figure out where that one came from."

Simpson added that he was planning to marry his longtime girlfriend, Nicole Brown, on Feb. 2. I asked if the rumor about him dating Theismann's ex-wife was a case of mistaken identity.

"No," he said. "My fiancée is a lot better looking than Joe's ex-wife." That was O.J. trying to be funny.

At the time, I liked O.J. When the Fresno Bee did a feature story on me in 1990, the reporter, George Hostetter, asked me about some of the sports celebrities I had interviewed. This is a quote that appeared in Hostetter's story: "O.J. is one of the nicest people you would ever want to meet."

He had a lot of us in the media fooled.

NBC hired O.J. to replace Ahmad Rashad on its NFL pregame show in 1989, only a few months after being arrested for spousal abuse at his home after a New Year's Day party. The arrest did not make the papers until a month later. In May he pleaded no contest and got a slap on the wrist – two years' probation. He also had to donate $500 to benefit battered women and undergo counseling.

In July, a few local sportswriters, including me, were invited by NBC to have lunch with O.J. at the Century Plaza Hotel. After the formal questioning period, I got O.J. off by himself to ask him about the New Year's Day incident.

He admitted there was a confrontation between him and his wife Nicole but called it a "bum rap" and claimed it never would have happened if they had not been drinking. I wrote what he told me in my next column. He later gave the same excuse to Roy Firestone on ESPN's "Up Close" show.

A few weeks after I wrote about the New Year's Day "confrontation" between O.J. and Nicole, I was back at the Century Plaza for a charity function. I was exiting through the lobby when a man I did not know stopped me.

"O.J. sent me over," the man said. "He wants to buy you a drink." The stranger took me over to a table where O.J. was sitting with Nicole. As I was standing there, Simpson laughed and said, "Hey, Nicole, this is the guy who reminded the public about our little spat on New Year's Day." Nicole was not laughing. She was looking at me with dagger eyes. I could tell she was angry, so I passed on the drink offer and walked away. I would later realize she was angry at her husband, not me.

Over the years, I talked with O.J., either in person or on the phone, maybe a couple dozen times. He was almost always gracious. One time, when I was in New Orleans for the Super Bowl in 1990, he was not so gracious.

I will have more on that later in this chapter.

In 1992, O.J., who by then was divorced from Nicole, invited me and other media members to a Sunday evening grand opening of a friend's sports bar/restaurant on Pico Boulevard in West L.A.

That afternoon I took my friend Gary McMillan, a Chicago native, and his then-wife Kate to a Dodger-Cubs game at Dodger Stadium. It was McMillan's 40th birthday. At one point I went up to the broadcast booths and introduced myself to the Cubs' legendary announcer Harry Caray. Fortunately, he was familiar with my column and was as gracious as could be.

I asked if he would mention my friend's birthday on the air. I knew Caray did such things. After writing down McMillan's name, he said he would mention his birthday first on radio and then the following inning on TV. It was a nice surprise for McMillan's mother, who was watching the game at home in Chicago.

I had told McMillan and Kate that, after the Dodger game, we were going to the opening of a sports bar/restaurant in West L.A. I did not mention O.J. would be there. I thought that could be a nice surprise.

When we got to the restaurant on Pico, I was surprised so few people were there. Doug Krikorian was the only other media person there. O.J. was at a table with his girlfriend Paula Barbieri and his friend A.C. Cowlings. When O.J. saw us at the bar, he got up and came over. He immediately hit on Kate. When O.J. saw he was not getting anywhere, he said to Kate, "Could you get me a Heineken?" He then turned his attention to us guys.

Kate, who worked as a bartender, told me later, "Who did he think I was, his personal bartender?" She added, "Something about him gives me the creeps."

On June 13, 1994, I got a call at home midday. It was from Eric Malnic, who was one the Times' top news reporters. He wanted a phone number for O.J.'s agent, Ed Hookstratten. He said O.J.'s ex-wife Nicole and a young man were murdered at the condo Nicole was living in on Bundy Avenue in Santa Monica.

"O.J. is not involved, is he?" I said to Malnic.

"I don't think so." Malnic said. "I believe he is in Chicago for a charity event."

I, along with the rest of the world, would soon know a lot more.

After O.J. was found not guilty of murder, he initially was keeping a low profile. So it was somewhat surprising that the day before the 1995 USC-UCLA football game O.J. was on the air with radio sports talk show host Joe McDonnell, who was then working for AM 1150.

McDonnell asked softball questions, which was unlike him. His on-air partner at KMPC 710, Doug Krikorian, often referred to him as "The Big Nasty." I saw McDonnell the next day in the Coliseum press box. McDonnell was livid. He had been ordered by station manager Roy Laughlin to only ask football questions.

"Anyone who knows me knows I would have unloaded on O.J. unless I was ordered not to," McDonnell said.

The radio station took so much heat that Laughlin issued a statement apologizing for having O.J. on the air. I followed up with a call to find out what Laughlin was thinking. He told me O.J. had just called up out of the blue.

"We put people on the air who call us," Laughlin said.

My story ran on a Tuesday, my day off. When I called in to the paper to get my messages at work, there was one from O.J. He asked me to call and gave me his home number.

When I first called, I got his daughter on the phone. I asked her to give O.J. a message that I called and gave her my home number. When O.J. called back, it was weird. This was not the O.J. I had known for years. In harsh tones, he told me he had not called the radio station out of the blue but rather the station manager had been asking him for months to come on the air during USC-UCLA game week. He talked to me as though he did not know me.

O.J. then began rambling, not claiming to be innocent but rather talking about people who believed him to be innocent. I recall at one point pulling the phone's receiver away from my ear in disbelief that I was having this conversation.

A month or so later, ESPN announced O.J. was going to be interviewed by Chris Meyers on "Up Close." Since I now had O.J.'s home number, I called him.

This time he was more abrupt. "They asked me to come on the show and I said I would," he said. "That is all there is to it."

That was the last time I talked to O.J. Simpson.

I loved Super Bowl Weeks. At least before they got out of control, attracting hordes of people who were not interested in attending the game, people who came to town just to party.

I first began to realize that was the case when I was in New Orleans for Super Bowl Week in 1990, when the Denver Broncos faced the San Francisco 49ers. My first night in town I noticed five women wearing Bronco gear walking in the French Quarter. I asked them if they were from Denver. They were all longtime friends, most of them living in different states. They told me they were just in town to party and bought the Bronco gear so they would fit in.

When I saw them again a few days later, they told me that a photographer for the Denver Post had taken their photo and asked if I knew how they could get a copy of that paper. I explained just because a photographer snapped a photo, it does not mean it will appear in the paper. "That photographer probably shot at least 100 photos that day," I explained.

In the press center, copies of the Denver Post and San Francisco Chronicle were made available to the media. As I walked past two stacks of those papers, I glanced down at the Post. To my astonishment, on the top of Page One, was a four-column photo of these five women. The photo caption identified them as Bronco fans. I grabbed a bunch of papers and took them to my hotel room.

I did happen to see this group again. They went nuts when I showed them that they had made Page One of the Denver Post.

That is just one thing that happened during what I regard as the best week of my career. One night there were so many parties that I had trouble deciding on which one to attend. First, I walked to a CBS Radio party. Then while walking to my next party, I came across Paul's Kitchen, a well-known New Orleans restaurant. There was a sign in front saying, "Private Party." When I looked inside, I noticed it was a party for ESPN personnel. I knocked on the door and was invited in. That was party No. 2, and the night was still young.

Another night, Steve Sabol, the president of NFL Films and one of my all-time favorite people, hosted a small group for dinner at the five-star Grill Room at the Windsor Court. At Sabol's request, I had invited my friend Michael Young, then a Bronco wide receiver. In the AFC title game against Cleveland, Michael had scored on a 70-yard pass play and set up another touchdown with a 52-yard reception.

After a marvelous dinner, we all went back to Sabol's hotel suite to watch the NFL Films' "Road to the Super Bowl." When Michael's touchdown catch was shown, Sabol was the most excited person in the room.

Before going to dinner that night, I met Michael at the Broncos' hotel. He was going to be interviewed there live by Channel 2's Jim Hill. After taking a seat at a nearby couch, I noticed a bowl of peanuts in front of me. While the interview was taking place, I was continually shoveling handfuls of peanuts in my mouth.

I had told Norma about the interview, so she and our daughters were watching. There I was, in plain sight in the background, first plopping down on a couch and then shoveling peanuts in my mouth. Meanwhile back home, Norma and the girls were laughing hysterically. This is now a part of family lore.

The next night, USA Today's Rudy Martzke and I were scheduled to appear on a segment of the Super Bowl special on the Prime Sports Network, which consisted of Fox-owned regional sports networks from across the country.

By coincidence, Michael Young and 49er receiver Mike Sherrard, teammates at UCLA, were also scheduled to appear on the same show, right before the segment with Rudy and me. Michael and Sherrard were getting picked up by a limo, so Michael suggested I come over to the Broncos' hotel and ride with them.

Apparently, players get limos while sports TV columnists are on their own.

On the limo ride to the set where the show was originating, Young and Sherrard started talking about their weeks. Bronco Coach Dan Reeves let his players go out on the town after they arrived on Sunday, but the 49ers, coached by George Siefert, had a curfew of midnight their first night.

By listening to Young and Sherrard, I learned that the Broncos made the most of their night of freedom but were paying for it at practices. The 49ers, meanwhile, got a good night's sleep their first night in town and were clicking at practices. I had good inside information here. But I am not a gambler, so I did not bet on the 49ers. I should have. They won, 55-10.

Another good thing about that week in New Orleans was becoming more than just an acquaintance of Don Klosterman. We became good friends.

I was a late addition to a crew of 11 reporters and two photographers the Times had in New Orleans. During the game, when the halftime score was 27-3, Jim Murray quipped to Dwyre, "I think you can now send half the staff home."

By the time Dwyre approved my request to go to New Orleans, all the rooms in the media hotel were full. I got lucky with a contact who got me a room at the more expensive and exclusive Monteleone Hotel. Dwyre got in a dig during a staff meeting, saying, "And then there is Larry staying at a $500-a-night hotel." That was a lot in 1990.

After arriving in New Orleans, while checking in at the Monteleone, I heard a loud voice coming from the bar adjacent to the lobby. "Larry Stewart, what are you doing here?" It was Klosterman. He was also staying at the Monteleone. We spent a lot of time that week going around in circles while having drinks in the hotel's famous Carousel Bar, which features a circus-themed merry go round.

We made a date to go out to dinner one night, just the two of us. "Come up to my room," he said. "I'll leave the door cracked open."

Although he was able to walk with the assistance of a cane, getting up out of bed was a chore. After making my way up from my third-floor room to his room on the fifth floor and walking in, I found Klosterman laying on his bed talking on the phone.

"Hey Juice, guess who just walked into my room?" Klosterman said. "Your buddy, Larry Stewart."

Yes, it was O.J. I had been critical of him following the recent AFC championship game. Doing post-game interviews, he botched a couple of names, had incorrect statistics, and overall came across ill-prepared.

"O.J. wants to talk to you," said Klosterman as he handed me the phone. I figured the conversation would be civil. It was not. O.J. was more than angry, he was threatening. I had never seen that side of O.J. But soon he flipped and started kidding around, becoming more like the O.J. those of us in the media knew.

Looking back, I think right there I got a glimpse of the other side of O.J. Simpson.

After that week in New Orleans, Klosterman and I frequently got together – golfing at Bel-Air or dining out at exclusive restaurants with famous people.

Mid-morning on June 7, 2000, on Wednesday, I was working at home when I got a call from assistant sports editor Dave Morgan. "Don Klosterman died last night, and we've got (Earl) Gustkey working on an obit," Morgan said. "Didn't you know him? I think Gustkey could use some help."

"I knew Klosterman very well, and know all his friends too," I said. "I'm coming into the office."

Once there, I started making phone calls and took over writing the obit.

Eddie Merrins, the long-time golf pro at Bel-Air Country Club where Klosterman was a longtime member, told me: "He was a friend to everyone from the lowly to the mighty."

"He wasn't one of my best friends, he was my best friend," said legendary Hollywood publicist Jim Mahoney, who was then the president of Bel-Air.

Said Dick Crane, another friend and fellow Bel-Air member: "He was the older brother I never had."

Klosterman, who had lifelong physical problems following that terrible skiing accident in 1957 that would have crippled most men, had major heart surgery six weeks prior to his death. I heard about the surgery and called him the night before to wish him good luck.

"I've got a 7:40 tee time," he cracked, cheerful as always.

That was the last time we talked. Six weeks after the surgery, he suffered a fatal heart attack at home on the morning of June 6. He died at Cedar-Sinai Medical Center at 11:15 a.m. June 7 without regaining consciousness.

The headline on the obituary read: "City Loses One of Its Best Friends." It was a perfect headline. He had many "best friends," including me.

A funeral was held on June 12, a Monday, at the Sacred Heart Chapel on the Loyola Marymount campus. It was a Who's Who event featuring celebrities from sports, the entertainment world, and politics. I was there to both pay my respects and cover it for the Times.

I arrived a little late, and the five people scheduled to give eulogies were waiting in the chapel's foyer. They were Sen. Ted Kennedy, former NFL quarterback and presidential candidate Jack Kemp, legendary football coach Bill Walsh, and two men I knew well, Frank Gifford and Al Michaels.

I also knew Walsh from interviewing him over lunch after he was hired by NBC in 1989 and seeing him several times after that. Gifford, Michaels, and Walsh all greeted me, and Gifford introduced me to Kennedy and Kemp.

"Larry wrote the obituary that was in the Times," Gifford told them.

First Kemp had some kind words. Then Ted Kennedy, as we shook hands, said, "Great story. You really captured The Duke."

Klosterman's nickname was The Duke, short for The Duke of Del Rey, a nickname bestowed on Klosterman many years ago by Bud Furillo. Doug Krikorian later tabbed him ``The Duke of Dining Out."

Ted Kennedy, in his eulogy, said, "There's a word that best describes Don, and it is friend. Don was a great friend to three generations of Kennedys, including my brothers John and Bobby. We love you, Don. We miss you and always will."

Klosterman initially met the Kennedys through Gifford.

The funeral was a star-studded affair. Among the noteworthy attendees at the funeral were Ethel Kennedy, Joe Namath, who flew in from Florida, Al Davis, actor Robert Wagner, Lamar Hunt, many former Rams, and Vin Scully and wife Sandi, who was Klosterman's assistant with the Rams in the 1970s. Klosterman introduced Vin to Sandi.

At the ensuing wake, held at the Bel-Air Country Club, I was sitting at a small table with Gifford when someone approached and said my obituary was in an ice statue at the center table where all the food was.

Frank and I went over to see it, and a photographer offered to take a photo of me in front of the ice statue. I asked Frank to get in the photo, and the photographer also invited Namath, who was standing nearby, and an attractive young blonde to get in the photo as well. Then Gifford stepped away.

"Larry, if I get in that photo it will end up in the National Enquirer," he said. He was serious. Three years earlier, Gifford was entrapped by the National Enquirer who paid a woman to lure him to a hotel room in New York.

I wish Namath had stepped away too. He ruined the photo by leaning over to flirt with the blonde, a friend of Klosterman's named Denise whom I had met before. At least I think her name was Denise. Don called her "Denise the Niece" or simply "the Niece." Klosterman kidded around so much it was often hard to tell when he was kidding or being serious.

At one point during the wake, people were invited to come up to a microphone and talk about Don. Someone came over and suggested I go up and say a few words. At first, I hesitated but eventually walked up the microphone in the center of the clubhouse dining room.

I introduced myself and said I had written the Times obituary on Don, then said a few words. When I was done, some of the people stood and applauded.

It isn't often an obituary gets a standing ovation.

When I returned to the table where Frank and I were sitting, I spotted Ethel Kennedy and told Frank about meeting Courtney on a dinner cruise in the Marina Del Rey marina in 1984.

"She's here," Frank said as he pointed to a table where Courtney was sitting.

I do not think I would have recognized her. She had changed considerably. As I mentioned earlier, she seemed more subdued than she was in 1984. But she was cordial. And, whether she meant it or not, I was moved when she gave me her address and suggested my wife and I come and visit sometime.

Chapter 33: An Earthquake and Other Jolting Events

One of the most memorable moments of my career was being at Candlestick Park when the San Francisco earthquake rocked the stadium just before the start of Game 3 of the 1989 World Series between the Giants and Oakland A's. I went to San Francisco to not only cover the TV coverage but also do a feature story on how the Bay Area media was handling a Bay Area World Series.

In the production trailer with me when the quake hit just after 5 p.m. were ABC Sports publicist Bob Wheeler, USA Today's Rudy Martzke, and special guest Timothy Busfield, one of the stars of the ABC show, "Thirtysomething."

The trailer rocked, but I did not think the quake was too bad until I went outside and saw people running out of the stadium. I knew almost immediately that I was now a news reporter.

I first went into the stadium to talk with fans who had remained in their seats. As I was returning to the TV complex, I spotted a worker off in the distance climbing down from one of the 100-foot light poles that surround the stadium. I had earlier noticed them swaying back and forth.

I sprinted to catch the worker before he could get away. At first, it was just him and me before a few other reporters arrived. His name was Benjamin Young, and he explained that he had volunteered to go up and unhook a decorative windsock that was caught in the lights. He had reached the catwalk at the top just as the quake hit. The light pole swayed back and forth like a tree in a windstorm.

"I went to my knees and hung on for dear life," he told me. "I thought I was dead. I've never been so scared in my life."

This was a good story which had literally dropped out of the sky. A year later, on the one-year anniversary of the quake, the San Francisco Chronicle had a special section. One of the feature stories was on Benjamin Young.

After my interview with him a year earlier, I hustled back to the TV complex to write. I was facing a 6:30 p.m. deadline for what was then an early edition of the Times. I had to dictate my story because phone lines were down. When I was done, I went back outside looking for more people to interview. I tracked down ABC commentator Tim McCarver, who told me what it was like in the broadcast booth when the quake hit. After that, I went around getting reactions from as many people as possible.

When I went to write my next story, there was no electricity in the dark TV production trailer. Luckily, I found an 8-year-old girl, Alyssa Dubin, who volunteered to hold a flashlight as I wrote for nearly three hours straight.

Fortunately, the batteries in my computer and the batteries in the flashlight kept on going. When I was done, I found a working phone line and filled my lengthy story. When I called the office to check in, Bill Dwyre got on the line and said, "We're going to divide your material up into three separate stories."

I said, "That's fine, do anything you want. I only ask one thing. There has been an 8-year-old girl holding a flashlight for me so I could write. Make sure her name is not cut out. I told her she was going to get her name in the L.A. Times."

Her name did get in print, thank goodness.

I had taken a cab from the Hyatt Regency hotel in Burlingame, where I was staying, and had no idea how I would get back there. There were no cabs available. When I told Wheeler, the ABC publicist, about my predicament, he pulled out a set of car keys and said, "Take my rental car. I can get back to the ABC hotel and will figure out things from there." He told me where his car was parked.

I found the car. It was now after 11 p.m. As I was driving back to my hotel, I wondered if the bar would be open. Of course, there was no chance of that. The hotel wasn't even open. When I got there, people were all over the lawn. The hotel across the street was missing part of a wall.

Around 3 a.m., some of us were given the option of returning to our rooms. We were told there was still no electricity, so we would have to be guided to our rooms. I opted to do that. When I went into the totally dark room, I felt a lamp and other objects on the bed. I cleared off the bed and slept in my clothes. At 6 a.m., a loud voice on the intercom announced the entire hotel was condemned and we had to leave.

In the lobby was free coffee, juice, and some food. There was a phone set up for guests, but the line to use it was long. I opted to just drive to the airport. I dropped off Bob Wheeler's rental car and then, with my suitcase in hand, proceeded to one of the long lines where people were waiting to make flight arrangements.

Ticket agents were walking up and down the lines. I lucked out and got booked on an 11:30 a.m. flight to Burbank, where my car was. I was somewhat relieved, so I went for a walk. I had plenty of time. Then I got even luckier. During my walk, still carrying my suitcase, I saw a sign for a departure to Burbank. It was now around 7 a.m. Amazingly, I got on that flight – just barely. The ticket agent radioed the pilot to hold up a minute before closing the airplane door.

I carried my suitcase onto the plane and put it in the seat beside mine. A flight attendant came by and said, "Sorry, we can't offer you anything. And I apologize for looking the way I do. I was awakened and told to get to the airport immediately. I had no time to wash my hair or put on any makeup."

I told her, "Don't worry about any of that. I'm just thrilled I'm on this flight and headed home. To me, you look great."

I went straight from the Burbank airport to the downtown Times Building. I still had writing to do. I was back at my desk by

9:30 a.m. when someone who knew me asked, "How in the world did you get back from San Francisco so fast?"

"That is quite a story," I said. "Someday I'll put it in a book."

Although not as jolting as an earthquake, an interview I did with CBS commentator Billy Packer in 1998 did shake up things at his network.

UCLA, in Steve Lavin's second year as coach, had managed to reach the NCAA basketball tournament Sweet 16, where the Bruins (24-8 at the time) would meet No. 5-ranked Kentucky on a Friday night. (UCLA lost, 94-68.)

Packer would be announcing the game with Jim Nantz, so I called him at his home in Charlotte, N.C. Toward the end of a routine interview, I mentioned to Billy that I was an alum of Fresno State.

The previous Sunday, on CBS' "60 Minutes," there was a segment reported by Mike Wallace about Fresno State and the criminal element involved with the basketball team, then coached by Jerry Tarkanian. When I asked Packer what he thought of that segment, that opened the floodgates.

He exploded, blasting "60 Minutes." He called the long-running news program "a cancer in our organization," adding, "You can quote me on that."

Packer was now on a roll. "They have done four college basketball stories around NCAA tournament time, and they always look for the most negative thing they can find. They go in with a preconceived plan and stay on it until they find what they want. About 99% of college basketball is positive and they look for 1% that is negative."

Insinuating that "60 Minutes" is not a team player, he said, "I wouldn't want to find them on my team in a foxhole."

The segment on Fresno State cited eight of 10 scholarship players who had missed games because they were suspended, ineligible, in rehabilitation or quit. Four were convicted felons.

After my interview with Packer, I needed to get a hold of Mike Wallace. The CBS publicist for "60 Minutes" gave me Wallace's phone extension. When I called it, I was surprised that Wallace himself answered. I had to call him back several times, and after answering he would say, "Larry, my friend, what's up?"

After my column ran, the story went national and CBS scheduled a conference call with reporters so Packer, if not apologizing, could at least clarify a few things. To Packer's credit, he stuck by his guns and not once complained about being misquoted or quoted out of context. I was on the call and toward the end, I was called on to see if I had a question.

"Larry, I didn't think you would be on the call since you already had the story," Packer said. "I have no problem with anything you wrote."

Sweet words to a reporter's ears.

As a reporter, you sometimes forget that a lot of people are reading what you write. It is not like where you are a performer or athlete and there is immediate gratification. But there were times during my career that made me realize that, yes, people are reading what I write.

In 1995, when I covered that national cable television convention in Anaheim, many new channels were being added to the TV landscape. To these new channels, this convention was a great place to get the word out.

The big draw at this convention was a live performance by the Eagles, the legendary band that had been on a self-inflicted hiatus for 13 years. Now they had reunited and were preparing for their "Hell Freezes Over Tour." It was called that because guitarist Don Felder had said they would get back together when hell freezes over. A near brawl between Felder and guitarist/lead singer Glenn Frey at a concert in Long Beach had caused the split.

Now the Eagles were going to have what was considered a dress rehearsal for their upcoming tour. It was scheduled for the Anaheim Marriott ballroom, and each registered participant at the convention got a free ticket.

I was never a huge fan of the Eagles, although I liked their music. Two women I met at a party that night convinced me to go to the concert. The ballroom was packed, shoulder to shoulder. Everyone stood. There were no seats.

I remember the name of one of the women, Helen Stubblefield. She was a former Dallas Cowboy cheerleader. I do not remember her friend's name, but I do remember her friend had enjoyed more than a few glasses of red wine. A good portion ended up on her white dress. But that did not slow her down.

I followed my two new friends as we worked our way up through the crowd all the way to the stage. There, the woman in the wine-stained white dress flirted with a member of the band who ended up inviting us backstage.

This was a hotel ballroom, so there was no real backstage. Just a side door.

We got through, and there was Glenn Frey. The well-oiled woman approached him while Helen and I held back. Soon Glenn started walking over to us. I was sure he wanted to meet Helen. But he walked up to me instead.

"Are you really Larry Stewart?" he asked. "I can't believe I am meeting you. I read your column every Friday." He went on to discuss several of the opinions I had stated in print. He did not like Keith Olbermann either.

This went on for what seemed like five minutes. I had never gotten a "fan" reaction like this one. And I never would again. I was totally blown away.

Before he walked away, he explained that if he were not a musician, he would have loved to have been a radio sports talk show host.

When Frey died in 2016, I wrote a letter to the Times, briefly summarizing my one experience with him. My letter got printed.

Chapter 34: More Stories that Stick Out

Speaking of being blown away, a story told to me by former USC basketball coach George Raveling did just that. I interviewed him when he was a basketball commentator for Fox Sports Net, a local cable channel.

My ensuing column, which ran Jan. 14, 2000, I rank as one of my best, not because of how I wrote it but rather because of the story behind it. It was not really a TV column per se, except that Raveling was working in the business.

A mutual friend, Jeff Fellenzer, gets a big assist here. He suggested I write a column on Raveling and told me to be sure and ask him about Martin Luther King's "I Have a Dream" speech. Martin Luther King Day was coming up the following Monday, so such a question seemed appropriate.

When I asked about the speech, Raveling proceeded to tell me his story.

In 1963, Raveling was two years out of Villanova, where he starred in basketball, and was then a graduate assistant coach. In late August of that year, he went to visit his best friend in Wilmington, Del., and the two of them drove to Washington to attend the scheduled civil rights demonstration.

They found a motel room and were walking among the crowds on the evening of Aug. 27 when a man approached them. Because of their size, the man asked them if they wanted to work security the next day. They were told to report at 8:30. They arrived a half-hour early, so were among 10 security people assigned to the podium in front of the Lincoln Memorial.

Martin Luther King was one of the scheduled speakers that day. Each speaker was limited to five minutes. King took 8½ to deliver his "I Have a Dream" speech.

After the speech, Raveling, stationed behind King, asked him if he could have the typewritten copy of the speech. King nonchalantly handed it to him.

Raveling, a collector, put the speech inside another important possession – a book signed by President Harry Truman and given to him when he played in an all-star game in Kansas City.

Raveling did not give it much thought for years after that.

This was not quite a scoop for me, although I believe this was the first time this story appeared in a major newspaper. It was first reported in the Gazette newspaper of Cedar Rapids, Iowa, in 1983, Raveling's first year of coaching at Iowa. He had previously spent 10 seasons at Washington State and, after a three-year stint at Iowa, was at USC from 1986 until he retired from coaching in 1994.

When a sportswriter from the Gazette asked Raveling if he had been involved in the civil rights movement of the 1960s, he initially said not really, then told his story about the King speech. The Gazette reporter realized this was an amazing story and gave it a good write-up. But since this was long before the internet, the story stayed in Cedar Rapids. But now I gave it national exposure and it has since been written up in Sports Illustrated and other publications.

After that 1983 interview with the Cedar Rapids Gazette, Raveling got his copy of the speech framed and preserved and put it in a bank safe deposit box. Last I checked, he had been offered $3 million for it.

Here is an excerpt from my column that reveals a largely unknown fact:

Raveling said the phrase "I have a dream," which King used throughout his speech, was not in the original speech. "He ad-libbed that," Raveling said. "He had just used it in a speech at a church in Detroit, and it had been well received."

The same week of my George Raveling column was a good one for me. On Tuesday of that week, Jan. 11, a story of mine featuring Steve Rosenbloom, the son of the late Rams owner Carroll Rosenbloom, ran on Page One of Sports.

A few weeks before the St. Louis Rams, coached by Dick Vermeil, defeated the Tennessee Titans in the 2000 Super Bowl, I spent parts of two days interviewing Steve Rosenbloom in Covington, La., a town then of 7,700 located on the other side of Lake Pontchartrain from New Orleans.

The 24-mile Causeway, the world's longest single-span bridge, connects New Orleans to Covington. In my story, I wrote that it was an appropriate place for Steve Rosenbloom because, for him, a lot of water had gone under the bridge.

Carroll Rosenbloom drowned in 1979 while swimming in the ocean north of Miami. His will left 70% of the team to his wife, Georgia Frontiere, who a year later fired Steve, her stepson, as the team's executive vice president.

Georgia moved the Rams to St. Louis prior to the 1995 season. The team returned to Southern California in 2016.

I could have written a book about the Rams family drama, there was so much material. This is a soap opera no one could have ever dreamed up. The headline on my story read: "As the Rams Turned."

I got to know Steve while making Ram trips when I was at the Herald. We are approximately the same age. He graduated from Georgetown with a degree in business administration in 1967. I graduated from Fresno State with a degree in journalism in 1968.

I liked Steve a lot. Just a down-to-earth good guy. No pretenses whatsoever.

He was hesitant to do the interview. He was concerned about damaging his relationship with his half-brother, Dale, who is better known as Chip, and half-sister, Lucia Rodriguez. Carroll fathered those two with Georgia.

I assured Steve I would tread carefully about anything involving them.

When I interviewed Chip for my story, I was impressed. He had changed from the teenaged Chip I remembered from Ram trips in the 1970s.

"I could never say anything bad about Steve," Chip the adult told me. "I consider him my brother, and I love him as a brother."

After Carroll drowned, Georgia took control of the Rams with her 70% ownership. Carroll's five children got 6% each. Steve, after much turmoil, ended up with about $2 million. Steve said his father frequently changed his will and that it just so happened that when he drowned the will in effect at that time left 70% of the team to Georgia.

Steve told me his father did that because of the widow's tax exemption.

"He didn't want to give all his money to Uncle Sam," Steve said. "But I can't imagine he meant for her to run the team."

Steve, who worked his way up from picking up jocks in the locker room, should have been the rightful owner, many people claim. The Rams are now valued at nearly $5 billion. When Georgia died in 2008, her net worth was estimated at $1.8 billion.

Steve told me he never would have moved the Rams to St. Louis, or anywhere else. "Why would you move the team?" he said. "My dad made the deal to acquire the Rams because they were in a bigger market. So why would you move them to a smaller market?"

Steve Rosenbloom stayed in Southern California for a year after being fired by Georgia. He then spent one year as the general manager of the New Orleans Saints, then got out of football.

"I got run over by a semi a few times," he said of that period in his life.

When I interviewed Steve, he seemed content. There was no sign of anger or bitterness. He owned a business involved in supplying equipment to oil drillers.

In talking about the year that he spent in L.A. after being fired, he said, "I would be at a restaurant, a function or someplace and total strangers would come up to me and tell horrific stories about their own family feuds. I guess they wanted to make me feel better."

"Were these feuds usually over money?" I asked.

"Just about 100% of the time, it was over money," Steve said.

I told him about a few family feuds I was familiar with, but none of them involved millions of dollars.

"The amount does not matter," Steve said. "Anything over a buck-fifty and you've got a problem."

I rank my Rosenbloom story as maybe the second-best story of my career. No. 1 is a story I did in 1997 on former UCLA quarterback and current broadcaster Matt Stevens and his battle with testicular cancer. The photo below shows me with Matt in January of 2020 when he was inducted into the Southern California Sports Broadcasters Hall of Fame.

Stevens, the last UCLA quarterback to win a Rose Bowl game

(1987), became a sideline reporter for Bruin radio broadcasts in 1994. In 1998 he moved up to the booth, joining play-by-play announcer Chris Roberts as the commentator.

I am a little fuzzy on the timeline, but sometime mid-season in 1997 I called Matt to do an interview. I knew about his three-year battle with testicular cancer and figured he might be worth a lead item in that Friday's column.

About 45 minutes into a phone conversation in which Matt gave me precise and moving details about his battle, I told him, "This is more than a column item. This is a full-blown Page One feature. We need to meet in person."

We met the following night at Phil Trani's restaurant. UCLA quarterback Cade McNown, then leading the Bruins on a 20-game win streak, was there that night, and he became our pseudo waiter. He brought food to our table but left us alone once he could tell we were deep into a serious topic.

(McNown would become a friend, and I last saw him at a ceremony on Oct. 22, 2021, when Tunnel 8 at the Rose Bowl was named after him.)

I left Phil's place late that night in 1997 knowing this story warranted a Page One spread. When I told Bill Dwyre what I had, he agreed. He scheduled it to run on Saturday, Nov. 22, the day of that year's UCLA-USC game. I worked hard on the story. I wanted it to be good – and accurate. I had my neighbor the hematologist, Dr. David Snyder, check over my medical terminology. In early 2021, David retired after 36½ years at City of Hope.

Like the Steve Rosenbloom story would a few years later, my Matt Stevens story dominated Page One. The layout included three photos of Matt, one as a UCLA quarterback, another of him with no hair during chemo treatment, and one, taken by a Times photographer, of him at work as a sideline reporter.

Matt deserves most of the credit for how well the story turned out. All I did was organize his words.

One night while undergoing treatment Matt and his then girlfriend decided to go out to a movie. But he got sick halfway through the movie and they left. "On the way back to the car, I threw up in an alley and collapsed in exhaustion," Matt told me. "I just lay there, my head in my vomit, next to a trash bin."

Of having to choose between delicate surgery or heavy-duty chemo, he said, "If I had to do it over again, I would not have chosen chemo. Anything would have been better. If I knew now what I did not know then, and they said, 'It's either chemo or we have to break your arm, I'd say, 'Here, snap that sucker.' "

The day the story ran, I went to the UCLA-USC game at the Coliseum. At the press elevator, I ran into Matt. He beamed when he saw me and gave me a hug.

This was an ideal situation for a reporter – the bosses liked the story, the readers liked it and the person I wrote about liked it.

When I mentioned the reaction to colleague Tim Kawakami, he said, "Sounds like you hit a trifecta," I added that Matt then also managed the Los Verdes Golf Course in Palos Verdes, where tee times were tough to get. "Make that a superfecta," Kawakami said.

A year later, when Hall of Fame baseball writer Ross Newhan and I were honored for our 30th and 20th anniversaries at the Times, I was presented with a slick, framed copy of the page with the Matt Stevens layout. For years, it hung in the family room at our home in Arcadia. Eventually I gave it to Matt.

On my birthday in 2019, July 22, Norma and I had dinner with Matt, his wife Andrea, and their son Matthew at the Fish Market in Del Mar. Six months later, when Matt was inducted into the Southern California Sports Broadcasters Hall of Fame, we discussed meeting again for my birthday in July. The pandemic nixed that, but we did celebrate my birthday with Matt and family in 2021 at the seaside restaurant Brigantine in Del Mar.

As I mentioned earlier in this book, reporters are not supposed to become friends with people they write about. I understand that thinking. But if you have normal human emotions, you can't help but make friends. To me, that has been the best part about being a sportswriter.

Here is a story with a different twist. In June of 2001 I co-wrote a profile of Laker owner Jerry Buss. What makes this story stick out is not only its content but also what I went through doing it.

Buss did not do many one-on-one media interviews. But I was able to arrange one through Bob Steiner, who was hired in 1979 as the head of publicity for Buss' sports interests. I had a good relationship with Steiner, and through a few late-night, off-the-record chats with Buss, I believe there was a good relationship there too. I was one media member allowed into Buss' Staples Center suite during games and into the exclusive Chairman's Room lounge after games.

Randy Harvey, then the executive sports editor, looked surprised when I told him I was going to interview Jerry Buss. A little later, Harvey called me into his office. "If anyone is going to interview Jerry Buss, it is Steve Springer," Harvey said.

Springer was in Las Vegas on a boxing assignment, but Harvey said he would fly back to L.A. to do the interview, then go back to Vegas.

I have a temper, like anyone else. But I rarely show it. But I did this time.

"What?! I set up the interview and now you are giving it to Springer?"

Harvey could tell I was more than just a little annoyed. I knew Harvey and Springer had a special bond, but this was ridiculous.

"Well, why don't both of you do the interview?" Harvey suggested.

I did not like that idea but agreed to it. A few nights later Springer and I sat down with Buss in a private area of Staples Center prior to an L.A. Sparks game. Buss owned the WNBA team at the time.

Springer opened the interview with quite a few questions, one right after the other. When I finally tried to ask a question, Springer, sitting next to me, put his arm against my chest and said, "Larry, I'll do the questioning here."

I ended up just sitting there, hoping nobody noticed the steam coming out of my ears.

But things would get worse.

Even though I was not a participant in the interview, I had a lot of material to contribute to our story, which we worked on separately for several days.

A few nights before the interview with Buss, I was in his suite when Hugh Hefner and his seven Playboy Playmate girlfriends were there. One kept jumping up and cheering after every basket, no matter which team scored.

Hefner was among the dozen or so people I interviewed by phone before typing up my share of the story. Hefner told me he wasn't a basketball fan, but added, "Jerry is a friend. What we have in common is we both like young women. Jerry comes to a lot of our parties at the mansion and dates some of our Playmates."

That was hardly a scoop, but a good quote to get in print.

"Just because I am a public figure doesn't mean I don't get to live my life the way I want," Buss told me.

After typing up all my material, I emailed it to Springer. He never said a word to me. He filed the story the next day, so I called it up on my computer screen. It included one paragraph of mine, a Jerry West quote. The rest was all Springer's, with only his byline on it.

I was angry before. Now I was livid. I burst into Harvey's office. Assistant sports editor Dave Morgan was there too.

I screamed, "Springer is a f-ing weasel!" I was just getting warmed up.

No one at the Times had ever seen me this mad.

When I went back to my desk, I started to call Springer. But I caught myself. I had to cool down. I went out to lunch with two co-workers, Pete Thomas and Kelly Burgess. But after I got back to the office, Springer called me. And I let him have it.

He tried to tell me the story was what Randy wanted. He attempted to appease me by suggesting I write a sidebar about Buss' role in the creation of the local sports channel Prime Ticket. That made me even angrier. It was a dumb suggestion.

I went in to Dwyre's office to yell some more, but he had no idea what I was talking about. I was too mad to explain it clearly.

Astonishingly, it was Harvey who came to my rescue. He told me that Springer's story was mostly just a rehash of old information Steve had used for a book he wrote on the Lakers. Harvey told me to rewrite what Springer turned in.

The result was a story that was now at least two-thirds mine.

It ran on June 15, the day of Game 5 of the 2001 NBA Finals, in which the Lakers beat the Philadelphia 76ers for the 13th of their 17 championships.

The byline on the story read, By Steve Springer and Larry Stewart. That day in the office, Harvey approached me and said, "I know it was mostly your story, but we used Springer's name first because S P comes before S T alphabetically."

Barely, but I certainly was not going to complain about such a minor issue.

I saw Springer that night in the Chick Hearn Press Lounge at Staples Center.

"I think the story turned out fine after all," he said. I did not respond.

I am not one to hold a grudge. I was mad, and certainly had a right to be, but I got over it.

Buss' connection to the creation of Prime Ticket in 1985 was strictly a financial one. Bill Daniels, one of my all-time favorite people, was the actual creator. After Daniels died at age 70 on March 7, 2000, I wrote, "He was the nicest billionaire I've ever known." His estate was valued at $1.1 billion.

Daniels and Buss were 50-50 partners in creating Prime Ticket, but Daniels bought out most of Buss' interest in 1988. Buss needed capital to invest in the Lakers.

I found Daniels, often called "the Father of Cable Television," to be a newspaperman's delight. Ask a question, get an answer.

When the Kings acquired Wayne Gretzky on Aug. 9, 1988, for $15 million in cash, I called Daniels to ask about his role in this monster deal. By then he owned 85% of Prime Ticket, which televised the Kings. Daniels laid out it all out for me

Kings owner Bruce McNall had called Daniels, reaching him on his private jet. McNall gave Daniels 10 minutes to agree to increase the television rights by one third, going from $1.52 million a year to $2.28 million, or the deal was dead. Daniels quickly crunched the numbers before saying yes.

When Daniels sold Prime Ticket in 1994, he once again answered all my questions with specific information. Daniels and Buss created Prime Ticket for $5 million each and nine years later, according to what Daniels told me, it sold for around $260 million.

Daniels gave me so much inside information that his communications officer, Bob Russo, and a company lawyer called and explained to me there was a confidentiality clause and if I printed all the information Daniels gave me, it could kill the deal. I called Dwyre at home and he told me to use my own judgment. A compromise was reached, and I still had plenty of solid details.

Another person I found to be a great interview was Michael Irvin, the colorful and controversial former Dallas Cowboy star. I first met him at a Laker game in the Chairman's Room in 2001. He had recently become one of the on-air personalities on Fox Sports Net's "Best Damn Sports Show Period," so I went over to introduce myself, not sure what to expect.

"I know who you are," Irvin said enthusiastically. "I've read your column in the Times. You and I need to get together. I want to pick your brain about this broadcasting business."

We exchanged cell numbers and talked several times after that. I told him I wanted to do a feature story on him. At first, he was hesitant, but eventually relented.

When I called to interview him, he said, "I know you are going to do a search and find a lot of bad stuff about me. I know you have to write it. I just ask one favor. I was once charged with rape, and I think that is the worst crime there is, short of murder. It was a totally bogus charge. Please do not write about it."

My research showed that in 1996, a Cowboy cheerleader accused Irvin and a teammate of sexual assault. The cheerleader later recanted her story, was found guilty of perjury, and was sentenced to 90 days in jail.

"The rest is all true," said Irvin as he went on to openly talk about his transgressions with women, drugs, drinking and partying that led to several run-ins with the law. He said he was never addicted to drugs or alcohol, that his addiction was sex, and it almost cost him everything until he finally hit bottom. That happened, he said, on Valentine's Day, 2001.

After coming home from a two-day binge of partying, he left again, but not before promising his wife Sandi he would be back in an hour. He ended up spending the night with another woman.

"I would always tell myself I was going to have only one drink," Irvin said. "Then a bad woman would come over, and sometimes she'd bring a friend. Bad women were always my excuse for having another drink."

It was at this point that Irvin, realizing he had a sex addiction, sought professional and spiritual help. He would then learn the root of his sex addition.

"It was all about self-esteem," he told me. "I lacked self-esteem, going all the way back to kindergarten (in Fort Lauderdale, Fla.). I could not read or write, but the white kids could. I thought, 'I'm just a dumb black kid.' I did not realize the white kids had been to preschool. That lack of self-esteem stays with you. You are always trying to prove to everybody how great you are, how perfect you are."

My ensuing story, which ran as a Page One feature, was certainly no puff piece. His many arrests and bad behavior were prominently noted. Thus, I was surprised when Irvin called to say thanks and offered to take me out to dinner.

I accepted and we picked a date and place. He asked me to pick him up at the Century City hotel where he stays while in L.A. He said he would meet me out front. True to his word, he was standing in the valet parking area when I arrived.

Over dinner at the Grill on the Alley in Beverly Hills, he talked more about his sex addiction, equating it to a drug addiction.

"The worst thing for a drug addict is for someone to offer them drugs," he said. "The worst thing for a sex addict is women making themselves available. When I was with the Cowboys, it was amazing. Women would come out of nowhere and hit on me."

Just at that point, a young woman came out of nowhere, sat down next to Michael and hit on him. He told the woman he had things to do, then, with a smile said, "How about Larry here? He is a famous sportswriter." She was not interested. Maybe she spotted my wedding ring. At least I told myself that.

"Come on, did you set that up?" I asked Irvin.

"No way," he said. "I'm serious. I did not set that up."

A couple of years later, I arranged for Irvin to speak at a Pasadena Quarterbacks Club luncheon, and he told the whole story about the woman at the Grill.

When I was doing Morning Briefing, I often attended Pasadena Quarterbacks Club luncheons on Fridays during football season. I usually got plenty of good material from the guest speakers.

Mike Garrett, a guest speaker when he was USC's athletic director, said Pete Carroll came up to him at a practice one day and said that Darnell Bing, a defensive back recruit from Long Beach Poly, wanted to wear his high school number.

"I asked Pete, so what is the problem?" Garrett told the luncheon audience. "Pete told me 20 was my number and it had been retired. I asked, 'Is this kid any good?' Pete said, 'Very good.' I said, 'Then give him that damn number'."

An editor replaced the word damn with an ellipsis (or a dot, dot, dot). That made it look like the word was a lot worse than damn.

Editing is not an exact science. A later Morning Briefing item that I feared might have been too off color did get past the editors.

It was about a 1960 tag football game involving Elvis Presley and his traveling crew playing a group of UCLA players at Beverly Glen Park. Elvis' team, featuring him at quarterback, included his bodyguards. Inevitably, the game got physical.

One of the UCLA players, running back Mitch Dimkich, recalled sacking Elvis and described it thusly: "I ended up on top Elvis and thought, 'Boy, I bet there are a lot of girls in the world who would like to be in my position right now'."

Chapter 35: Wrapping Thing Up

I mentioned in an earlier chapter that former UCLA football coach Terry Donahue was a close friend. On July 4, 2021, my wife and older daughter Kelly went out to watch fireworks. After we dropped Kelly off at her apartment and returned home, I looked at my cell phone, which I had left behind. There were a dozen or so text messages alerting me that Terry had lost his two-year-plus battle with a rare form of cancer. The first text was from Terry's younger brother Pat. Terry had died at 6:30 p.m.

Terry told me in February of 2020 that chemo treatments were keeping him alive. "When that no longer works, I will pass on," he said, off the record.

That hit me hard. It reminded me of the time Bob Chandler told me we wouldn't be able to do a story on how he had beaten cancer.

My conversation with Donahue took place at an annual event he had hosted since 2012. Called the California Showcase, it is a one-day free football combine in Orange County for high school players passed over by Division I schools. I was there, as usual, covering the combine as a freelancer for the Southern California News Group, which consists of 11 suburban newspapers, including the Orange County Register. I always volunteered to cover this worthwhile event, which draws coaches from Division II, Division III and NAIA colleges from throughout the country.

Created by Terry and Pat Donahue, backed by the National Football Foundation, and made possible by hundreds of volunteers, the combine, in its first eight years, led to some 1,100 young men making it onto a lower division college roster. Most have also received financial aid. The average is around $29,000 per player.

Terry sought to make the California Showcase as much a part of his legacy as his school record 151 victories, his conference record 98 wins, and his eight bowl victories, including seven in a row. The plan is to keep the combine going for years to come.

My friendship with Donahue goes back to mid-December 1995. After working a night desk shift, I received a phone call from Angelo Mazonne, Donahue's friend and confidant, at 7:30 a.m. "Can you meet me and Terry Donahue for lunch today?" Angelo asked. I was taken aback. I barely knew Angelo at the time, although my friends Terry Moore and Mike Izzi were close with him.

The lunch took place at Monty's in Westwood. It lasted about two hours as Terry asked questions about broadcasting and took

extensive notes. Off the record, he told me he had an offer from CBS to be the network's lead college football commentator. That meant he would work with Jim Nantz.

It was pretty much a done deal that Donahue was going to retire after 20 years as UCLA's football coach. At the end of our off-the-record lunch, I said, "I am going to have to write something." He agreed that without quoting him, I could write that it was close to happening. After that lunch, we often met for a meal, a beer, golf – or all three. The photo here was taken on Balboa Island.

I think he liked playing golf with me. He was just starting out and I was one golfer who was worse than he was. Donahue's retirement present from his players was a membership at Wood Ranch Country Club in Simi Valley. But after he and his family moved to Balboa Island in Orange County, he was able to switch that membership to the Newport Beach Country Club. Terry eventually became a proficient golfer. He was a perfectionist in every way, and golf was no exception.

We played a lot at Newport Beach, but also played elsewhere. We once played at Del Mar Country Club as a guest of announcer Charlie Jones. Another time we were at Rancho La Quinta when hardly anyone else was playing. At the turn we ran into former USC basketball coach Bob Boyd, who joined us for lunch. We also played at Pebble Beach on a media day, and Nantz was in our foursome.

I got invited back for another media day at Pebble the next year. After I arrived, CBS publicist Robin Brendle informed me that because of recent rain we would be playing Spanish Bay instead of Pebble. That was fine by me. Pebble is too tough for me.

Then Robin informed me that actor Jack Lemmon would be in my foursome, which was awesome.

I think it was the 15th hole on the back nine at Spanish Bay where Lemmon and I decided to walk after hitting our tee shots about the same distance. The sun was glistening off the ocean and two deer ran across the fairway in front of us as we approached our tee shots. "Lock this into the memory bank," I told myself. Playing golf with Jack Lemmon was one of my all-time pinch-me moments.

Another came in October of 2018 when I was involved in organizing a UCLA quarterback reunion to honor Donahue. This was before the cancer diagnosis in May of 2019. The reunion, mainly organized by former quarterback Pat Cowan, took place at Trani's in Long Beach. Seventeen former UCLA quarterbacks showed up.

Donahue thought he and his brother Pat were meeting me and my friend Don Rodriguez for lunch. When Donahue walked in, he immediately noticed a lot of people in the bar area. He walked up to me and said, "Is that Gary Beban over there?" It was.

"Look around, Coach," I said.

"What in the world is going on here?" Donahue asked me.
"They are all here to honor you," I said.

My next anecdote shows how things can change over time.

In 1988, Dennis Swanson, then the president of ABC Sports, banned all ABC personnel from speaking to me after I heavily criticized the coverage of the 1988 Winter Olympics in Calgary. Much of what I wrote came from an on-the-record interview with Jim Lampley, who had been fired by Swanson and was working as a news anchor at Channel 2 in L.A.

The ban really did not have much impact on me. Swanson had no way to monitor who talked to me.

He was particularly upset because he thought I did not contact

him or anyone else at ABC to get a response to Lampley's remarks. But I had called Bob Wheeler, the head of ABC Sports publicity at the time. I could not tell Swanson that because Wheeler, already on thin ice, would surely have been fired. I kept mum to

protect Wheeler. Twelve years later, in 2000, Swanson was with NBC and in charge of the cable TV coverage of the Sydney Olympics. I was invited by NBC to an Olympics press function at a downtown L.A. restaurant. When I walked in, there was Swanson greeting guests.

After we reluctantly shook hands, I said, "Dennis, you might not remember this (knowing full well he would), but I know you were upset with what I wrote during the Calgary Winter Olympics and that you thought I didn't attempt to call anyone at ABC to get a response. Just thought I would let you know that I did call Bob Wheeler. Not sure what happened there."

I could see the tension disappear from Swanson's face. And soon Swanson and I were laughing it up with, of all people, Jim Lampley, as the photo on the previous page shows. Lampley was there because he would be hosting some of the cable coverage from Sydney. The photo of the three of us was among several Swanson mailed to me. Included with the photos was a note that read: "Larry – Enjoy the pix. Thanks for attending that evening. Dennis."

In 1988 I could never have envisioned ever laughing it up with Dennis Swanson and Jim Lampley.

People familiar with my column know Keith Olbermann was a frequent target. It started shortly after Olbermann came from CNN to KTLA Channel 5 in Los Angeles as the main sports anchor in 1986. The other sports anchor there, Steve Roah, complained to me about Olbermann, saying that he was not the flippant, light-hearted person people saw on TV. Roah said Olbermann was almost nightly sending him critical memos about his work.

As Olbermann moved on to KCBS, ESPN and eventually Fox Sports Net, I kept hearing negative stories about him. One was that he sent memos to workers not to bother him with idle chit-chat. Another one was that he had a popcorn machine removed from a studio because the smell bothered him, depriving everyone else.

Often Olbermann fought back with emails to Dwyre demanding I be fired. In one, Olbermann claimed that I was sitting on a story about KNBC Channel 4 sports anchor Fred Roggin's cocaine addiction.

I will admit I let myself get too close to Roggin, but I was on top of the story. When Roggin checked himself into a drug rehab facility in Orange County, I had the exclusive.

However, longtime morning radio host Robert W. Morgan, who had also battled drug problems, ripped me for writing about Roggin's drug issues. Morgan, saying I wrote "only once a week and was a part-time floor sweeper the rest of the time," claimed I only wrote the Roggin story in order to get my name in the paper on some other day besides Friday.

This was a case where I was getting hit from both sides.

In the interest of fairness, I did get a few nice emails from Olbermann. One was dated Feb. 9, 2001, and it was in regard to a column I did on the XFL and announcer Matt Vasgersian. The subject line read: "I hope you are sitting down." After three paragraphs of praise, the email ended with: "I'll spare you all the cutesy jokes about the irony of this email."

Yes, I was tough on Olbermann, but I think my toughest column may have been one in February of 1989 on longtime L.A. sports anchor Jim Hill. He went from Channel 2 to Channel 7 in July of 1987 before returning to Channel 2 in 1992.

I wrote in my column that he did too many soft, in-studio live interviews rather than putting together edited features. I also wrote about complaints that he did not always follow through on promises he made to charities and school children. I noted that Hill once spoke at a middle school and promised every student an autographed photo. The station's promotion department printed 400 photos, which remained in boxes and were never signed.

Hill and I did not talk to each other for a year and a half. One day his agent, Ed Hookstratten, called to invite me to dinner in Beverly Hills. I thought it was going to be just Ed and me, but I knew what was going on when I saw Hill arrive at the restaurant at the same time as I did. We talked things out to the point where at least we resumed talking to each other. I was glad about that. Personally, I liked Jim. And I think most people who know him do too.

Someone else I had an up-and-down relationship with was sports reporter Jim Gray. I first met him in 1983. I initially liked him.

But I came to realize that he was abnormally obsessed with being a success. He worked very hard at connecting with the right people.

He broke an unusual number of stories, including the Rams trading Eric Dickerson to Indianapolis and the L.A. Raiders firing coach Tom Flores. While writing a column on Jim after his Flores scoop, I learned that his father was a real estate partner of billionaire Marvin Davis. Not sure what role, if any, that played in Gray's career. All I know is that he begged me not to write about that connection.

Gray was always suggesting we go out to dinner. I finally acquiesced in 1987, the day of an NBA Finals game between the Lakers and Celtics. I was going to be on the west side, I suggested we watch the game and then have dinner.

Gray liked that idea and invited me to his townhouse. While we were watching the game, Mike Madden, John Madden's son, joined us. Then Al Davis called Gray and invited those two to dinner. Gray accepted the invitation.

"I thought we were going out to dinner," I said.

I was hungry. I hadn't even eaten lunch.

Gray suggested I come along. I agreed but said I was taking my own car because it did not sound as though I was invited.

Al Davis arrived at Mateo's in Westwood at the same time we did. Davis and Gray talked after they gave their cars to the parking valet. Then Davis came over to my car and greeted me warmly. That seemed encouraging. I thought maybe I could help create a better relationship between the Times and Davis.

But that did not happen. After the valet took my car and I was approaching the restaurant, Gray came out the door and said, "I don't know how to tell you this, but Al doesn't want you in the restaurant."

I was furious, beyond furious, as I drove home on an empty stomach. Gray called the next day to apologize. I was still angry.

"What was I supposed to do?" Gray asked.

"You were supposed to tell Al you already had dinner plans," I explained in no uncertain terms.

NBC's Mike Weisman once told me, "Jim Gray is the type of person who, in a room with other people, will always be looking over his shoulder for someone more important to talk to."

In 2004, assistant sports editor Dave Morgan assigned me to do a profile on Gray and see how he got so close with athletes. Morgan specifically had Kobe Bryant in mind.

I met with Gray and his wife in Santa Monica. During a one-hour-plus interview, Gray denied he used his father's partnership Davis to connect to sports figures. After that ingterview, Gray called me every day, asking what I had written. He begged me to read him the story, but of course that was not going to happen.

"Just tell me the worst part," he pleaded.

"Okay, I think it is the night Al Davis had you ban me from entering Mateo's," I said.

"Fair enough," Gray said.

I believe somehow Gray got the story killed. It just disappeared. I could not find it and never heard a thing about it. Usually when editors don't like a story, the reporter is asked to do a rewrite. That did not happen in this case.

While writing his book, I called Dave Morgan to see if he could provide any insight. He could not recall what happened.

Switching to people I truly admired, I first met Pat Haden when I did a feature story on him in the summer of 1971. He was the starting quarterback for the South team in the annual high school all-star Shrine Game at the Coliseum. This was after he and J.K. McKay led Bishop Amat High of La Puente to a CIF championship.

Haden and McKay capped off their college careers at USC by being named co-MVPs of the 1975 Rose Bowl game, a classic in which the Trojans upset Ohio State, 18-17. And it was their senior year when USC, trailing Notre Dame, 24-0 late in the first half, came back to beat Ara Parseghian's team, 55-24.

Years later, Haden and I became golfing buddies. Once we played at the exclusive Valley Club in Montecito, but we usually played at the Los Angeles Country Club or occasionally at the San Gabriel Country Club.

One time at San Gabriel, it was three of us – me, Pat, and J.K. After nine holes, the scores were me 43, Haden 44, and McKay 46. While standing on the 10th tee, a foursome that included Merlin Olsen stopped to visit. As they drove away, I called out: "Hey, Merlin, guess who is leading this group?"

Big mistake. Haden went two under on the back nine, McKay did better on the back nine and of course I did much worse. In a thank-you email to Pat, I wrote, "It was just a thrill to be leading at halftime."

Replied Pat: "That is what Ara Parseghian said."

McKay and I became close in 2001 when he was general manager of the L.A. Xtreme of the ill-fated XFL, co-created by Vince McMahon and NBC. Dwyre had me cover the Xtreme, saying, "It is more a TV story than anything else."

One day McMahon was to meet Dwyre and I for lunch at a restaurant near the Times. I called to make a reservation for three, but it turned out there were four of us. I was the first to arrive at the restaurant and was taken to our table. Sitting there was a man I did not know. The man introduced himself. He was an attorney named Tony Capozzola.

After Dwyre and McMahon arrived, Capozzola made an impassioned pitch to McMahon about what he thought might save the XFL. He talked for maybe 15 minutes, handed McMahon a business card and left.

When we were done with lunch, I invited McMahon to walk over to the Times Building for a tour. He gladly accepted. As Dwyre, McMahon and I made the one block walk, we figured out that Capozzola was an uninvited guest.

"Did you invite him?" Dwyre asked me. I said I did not. McMahon said he did not know him.

What we learned later was that he somehow found out with whom McMahon was meeting for lunch, guessed where, called the restaurant and learned there was a reservation in my name, then just showed up and was seated at our table.

I believe the word for that is chutzpah. Or sleazy.

CBS broadcaster Verne Lundquist ranks high on my nice-guy list, even though I did not have many dealings with him. I knew that he was beloved by everyone he worked with, which included Haden, both on college football at CBS and the NFL on TNT. When Terry Bradshaw was inducted into the Pro Football Hall of Fame in 1989, he chose Lundquist to present him.

I went to the 2006 Masters on my own with a friend, Rick Odekirk, who made the arrangements and we split expenses. I made sure to tell Dwyre about my plans. I did not want my boss hearing second hand I was at the Masters.

We went for the weekend only. Once there, CBS publicists LeslieAnne Wade and Robin Brendle got us into the TV complex. Lundquist was there and to my amazement he invited us to sit with him in the 16th tower during Sunday's round.

We did not do that, and I only bring it up to solidify Lundquist's reputation as being among the all-time nice guys in the business.

I just mentioned another favorite of mine, Terry Bradshaw. When Fox began televising the NFL in 1994, the "Fox NFL Sunday" one-hour pregame show was inaugurated. David Hill, the brilliant and personable chairman of Fox Sports, and Ed Goren, the executive producer and president, gave me a standing invitation to visit the show's studio, first located in Hollywood and later at the Fox Plaza on the Twentieth Century Fox lot in Century City.

I often took advantage of that invitation. And years later, after I got into charity work, I would auction off a visit to the set and the adjacent green room. I got bids as high as $5,000, and never had an unhappy bid winner.

Fox picked up on what I was doing and eventually the only way visitors were allowed was via a charity auction.

I was always concerned that my guests would enjoy the experience, and the person who made sure they did was Bradshaw. He would spend time entertaining my guests with stories, pose for photos and autograph whatever they wanted autographed. And he always gave me a big buildup. One time when he saw me, he got down on his hands and knees and crawled over to kiss my shoes.

I am not making that up.

Someone else who was always particularly kind to my guests was the show's original host, James Brown. He ranks among the nicest guys I ever met. J.B., as everyone called him, was with Fox for 11 years before returning to CBS, where he began his network broadcasting career in the mid-1970s.

Whenever he met a young person, J.B. always took time to talk to that person, find out about their ambitions and offer to help in any way possible.

As for Bradshaw, another thing I liked about him was his openness about his battles with hyperactivity, depression, and attention deficit disorder, or ADD.

I interviewed Terry on the phone in January of 2003 when he was at his farm in southern Oklahoma. Here are excerpts from the ensuing column:

"My mother used to call me a fireball. She would say, 'He's a very energetic young man who likes to hang from the ceiling.'"

"I'm always starting projects – designing a house, building a barn, remodeling, building a lake, changing a driveway, straightening out everything in the house. I rarely finish any of them."

"I have tremendous mood swings. It is so bad, there is a joke about me around here. The workers are always asking, 'Did he take his pill today?'"

To me, Terry Bradshaw is more than a four-time Super Bowl winning quarterback for the Pittsburgh Steelers. He is also a super guy.

In 1990, I had an assignment that took me to New York. I decided to stop in St. Louis on my way home to interview Jack Buck, who had been named CBS' lead announcer on baseball following the firing of Brent Musburger in the middle of that year's Final Four in Denver.

I was in Denver on vacation when Musburger was fired and got called into duty, first writing a new story and then a follow-up column after the championship game. Thank goodness for my friend Bob Russo, Bill Daniels' right-hand man. Bob loaned him his laptop and gave me a quick lesson in how to use it.

As for Jack Buck, I had called him more than a week earlier to set up the interview. I told him the date, and he said he would meet me in the Busch Stadium offices at 5 p.m.

I was staying at the old Adam's Mark Hotel, now a Hyatt Regency. The hotel is adjacent to Busch Stadium. I headed over to the stadium a little early, hoping Jack had remembered our date. I was kicking myself for not calling to confirm it.

I arrived at the stadium offices at 4:45 and there was Jack, sitting there waiting for me. He took me around, introducing me to everyone from elevator operators to a state senator. Jack knew everyone's name. We went down on the field, where I met Manager Whitey Herzog and most of the players on the roster.

We then went up to the press box to have dinner and do the interview. When I was done, I thanked Jack.

"Where are you going?" he said. I explained I'd just stay in the press box.

"No, we have a seat for you in our booth," he said. "You'll be sitting between me and my partner, Mike Shannon."

And that was a blast.

NBC's Charlie Jones called me a lot to plant items about himself and an upcoming event he would be calling. I did not mind. I often told broadcasters it was okay to call me directly rather than rely on a PR person. Some did, but others told me they felt awkward about doing that.

Jones gave me more than just items about himself. He was a good source for me. So was his agent, Martin Mandel, not to be confused with ABC Sports publicity director Mark Mandel.

Martin Mandel was pleasant to deal with and always grateful when I mentioned one of his clients. He sent more thank you notes than anyone, although Vin Scully was a close second in that department.

Charlie Jones died of heart failure at his home in La Jolla on June 12, 2008. I attended his memorial at the La Jolla Tennis Club. There were no speeches, just friends mingling and talking. It was the way he would have wanted it. Bill Walton and Merlin Olsen, and their spouses, were among those I mingled with.

I recall a phone conversation I had with Merlin before he died not quite two years later at age 70. I was doing a story for a local website on the gym I used, Arcadia All-Pro, and members there believed Merlin was among the original investors. "No, that was my brother Phil," Merlin told me. "But we didn't bother to correct anybody who thought it was me."

I was among hundreds who attended Merlin's memorial on March 17, 2010, at All Saints Church in Pasadena. Sitting in front of me in one of the back rows was NFL Commissioner Roger Goodell.

The sports broadcasting beat changed drastically during my tenure. When I first began writing my Herald Examiner TV column, there was no ESPN, no cable TV sports at all, no Fox Sports, and only a smattering of Dodger, Angel, Laker and USC and UCLA football games televised. Sports talk radio was in its embryonic stage. I would get one press release per week from each of the three major networks regarding sports programming.

By the end of my run as a TV sports columnist, some 100 press releases a day arrived via email. They came from everywhere.

When I started on the beat, I was one of only a few TV sports columnists at major newspapers in the country.

I believe Jack Craig of the Boston Globe was the first full-time TV sports columnist. His 29-year run on the beat began in 1967. Gary

Deeb, an acerbic television critic for the Chicago Tribune, often took on sports topics in the '70s. And Howard Rosenberg, the L.A. Times' Pulitzer Prize winning television critic, would touch on sports from time to time.

With the arrival of ESPN in 1979 and the growth of sports on cable television, more newspapers started running weekly sports TV columns. USA Today, which began publishing in 1980, two years later assigned Rudy Martzke to write a daily column covering sports television. That led to almost every major newspaper in the country having a sports TV columnist.

Another change was the advent of the press conference call. Network publicists liked them because instead of having to set up a bunch of individual interviews to promote a televised sports event, it could all be done with one call. There could be as many as 30 to 40 sports TV newspaper columnists on one conference call. Sometimes there would be two, maybe even three, conference calls in one day.

I grew to hate conference calls. Some involved major news events and were mandatory. But many were for simply promoting a weekend event. I could spend an hour on a conference call and end up using a sentence. Or nothing at all.

There were two reasons I felt obligated to be on conference calls. One, the publicists appreciated participation from the L.A. Times, and two, I might miss something important. If John McEnroe was on a conference call, I had to be on it. He almost always managed to stir up a controversy or at least say something provocative.

In 2016, I ran into McEnroe and Pete Sampras at Bel-Air Country Club and told McEnroe, "No one does press conference calls better than you."

"Is that supposed to be a compliment?" he said dryly.

Quite by accident, I finally got help with conference calls.

In 1994, Mike Izzi connected me with David Schwartz, a recent Stanford grad with a 3.8 grade-point average who had been sports editor of the Stanford Daily. He was now living in Santa Monica. "Couldn't you use a personal intern?" Izzi asked.

I explained that it didn't work that way, but of course I agreed to at least talk with David. He wanted to be a sportswriter and learn more about my job. In turn, he asked what he could do for me. The light bulb went off. I explained press conference calls and suggested I could use help with the routine ones. As an enticement, I told him there were usually famous people on these calls.

David took the non-paying job and was great at taking notes for me. But about six months later he went off to law school at Penn. He is now a partner in a Century City law firm specializing in intellectual property rights.

In 1999, I recruited another "personal intern" to help with conference calls, Jenny Jackson. I met her when I spoke in Jeff Fellenzer's USC sports media class and was impressed with her questions and her observations about announcers and sports in general. Jenny helped me for several years and accompanied me to various events and functions. She did a fantastic job and was well-received by those who met her. I often took her with me to the Fox Studios to visit the set where "Fox NFL Sunday" is televised, and whenever I went there without her, Terry Bradshaw, in particular, would ask, "Where is your intern?"

Now Jenny Jackson Koch is the mother of two and lives in a beautiful home in the Hollywood Hills with her husband Christian, an

anesthesiologist at Huntington Hospital in Pasadena. Jenny owns her own interior design company. Jenny and I lost touch until she sent me a Christmas card in 2015. In 2016, she invited me to go with her family to a Ram game at the Coliseum and I later invited her to attend a Southern California Sports Broadcasters luncheon. The photo here is of us at that luncheon.

My third intern was Steve Rom, whom I met in 2002 through my neighbor, Dr. David Snyder. Steve, who was being treated at the City of Hope for his second bout with leukemia, was a Michigan grad and sportswriter at the Ann Arbor News. Steve did conference calls plus short book reviews for what was called "The Hot Corner." And he wrote two freelance articles for the Times. One was about meeting

his bone marrow donor, a 32-year-old German woman, at a City of Hope media event in 2005. The other was about his odd-couple relationship with his best friend, Rod Payne, an All-American center on the Michigan football team who also played in the NFL for the 2000 Super Bowl champion Baltimore Ravens. Steve turned that friendship into a 228-page book, "Centered by a Miracle," published in 2006. The photo here shows Steve and Rod, along with Dr. Snyder and me, as Steve awaits to meet his donor.

I lost contact with Steve and was saddened to hear that he passed away from another form of cancer.

In February of 1990, a weird thing happened, mostly in a good way for me.

After the Herald Examiner folded on Nov. 2, 1989, the Times picked up a significant number of writers and editors from that paper. In Sports, that included columnists Melvin Durslag and Allan Malamud, horse racing handicapper Bob Mieszerski, and desk personnel Steve Horn, Jay Christensen, and Fred Robledo.

On Sunday, Feb. 18, 1990, at the top of the comics section that wraps around the front section, there was this: Sports in the '90s, followed by Southern California's all-star team of sportswriters. There were six names listed, including Durslag, Malamud and Mieszerski. Also listed were the Times' featured sports columnists Jim Murray and Mike Downey. The sixth name was mine.

Since the Sunday comics are pre-printed, I saw it prior to distribution.

When Bill Dwyre walked by my desk, I showed him the comics section and said, "Did you have anything to do with this?" He became visibly upset and said, "I certainly did not."

I guess I had a fan in the promotions department.

I could understand why Dwyre was upset. He had not been consulted.

Durslag retired after one year, while Malamud's "Notes on a Scorecard" column on Page 2 became maybe the best-read thing in Sports. Malamud, who battled lifelong weight-related issues, tragically died of natural causes in 1996. Allan was only 54. He was found by a maid in his apartment on a Monday morning. On the previous Saturday, he left a USC football game at halftime, telling people in the press box that he was not feeling well.

Malamud was a brilliant writer whose style I attempted to follow but could not match. Word economy is something he tried to teach me. "Always use as few words as possible," he would say.

I can imagine his reaction to this book. He would shake his head, make a face, whine a little and say, "Oooh, it's way too long."

And I would say, "I know, Allan, I know."

Chapter 36: Strathmore Football Revisited

My first bylined stories of my career, back when I was 14, were about Strathmore High football. In 2017, 57 years later, I was again writing about Strathmore High football. That is when my tiny little high school won a lower division state football championship against a larger school in Orange County.

I knew Strathmore went through some terrible losing seasons in the 1970s and '80s and at one point during an 0-32 losing streak dropped varsity football altogether. A turning point for Strathmore football was the creation of a Pop Warner League in 1987. The sons of Hispanic farm workers began playing football instead of soccer.

Now, in 2017, Strathmore was playing for a state football championship.

There was a good story here, much like the one featured in a critically acclaimed 2015 Disney movie, "McFarland, USA," starring Kevin Costner. That was about McFarland High, a former league rival of Strathmore High, winning a state championship in cross country. The McFarland consisted of mostly sons of Hispanic farm workers.

The difference was the Strathmore story was football.

The creation of the Pop Warner League was in part made possible with funds raised during bingo nights at the high school.

Since Strathmore would be playing Orange High for a state title, it was easy to pitch a story to the Orange County Register.

My story ran on the Register website with this headline: *Bingo nights set in motion tiny Strathmore's movie-worthy journey to state football title game.*

I attended the game in which the Strathmore Spartans beat Orange High in thrilling fashion, 31-29, to complete a 16-0 season.

Because I had a press credential, I was allowed on the field and like in the early 1960s I was again walking the sideline at a Strathmore High football game.

The whole story felt like a movie, so I decided to write a movie treatment, which is basically an outline of what the movie story would be. This involved several trips to Strathmore, and one to a road game in Boron, of all places, with Strathmore football historian Bob Greenamyer, a 1968 Strathmore graduate.

I pitched my treatment to one of the producers of the McFarland movie. I also sent it to director-screenwriter Ron Shelton, a friend whose credits include "Bull Durham," White Men Can't Jump," and "Tin Cup." Shelton responded favorably but explained the difficulty and expense of making this story a movie.

I talked to other Hollywood types. I pitched CBS, hoping my story might be a nice feature on the Super Bowl pregame show. I pitched the story to ESPN, and to HBO via Bryant Gumbel. I pitched it to Sports Illustrated and the New York Times.

I had some nibbles but no solid bites.

When I voiced my frustration to one of my Strathmore friends, Byron Tillery, he said, "Why don't you write a book about yourself and your career and include a chapter on Strathmore football?"

That sounded like a plan, and well, here we are.

Although Byron was three years behind me in school, he and his classmate John Duboski are two of my closest Strathmore friends. Duboski was a star quarterback at Strathmore High and then Porterville College. Byron, his best friend, was his favorite receiver at both schools.

I became close with Duboski mainly through Byron, whose father Hugh employed my brother as truck driver at a young age. Byron and I also worked together for Bud Wyatt.

What follows here is an edited version of my Strathmore High movie treatment. The working title is *The Strathmore Story*.

The city limit sign says the population of Strathmore is 2,810.

For years, the hotspot in Strathmore was the appropriately named Dinky Diner – a dinky place in a dinky town – located kitty corner from Strathmore High School. The place is now called El Portal, a rundown fast-food eatery offering Mexican cuisine. The only thing hot about it now is the hot sauce.

Orange groves and olive orchards are the lifeblood of the area, where most people are either property owners or farm workers of some sort. Neither group has escaped economic blight. Almost everyone has been impacted by California's years-long drought.

In the small farming communities that dot the vast San Joaquin Valley, the main source of civic pride, often the only source of civic pride, is high school football.

On a Saturday morning, Dec. 16, 2017, an extraordinary amount of pride was on display when Robert Garza, his wife Diana and two teenage boys pulled into a parking lot at Strathmore High.

There were people everywhere; many of them holding up signs of support for Strathmore's beloved football team: "Go Strathmore," "Go Spartans" "16-0 is the goal," "State Champs!" The crowd was there to send off the team and the band, along with some students and boosters, to Orange County on three rented modern motor coaches, equipped with TV monitors and large comfortable seats.

There had never been an event of this magnitude in this hard-bitten town.

Robert Garza, the team's longtime offensive line coach, and his wife Diana were at the high school to drop off Diana's son Nick Salas, the 6-foot-6 starting quarterback, and Nick's stepbrother, Robert's son Anthony, the team statistician. Robert and Diana would be driving to Orange County so that they could spend the weekend in Southern California, a rare treat.

Head coach Jeromy Blackwell and his wife and many others were driving down as well. All told, the Strathmore contingent numbered nearly 1,400 – or half the population of the town proper.

The destination, some 200 miles and nearly four hours away, was a high school stadium located not far from Disneyland. For the Strathmore team and its supporters, all this was Fantasyland.

For the second year in a row, Strathmore would be playing for a state football championship. A year earlier, Strathmore, representing the southern part of the state, hosted a state title game against a Bay Area team from a private Catholic school, St. Patrick/St. Vincent, in its tiny stadium. In front of an overflow crowd of 2,000, Strathmore lost by a point on a field goal with 12 seconds left.

Strathmore, now representing Northern California due to a realignment, was headed south to play Orange High for the California State VI-AA championship. The game would be played at nearby El Modena High, which has a stadium big enough to more than accommodate the expected crowd of some 4,000.

There was a time in the 1980s when any kind of football championship game involving Strathmore High, let alone one for a state title, would have been unfathomable. Strathmore went more than three seasons without winning a game. And the outlook for the future was bleak. With the area's Hispanic population increasing, soccer was the sport of choice for the community's youth. Strathmore didn't even have youth football.

The high school's head football coach, Dave McDaniel, knew that, if there was going to be any kind of turnaround, the town needed a Pop Warner League. After the 1986 football season, he solicited the help of two prominent boosters, Jerry Crawford and Joe Vidrio, who became friends playing recreational softball years earlier. To start a league would take an initial investment of at least $5,000.

Crawford and Vidrio set out to raise money through a charity golf tournament. But a tournament at a nine-hole course in Three Rivers, located 30 miles away, barely raised $1,000. The next year a tournament at an 18-hole course in Tulare raised even less. But there was enough money to stage bingo nights at the high school.

Bingo, that did the trick.

In 1987, Strathmore was able to field one rag-tag Pop Warner team of seventh and eighth graders.

Meanwhile, at the high school, the 1987 season was a disaster.

Strathmore was coming off a 1986 season which ended with a five-game losing streak. The 1987 season began with a 12-0 loss to Corcoran. Coach McDaniel thought the seniors on the team had put out a weak effort. Next up was a home game against Riverdale, and during the week McDaniel announced that the team's underclassmen – the juniors and sophomores – would lead the pregame calisthenics, which is a somewhat important ritual in high school football.

The seniors responded by quitting the team. Left with only 13 players, Strathmore lost to Riverdale, 43-8. That was followed by a 45-0 loss to Laton, a perennially weak team, and a 25-0 loss to Chowchilla. McDaniel, thinking of the health and safety of his younger players, decided to drop varsity football. Strathmore forfeited its remaining six varsity games, and the juniors on the team were relegated to the JV team, along with the varsity coaches.

"That allowed our school to at least see some success at the lower level," McDaniel says. "But, looking back, I didn't handle that situation very well."

After the disastrous '87 season, varsity football was restored. However, the team had 0-9 records in both 1988 and '89. Going into its second game of the 1990 season, Strathmore had gone 0-32, if you count the six forfeits as losses.

On Sept. 14, 1990, in a non-conference game at McFarland, the losing streak ended. After winning, 20-6, the Strathmore players celebrated as if they had just won a state championship, throwing helmets in the air.

Robert Garza was then a junior guard/linebacker on that team. He had starred on both offense and defense. With tears of joy in his eyes, he would tell McDaniel: "I've never experienced winning a football game before. It is one of the best experiences of my life."

Strathmore won only twice more that season, but more importantly Garza could see McDaniel was a different person. Others could as well. Said McDaniel: "I think it was in 1990 that I reconfirmed my faith in Jesus Christ and totally changed my personality. I became a different person, a different coach."

He began holding Bible study classes at his home, inviting all students, including football players. "I wasn't trying to convert anyone," McDaniel says. "I wanted to show how God gives us the inner strength to overcome obstacles in our lives to reach our potential and become better people, better fathers and better citizens. I knew because I had overcome a lot myself. I also wanted these young people to get to know each other, to create a family unity."

Garza was among the regular attendees.

"My father left when I was three months old," he says. "Coach McDaniel became the father figure I never had.

"I can't say that I now attend church regularly, but back then those classes were inspiring to me. Coach McDaniel made each of us see the potential in ourselves and brought us closer as a group. We became a family, particularly those of us on the football team."

Familiarity doesn't always breed contempt – it can also breed friendship. Strathmore players began calling each other brothers and talked about being one family, something that would continue through the years. "Coach McDaniel made me realize I had the potential to be a good person," Garza says. And McDaniel, recognizing Garza's strong character, envisioned him as a team leader as a senior in 1991.

But, as fate would have it, Strathmore went 0-10 that season, and lost to Lindsay in its final game, 51-0. Garza was injured on the first series of that game and was unable to return. It was a bad way for his playing career to end, but it didn't dull his enthusiasm for Strathmore football.

When McDaniel learned Garza planned to attend nearby Porterville College after graduating, the coach talked to him about joining his staff as a volunteer assistant coach.

Garza was thrilled about the possibility.

It became a reality the next year, Garza's first at Porterville College. Garza started out helping coach the Strathmore JV team's offensive line. By midseason, he was brought up to the varsity and named a full-fledged assistant.

Garza worked with another assistant coach, Rick Anderson, who became a mentor. New blocking techniques were introduced, and Strathmore's football fortunes were about to greatly change. McDaniel began getting administrative support, and that enabled him to make some key hires. One was Anderson, a teammate at Porterville College who went on to become a scholarship player at UC Berkeley.

"A key figure in this story is Anneli Crawford," McDaniel says. "After she became school superintendent, she told me, 'Whatever it takes, you have my full support.' One reason for that support was that her and Jerry's son Duke was on his way to becoming the varsity's starting quarterback.

Anneli Crawford died in 2016 at the age of 74 after a 10-month struggle with ovarian cancer.

In 1992, Duke Crawford and the other players who started playing Pop Warner football as seventh graders were now seniors. The '92 Strathmore varsity lost its first four games, then started winning – and winning.

Strathmore ran off seven straight victories to earn the right to play for the 1992 Central Section small-school championship, or Valley championship, which is common terminology in the San Joaquin Valley.

The opponent in the title game was Fowler, which is located just south of Fresno on U.S. Highway 99.

The game was tight throughout, with Fowler taking a 19-15 lead after kicking a field goal with time running out. Strathmore had one more chance to score a winning touchdown, but it appeared that chance was lost when a Fowler player picked up a Strathmore fumble at the Fowler five-yard line and had clear sailing to the end zone at the other end of the field. However, for some unexplainable reason maybe divine intervention – the Fowler player simply dropped the ball after running about 30 yards. Strathmore recovered and had time to run one play from the 35-yard line.

Duke Crawford hadn't completed a pass all game. But that didn't keep McDaniel from calling a pass play. Good decision, as Crawford was able to find Jason Horn in the end zone as time ran out.

Fowler's coaches argued Horn had pushed off a defender, but to no avail. Final score: Strathmore 22, Fowler 19

The Spartans would return to the small schools Valley championship game again in 1998. Strathmore, with an 11-1 record, again played host to Fowler. With almost no time remaining in the game, Fowler scored to take a 16-14 lead. All Fowler had to do now was prevent a touchdown on the ensuing kickoff.

An old friend of McDaniel's, Steve Brown, was in his second season as Strathmore's co-head coach. A star at Porterville High, Brown became an All-American linebacker at Oregon State. He was a semifinalist for the College Football Hall of Fame in 2015.

At the end of practice on Thursdays throughout the season, Brown had the kickoff return team run a play that involves one kick returner on one side of the field pretending to fumble in hopes of drawing all the defenders toward him. He then passes the ball backwards across the field to the other kick returner. Ideally, the other kick returner goes all the way for a touchdown.

"We hadn't run that play all year," Garza said. "Coach McDaniel was afraid to try it, but Steve convinced Coach that it was our only option."

The play got off to a shaky start. Instead of pretending to fumble, the first kick returner fumbled for real. He barely picked the ball in time, but he got the pass off and, after that, the play worked to perfection. Final score: Strathmore 21, Fowler 16.

McDaniel left Strathmore High in 2001, becoming an assistant coach at Delano High, which, like Strathmore High, is predominantly Hispanic although much larger with an enrollment of 3,600. Delano, located a few miles up Highway 99 from McFarland, is the second largest city in Kern County behind Bakersfield.

Prior to Strathmore's 2000 season, Jeromy Blackwell became an assistant coach under McDaniel. Blackwell's father, a 1967 graduate of Strathmore High, worked as a school janitor in Lindsay. Jeromy was a star fullback at Lindsay High and in junior college at the College of the Sequoias in Visalia. He made the Fresno State team as a walk-on, playing for then-coach Pat Hill.

After graduating from Fresno State with a teaching credential, Blackwell, recently married, was desperate for a job where he could teach history and coach. He potentially had one lined up at a middle school in Porterville. Driving from his home in Exeter, located 14 miles northwest of Strathmore, Blackwell decided to drop off his resume at Strathmore High on his way to a scheduled job interview at the middle school in Porterville.

Coach McDaniel heard that Blackwell had applied for a job. He knew Blackwell as a tough player and a person of good character. He called Blackwell and told him there was an opening for a position as a history teacher and football coach at Strathmore and he should take it. McDaniel told Blackwell that he might be moving on after one more season, meaning Blackwell likely would become the head coach. "Wow, a head coach at my age?" Blackwell thought. "I didn't care where it was, I was taking that job," he said.

Blackwell years later would say, "I took a job I never intended to take and ended up with a job I never intend to leave."

McDaniel did leave Strathmore and Blackwell did become the head coach. Blackwell did not get off to a good start, and he takes some of the blame for that. For one thing, he obviously was inexperienced. For another, he had trouble controlling his temper.

He got ejected more than once by game officials. He admits that he needed to mature. And he did. Earlier during the 2017 season, an official who had ejected Blackwell early in his career wrote him a letter. In the letter, the official complimented Blackwell, his staff, and his players for how they conduct themselves and the sportsmanship they show.

Said Garza: "Jeromy was really proud of that letter. And it was all true. With our team, there's no swearing, there's no complaining, and there is always good sportsmanship."

When Blackwell first took over as the high school's head coach, Strathmore's Pop Warner League had grown to two age-group teams. But in 2001, the youth league went dormant and stayed that way for seven years.

In the summer of 2008, Garza literally went knocking on doors, looking for donors and players. As he always had as a player and a coach, he gave it his all.

At the time, Garza was commuting some 35 miles to his full-time job in Corcoran, where he was a correctional officer at the state prison there. Still, Garza found the time to not only restart the youth football program, but also run it. Under his leadership, the league grew to five age-group teams, annually attracting some 150 players from ages 5 through 13.

Garza spent 17 years (1996-2013) working in the prison's transportation department. Initially, Garza took three years off from coaching but returned after deciding he could handle both jobs. He eventually left the prison job, going on disability after injuring both knees while chasing an escaped prisoner.

After that, in addition to coaching, he became a behavioral special education aide at Strathmore High. But during the week of the '17 state title game, he learned he was losing the aide job because another aide was returning from a long leave of absence and an opening was needed to place her.

Garza would soon take a job with a farm management company to make ends meet. Of his stipend as Strathmore's offensive line coach, he says, "It figures out to be about 10 cents an hour."

Running the Pop Warner League, although almost a full-time job during the season, pays even less. It is a voluntary position. However, it pays dividends in other ways.

He likes to tell what happened in 2008 when an attractive woman, Diana Salas, whom he knew from high school, showed up with her lanky 8-year-old son Nick, wanting to sign him up for Pop Warner football. Garza knew her from high school and had a crush on her. Now it was difficult for Garza to look this woman in the eye and tell her that the roster for her son's age-group team was at its limit of 25 players. Diana, a strong-willed woman, didn't take no for an answer. She pleaded her case, saying that her son had lost his father a year earlier to a brain aneurysm and needed direction in his life.

Garza found a way to make it work by creating a new team to make room for Nick Salas, who would eventually become Strathmore High's starting quarterback. And Nick's mother would become Mrs. Robert Garza. The couple got married not long after Garza found room for Nick to play Pop Warner football. "I created a team and gained a wife," Garza laughs. "And a great stepson."

Strathmore High, which has been around since 1920, has an enrollment of approximately 400, with 85% of the students being Hispanic. Strathmore's opponent in the 2017 state title game, Orange High, has an enrollment close to 2,000.

Since 2004, Strathmore High has been part of the Porterville school district, which consists of seven high schools and 21 schools overall. When Strathmore High finally joined the Porterville district, it enabled the school to pay considerably higher teacher salaries, upgrade its facilities, and expand its agri-business department so that it can serve the entire district. Any student who expresses an interest in agri-business can transfer to Strathmore. Interestingly, a good number of these students are also football players.

Who wouldn't want to be a part of the team that rarely loses?

Another plus was the opening of the Harmony Magnet School in 2008. Located adjacent to Strathmore High, the magnet school, known for its academic standards, also draws students from throughout the district, in this case mainly those interested in engineering and performing arts. The Harmony orchestra, led by nationally known and much-honored conductor Michael Allard, performed at New York's Carnegie Hall in the summer of 2017.

Harmony has an enrollment of 520, but, generally, Harmony students aren't that interested in athletics. Only a few play football.

Most of the Strathmore players on the 2017 team came from Plainview, a poor Hispanic settlement of 945 located three miles west of town. That includes do-everything running back/defensive back Joseph Garcia, a three-year starter.

Since the age of 3, Garcia has lived with his father Juan and stepmother Lorenza in Plainview. Juan works as a welder and Lorenza is a manager at a Carl's Jr. in Porterville. Garcia's biological mother still lives in the area, but he rarely sees her.

Garcia began playing youth soccer in Porterville at age 4. People familiar with youth soccer know that, at ages 4 and 5, there are usually one or two kids on a team who dominate. Garcia was one of those kids.

His coach was his father, who admittedly pushed him, hollering such things as "you're not giving 100%," or "don't ever quit." Juan Garcia signed his son up for the new Strathmore Pop Warner League when Joseph was 7. From that point on, it was football instead of soccer for Joseph Garcia.

That first year of Pop Warner football, Garza was Joseph's coach. Then Joseph moved up a division the next year, and his new coach thought he was too small. Garcia didn't play for two games. He finally got to play in the third game – and scored five touchdowns. A star was born.

Garcia finished his senior season at Strathmore High with 2,849 rushing yards and 49 touchdowns while averaging 8.4 yards per carry. As a junior he had 40 touchdowns and 2,345 rushing yards, including 470 in a state semi-final game. He had 13 touchdowns as a sophomore, giving him a three-year total of 102. He is only the sixth Central Section player to score 100 or more touchdowns.

Garcia was also a three-year starter in the defensive backfield. As a senior, he made 54 solo tackles and assisted on 25 others. He continually made big play after big play, both on offense and defense.

On the 2017 Strathmore team, Garcia was among a core of eight mostly two-way players who all started out together in Pop Warner football at age 7. They all lived in Plainview. Some of them were brothers, others were cousins.

Amando and Cristian Rodriguez made up one set of the Plainview brothers. In 2017, Amando, a junior, was a wide receiver and free safety, while Cristian, a sophomore, was a free safety. In 2018, with Nick Salas having moved on to Fresno City College, Cristian took over as Strathmore's starting quarterback before an injury ended his season.

The Rodriguez brothers were raised by their grandmother, Francesca Barrientos. When the boys were in third and fourth grade, the grandmother left to visit family members in Mexico and their unstable mother moved in and took charge. When she started screaming at her sons for being on their cellphones too late at night, their older sister, 14 at the time, came to their defense. Things got out of hand, and the sister called the sheriff's department.

The next day at Sunnyside Elementary School, social workers showed up looking for the boys. They found Amando in his class but Cristian, still upset, didn't go to school. He stayed home. The boys were rounded up and taken to a county facility in Tulare, where they were held all day and into the evening. They ended up in foster care, but fortunately were placed with a nice family in Lindsay. Their foster mother was a nurse, their foster father worked in maintenance at an orange packing house.

After a year-and-a-half, the boys moved back in with their grandmother in Plainview after their mother, who battled a drug addiction, passed away. Although their biological father is around, the boys rarely see him.

Through it all, Amando and Cristian continued to play Pop Warner football. They say it was football that kept them grounded and disciplined. "Without Pop Warner football, I would have quit school and ended up on the streets," Cristian said.

Then there is linebacker-fullback Damien Valencia, who became a starter as a freshman. When he went to sign up for Pop Warner football, he did not have the money to pay the registration fee. Garza waived the fee.

Said Valencia: "I give a lot of credit to coach Garza. Without him, none of us young guys would be here. When we didn't have enough money to participate in Pop Warner, he would go to our mothers and tell them, 'Send them over. I got them'."

In Strathmore's Pop Warner League, young players learn the basic system they will use through high school, a system that features a strong, uncomplicated running game and emphasizes execution. There are basically only four running plays – over right guard, over left guard, around right end, around left end.

Says Blackwell: "We run with unconscious competence. We pound the ball." Also, the players abide by Blackwell's philosophy of "1-0 football: one play, one assignment, one situation at a time."

Another factor in Strathmore's success is unity. The players, to a man, talk about brotherhood and being a family. And as far as the players are concerned, there are no stars. They're all equal.

In a tradition started by McDaniel, they all participate in pre- and post-game prayers. And, in a tradition started by Blackwell, who also has an evangelical background, gather at midfield after every game, win or lose, and hold hands while reciting the Lord's Prayer.

A key player on the 2017 team who returned as a senior in 2018 was offensive and defensive lineman Jadon Guire, a three-year starter. He is 6-2 and 220 and built like a college linebacker.

Guire's father works for Kiwanis International, and his mother is a third-grade teacher at Strathmore Elementary School. Guire, who had college potential, attended Terry Donahue's 2019 California Showcase combine in Orange County. Guire did well there but lingering back and ankle injuries put his football career on hold.

Strathmore's 2017 season included a 56-14 victory over rival Lindsay. Other scores included 42-6, 55-20, 55-22, 69-8, 63-14, 42-0 (back-to-back), and 40-9 wipeouts. Often a running clock was employed when the scores became too lopsided. The coaches did not seek to run up the score. The kids were just that good.

Strathmore easily won its first two playoff games and claimed another Valley title by beating Rosamond, 42-32. Then came a tough double-overtime, 53-52 victory over Hilmar, a small school powerhouse who would overpower Strathmore the next season in the state championship game.

To advance to the 2017 state title game, Strathmore had to get past St. Patrick/St. Vincent of Vallejo, the team that beat Strathmore in the 2016 state title game. This time Strathmore won, 49-35.

Next was the title game in Orange County. When Strathmore fans arrived at the game site and were walking into the stadium, they heard Orange High fans asking: "What's Strathmore?" "Where's Strathmore?" "Who's Strathmore?" A young Strathmore fan responded: "You're about to find out."

These people, who obviously had not read my Orange County Register story, soon found out when Strathmore won, 31-29.

A week later came a victory celebration parade, the first parade of any kind ever held in Strathmore. That was followed by a sign, painted on the side of a 20-foot shipping container in letters three feet high, being put up outside of town that lets travelers know that Strathmore, once a football doormat, is a community proud of its 16-0, 2017 state championship football team.

On the trip back to Strathmore from Orange County, the three rented motor coaches and a motorcade of fans were greeted by about a dozen sheriff department vehicles. With red and blue lights flashing, the team and its supporters were escorted back to town in the middle of the night.

Strathmore High has continued to excel in football, despite now facing larger schools and tougher competition in non-conference games and the playoffs. The 2021 team was 11-0 before losing in the second round of the playoffs to a Bakersfield school.

IN CLOSING

It has been quite a journalistic ride for me, from covering Strathmore High sports to working part-time at the Fresno Bee during college, to the Visalia Times-Delta and then Los Angeles. It really does boggle my mind. Here is one more anecdote.

I never had the Lakers as a beat but often covered practices to give the beat writer a day off. In 1997, Shaquille O'Neal's first season with the Lakers, I covered a practice at the Forum. Shaq, who was nursing a sprained ankle, at first refused to talk to me. Then, moments later, I felt a big hand, a very big hand, on my shoulder. I turned around and looked up. It was Shaq. "What can I do for you, my man?" he asked. We shook hands and he gave me what I needed.

That day, Shaq's agent, Leonard Armato, was sitting courtside with Jerry West at the Forum. I always wondered if Armato was responsible for Shaq's change of heart.

Some 10 years later, I was having a business dinner at the Palm downtown with Armato, who was now the head of AVP pro beach volleyball. Amazingly, Armato remembered the incident with Shaq.

"Did you say anything to him?" I asked.

"I certainly did," Armato said. "I told him you are a very important writer in this town and that he should talk to you."

I planned to end this book with that line. But then Norma and I attended a memorial service on Oct. 26, 2021, for beloved and talented sportswriter colleague Chris Dufresne. The memorial was held 17 months after Chris died on May 25, 2020, at the age of 62 after a recurrence of late-stage melanoma. At the memorial I learned that Chris had a favorite saying about our profession that I find fitting.

"Sometimes it is great to be us."

ACKNOWLEDGEMENTS

First, thanks to my family, particularly Norma. Thanks to the main editors of this book, Strathmore High and UCLA graduate Bob Greenamyer, who in 2020 published an amazing book, "100 Years of Strathmore Spartan Football," and my daughter Jill, an Arcadia High and UCLA grad. Huge debt of gratitude to Arcadia High grad and USC student Jeffrey Lee, a tech whiz and communications major, for helping me self-publish. A bright future awaits Jeffrey. I also need to thank design wizard Steve Benke for creating the book's cover.

MY IMMEDIATE FAMILY

From left, Courtney Sanford, Norma, Jill Sanford, Kelly with grandson Teddy, then 3, at my 70th birthday in 2016.

Photo credit: Martin Leon

Made in the USA
Coppell, TX
03 April 2022